LONDON'S
CURSE

I have never heard such dreadful, horrible, blasphemous and abominable stuff as that which has been produced by this man who describes himself as the greatest living poet.

Mr Justice Rigby Swift on Aleister Crowley

An insatiable sexual athlete, a pimp who lived on the immoral earnings of his girl-friends, and a junkie who daily took enough heroin to kill a roomful of people.

Francis King on Aleister Crowley

The parallel with Macbeth inevitably forces itself upon the mind. Here was a man of action and endurance, a man capable of climbing Himalayan mountains and trekking in the scorching desert; but also a man eaten up by ambition; impatient, envious of any praise or reward that may have gone to the next (if lesser) man; and, withal, a poet. Like Macbeth, Crowley turned to the 'secret, black and midnight hags' when things did not go well for him. He was a poet, black magician, and impresario of the Ragged Ragtime Girls.

Guy Deghy and Keith Waterhouse on Aleister Crowley

He is a man about whom men quarrel. Intensely magnetic, he attracts people or repels them with equal violence. His personality seems to breed rumours. Everywhere they follow him.

Henry N. Hall on Aleister Crowley

LONDON'S CURSE

CURSE

MURDER, BLACK MAGIC AND TUTANKHAMUN IN THE 1920s WEST END

MARK BEYNON

To the memory of John Beynon (otherwise known as 'Grandall'), a true
gentleman in every sense of the word, and to Chris Simmons for piquing my
interest in the macabre.

First published 2011

The History Press
The Mill, Brimscombe Port
Stroud, Gloucestershire, GL5 2QG
www.thehistorypress.co.uk

© Mark Beynon, 2011

British Library Cataloguing in Publication Data.
A catalogue record for this book is available from the British Library.

ISBN 978 0 7524 6312 4
Typesetting and origination by The History Press
Printed in the EU for The History Press.

Contents

Acknowledgements

In writing this book it has been my good fortune to have worked alongside the fine people of The History Press who have breathed life into the project. I am indebted to my publishers, Laura Perehinec and Jay Slater, for believing in this book and for championing it when it looked like a lost cause; to my trusted editors, Chrissy McMorris and Matt Keefe, for their keen eyes and encouragement; and to my proofreaders, Chris Paull and Nick Mann, for their enthusiasm and their candid and valuable input.

On a more personal note, I would like to thank my friends and family for not only putting up with my endless stream of tedious conversation, but for also being stalwarts and saviours; in particular my sister, Anna, and brother, Ali, who provided an unrivalled proofreading service and constant support. Furthermore, I would like to extend my heartfelt love and gratitude to my partner, Vicky, for enthusiastically reading everything I put in front of her, for her unwavering patience and bearing the brunt of my incessant, often sleep-deprived ramblings, and for prudently suggesting that faking my own death and attributing it to the 'Curse of the Pharaohs' in order to drum up publicity wasn't in my best interest!

Mark Beynon
London
February 2011

Author's Note

Throughout the 1920s and 1930s the newspapers and print media referred to the pharaoh Tut-Ankh-Amen. For the purposes of consistency, I have seen fit to change these and use the modern and more familiar spelling of Tutankhamun in all references.

Timeline of Key Events

21 January 1907   Shortly after writing a report into the supposedly cursed 'mummy-board' at the British Museum, Bertram Fletcher Robinson dies at his home at 44 Eaton Terrace, Belgravia. The official cause of his death was recorded as typhoid fever.

4 November 1922 The 30ft sloping passageway leading down to the tomb of Tutankhamun is discovered.

16 February 1923 Howard Carter opens the sealed doorway to the tomb of Tutankhamun. Raoul Loveday dies at the Abbey of Thelema in Cefalù, Sicily.

5 April 1923   Lord Carnarvon dies at the Continental-Savoy Hotel in Cairo. Numerous other deaths attributed to the 'Curse of the Pharaohs' soon follow.

10 July 1923   The 'curse' appears in London's West End for the first time when Ali Kamel Fahmy Bey, a wealthy Egyptian prince, is shot dead by his wife, Marie-Marguerite, at the Savoy Hotel.

23 September 1923 Colonel Aubrey Herbert, the half-brother of Lord Carnarvon, dies of blood poisoning at the Harold Fink Memorial Hospital, Park Lane, following a routine dental operation.

January 1924   The body of Said Enani, Ali Kamel Fahmy Bey's personal secretary, is discovered in Paris. The official cause of death is listed as pneumonia.

15 November 1929 Captain Richard Bethell, private secretary to Howard Carter in Luxor and one of the first men to enter the tomb of King Tut, dies in suspicious circumstances at Mayfair's Bath Club.

20 February 1930   Lord Westbury, the father of Richard Bethell and a keen amateur Egyptologist, reportedly throws himself from his seventh-floor apartment at St James' Court.

24 February 1930   Edgar Steele, a sign-writer at the British Museum in charge of handling the Ancient Egyptian artefacts, dies at St Thomas' Hospital following an operation for internal trouble. On the same day, 8-year-old Joseph Greer is knocked down and killed by Lord Westbury's hearse in Battersea as it is carrying him to the crematorium at Golders Green.

13 October 1930   Henry (Harry) Reginald Holland Hall, the Keeper of the Egyptian and Assyrian Antiquities at the British Museum, dies at his London home after catching pneumonia.

2 January 1934   Arthur Weigall, the respected English Egyptologist with extensive links to the British Museum and who reported on the opening of Tutankhamun's tomb in Luxor, dies at the London Hospital in Whitechapel.

23 November 1934 Sir Ernest Wallis Budge, the second Keeper of the Egyptian and Assyrian Antiquities at the British Museum to succumb to the supposed curse, who had spent over thirty years in his position at the museum, dies at his home at 48 Bloomsbury Street.

5 April 1935   Two women reputedly disappear from a platform at Holborn underground station where the screams of an Ancient Egyptian ghost are said to echo. The women are never to be seen again, and strange, indecipherable marks are later found on the tiled walls belonging to the disused British Museum station a mere stop away.

2 March 1938   Howard Carter passes away at his home at 19 Collingham Gardens, Kensington, following a battle with lymphoma.

1 December 1947   At 72 years of age, Aleister Crowley succumbs to a respiratory infection at Netherwood boarding house in Hastings. His physician, a Dr William Brown Thompson, dies within twenty-four hours of his patient at his Mayfair apartment – Crowley having allegedly placed a curse on him three months earlier.

30 March 1972   The 'Treasures of Tutankhamun' exhibition opens at the British Museum in London. Numerous tales of curse-related goings-on are reported.

7 May 2000   Edward Crowley murders 12-year-old Diego Piniera-Villar at London's Covent Garden in the West End.

15 November 2007 The 'Tutankhamun and the Golden Age of the Pharaohs' exhibition arrives at London's O2 Arena.

PART I: THE CURSE

Prologue

London, 16 November 1929

Do what thou wilt shall be the whole of the Law
Love is the law, love under will

A rampaging, opaque pea-souper had rolled in off the Thames, engulfing all of
the concrete, glass, steel and tarmac that stood in its path. It was a suitably grim
milieu for something devilish. As dusk began to settle over the bustling metrop-
olis, dark, narrow alleyways had all but disappeared into the vortex of freezing
vapour, leaving only the main thoroughfares lit by dull beacons of lamplight.
Even the world-famous lights of Piccadilly Circus had become shrouded by a
fog so vast that they were barely visible through the thickening cluster of yel-
low-hued smog. The giant signs belonging to Bovril, Guinness and Schweppes,
previously drawn into the sharp relief of neon clarity, had become little more
than a mass of indistinguishable colour consumed by the pall of dense miasma.
Dim neon reflected and shimmered off puddles forming in the potholes of
the road as if they belonged to some liquid fantasy. Tourists looked on in won-
derment as their raincoats billowed in the gathering storm and their trilbies
became saturated by the sudden deluge. The outline of the buildings looked
timeless in the half-light; a gothic and ethereal quality set against the murky
light pollution. The once thunderous drone of automobiles and buses tearing
along Victoria Street had turned into nothing more than a gentle hum as the
Londoners, patently familiar with such singular weather changes, sagaciously

vacated the streets and took refuge in their domiciles, taverns, restaurants and private clubs.

Lord Westbury stirred in his grand high-backed chair. He noted from the ornate marble clock on the mantelpiece that it was a little after seven in the evening, thus he could only have procured himself a mere half an hour of sleep. But what strange and disquieting dreams those thirty-odd minutes of slumber had brought him. Westbury ran a tired hand down his long, wrinkled face, and could feel a gathering sheen of sweat across his brow and unkempt beard; no doubt a legacy of the appalling dreams.

The night nurse had prescribed him a dram and a half of bromide mixed with a fraction of a grain of heroin for his insomnia. Although he was grateful for the slumber the sour concoction induced, Westbury had decided against taking any further doses; the symptoms of the powerful potion, most notably the nightmarish dreams and visions it seemed to provoke, were just too terrifying to endure. He had come to the conclusion that he would rather be awake and drowsy, even though the prospect filled him with dread, than asleep and dreaming and at the mercy of the medicine.

The last of Westbury's party had reluctantly left, leaving him alone in the unnerving tranquillity of his seventh-floor apartment at St James' Court – a spacious courtyard encompassed by some of the finest flats that money could buy in one of the most desirable postcodes in London. He had given his valet, Chester, the rest of the evening off once he had finished tidying away the jumble of cups and saucers. His friends and family had arrived in their droves to pay their condolences after his son had died mysteriously in his sleep only twenty-four hours earlier at Dover Street's exquisite Bath Club. The terrible news had arrived with the timid policeman – little more than a boy – late the previous evening, and although it had yet to sink in, many bitter tears had been shed throughout the course of the day.

Feeling his arms trembling from the sudden cold, Westbury hauled himself up awkwardly in his chair. With the late autumnal chill penetrating his bones and pricking at his marrow, he threw a cursory glance around his glacial apartment; the vast array of Egyptian artefacts strewn about the room made it appear more of a museum than a study – a veritable den of antiquity. Walls and ceiling were smothered by hundreds of peculiar relics from Cairo and Luxor. Lean, angular figures, bearing vicious-looking weaponry, were placed with consummate care upon the dark mahogany shelving that gleamed with the shine and smell of expensive polish. Above were intricately designed almond-eyed monarchs and strange deities cut and chipped out of the blue Egyptian lapis lazuli. The Ancient Egyptian gods Osiris, Horus and Amen-Ra, and the goddess Isis, glared at Westbury with their wicked, unforgiving eyes, while in the centre of the extraordinary chamber was a sturdy oaken table, scattered with papers, bottles, pots and the dried leaves of an elegant, palm-like plant. The bookshelves, which seemed to creak and groan under duress, were crammed with leather-bound volumes of biblical proportions, string-fastened parchment manuscripts and Egyptian papyrus. The solitary ticking clock was the only noise Westbury could discern amidst the anomalous silence.

The apartment had been plunged into semi-darkness following the onset of fog. The fading orange embers of the fire began to spit and crackle in the grate, occasionally leaping from within and landing on the hearth in front of it. The incense candles discharged an acrid scent of balsamic resin that pervaded the room, although they too were in the process of emitting their final wisps of smoke.

Westbury peered down at the empty cut-glass whisky decanter and soda siphon that sat upon the scrupulously polished coffee table beside him. Force of habit demanded he call out for Chester to remedy the wretched state of affairs, but he checked himself before he did so. It alarmed him to think of how dependent he had become on the blasted man.

Drink and warmth were the two commodities Westbury most desired so he set about rectifying the hopeless situation himself. Shuffling across the wooden floor with the aid of his trusted ivory-handled walking cane, he got as far as the doorway to the kitchen before the shrill cries of the sentinel, hawking his wares from the frigid street below, stopped him dead in his tracks.

'EXTRA! EXTRA! READ ALL ABOUT IT! GET YER STANDARD 'ERE!'

Westbury started. He had never heard a sentinel stray so far from Victoria, certainly not to the limited confines of St James' Court, and most certainly not in such hellish weather. He wondered what could have brought him to his door on this night of all nights, knowing full well that it couldn't have been the flood of custom.

'THE CURSE OF TUTANKHAMUN STRIKES IN LONDON ONCE AGAIN!'

A sudden chill coursed down Westbury's spine. His eyes were immediately drawn to the lonely alabaster vase that was sat on the windowsill. Seemingly innocuous, it was the vase his son had pillaged from the tomb of Tutankhamun in Luxor and was subsequently presented to him as a gift – the showpiece of his collection. There was also something strikingly forbidding about the sentinel's voice. Westbury couldn't place it, although the gravelly rasp seemed strangely familiar to him.

'LORD WESTBURY'S SON IS FOUND DEAD AT MAYFAIR'S BATH CLUB!'

Dumbstruck, Westbury rested a trembling arm against the wall to support himself, taking in short gasps of the cold air in an effort to catch his breath. He had witnessed it in his vivid, terrifying dreams not five minutes earlier; he had seen himself falling to his death from the very window that was facing him. Deep down, in his heart of hearts, he knew that he would be the next to succumb to the dreaded curse that had seemingly infiltrated the city.

It was surely only a matter of time …

London, 20 February 1930

To the naked eye, the Beast almost seemed to sashay and float his way down St James' Street, his long, mustard-coloured cloak, covered in occult symbols, acting as a sponge, soaking up the puddles of rainwater as it trailed behind him. He disregarded the errant looks and sneers that came his way from the astonished tourists unaccustomed to his eccentric ways. The bizarre conical hat that covered his shaven pate seemed to attract the most attention and the odd muttered, derisive comment from those brave enough to risk his scold. *Indeed, if they see me, why does nobody speak to me?*

Against the pale glow of neon, the Beast looked like a deranged and spectral wizard on the warpath; his heaving bulk, which let off a pungent odour of scented oil and saffron, sweated profusely beneath his numerous layers of clothing. Tonight he was invisible; his special power having been granted him after the sacrifice of Richard Bethell – his third victim – at the carefully selected Bath Club on Dover Street. The man Bethell had put up little fight; the Beast knew the same would not be said about his tenacious father. *But the pentagram is almost complete …*

He was grateful that his cloak shielded him from the monotony of everyday life – the same monotony that had sucked the life and soul out of the men and women he witnessed going about the daily grind of their prosaic, workaday and pitiful existences. He couldn't bring himself to settle for the same mediocrity, and now, having come so close to completing his assignment, he would never have to. He allowed himself a sly, sardonic grin as he remembered all he had sacrificed for the cause. *Aiwass was right to choose me, for I am the Magus.*

The Beast stepped blindly across the road, ignoring the sudden screeching of tyres, the piercing car horns and the abusive cries from agitated motorists forced into sudden stops to make way for the peculiar creature in front of them. Directly ahead of him was the Mall, then St James' Park, and beyond that was beautiful, saccharine emancipation. St James' Park was darker than it usually was in February. The overhanging trees and their skeletal branches seemed to belong to some long-forgotten and overgrown graveyard. Indeed, to the Beast it seemed the most apposite of settings for him to conduct his devilry.

A short stride through the park, past the whispered conversations taking place in dark corners, took the Beast up towards Petty France and along the seemingly deserted Buckingham Gate. He suppressed a smile as he remembered his previous foray to St James' Court, when he masqueraded as the pathetic sentinel. There would be no play-acting this time – only cold-blooded, ruthless, perfect murder.

INTRODUCTION

The Origins of a Legend and 'Wonderful Things'

Smith stepped over to the table and looked down with a professional eye at the black and twisted form in front of him. The features, though horribly discoloured, were perfect, and two little nut-like eyes still lurked in the depths of the black, hollow sockets. The blotched skin was drawn tightly from bone to bone, and a tangled wrap of black coarse hair fell over the ears. Two thin teeth, like those of a rat, overlay the shrivelled lower lip. In its crouching position, with bent joints and craned head, there was a suggestion of energy about the horrid thing which made Smith's gorge rise. The gaunt ribs, with their parchment-like covering, were exposed, and the sunken, leaden-hued abdomen, with the long slit where the embalmer had left his mark; but the lower limbs were wrapt round with coarse yellow bandages.

Sir Arthur Conan Doyle, *Lot No 249*

The name Tutankhamun is synonymous with Ancient Egypt, archaeology and, probably most significantly, the 'Curse of the Pharaohs'. When his tomb was initially discovered in 1922, few would have prophesied the lasting effect this long-dead pharaoh and Egyptian boy-king of antiquity would have on modern society and culture, and quite how the curse of King Tut would become a worldwide phenomenon. Inspiring renowned writers such as Sir Arthur Conan Doyle, Bram Stoker, H.P. Lovecraft and Marie Corelli to pen ghost stories based around the themes of Ancient Egypt and retribution, the legend and legacy of Tutankhamun continues to encourage filmmakers and authors to embrace Ancient Egyptian curses and mythology in their creative aspirations today – much as it did almost ninety years ago. Directly inspired by the curse of Tutankhamun, a character loosely based on King Tut originally emerged in movies such as Universal's *The Mummy*, *The Mummy's Tomb* and *The Mummy's Curse* – thus beginning cinema's fascination with 'the curse of the mummy'.

Frequently reappearing in contemporary film, television, books and comics in many guises and semblances, most notably in Stephen Sommers' *The Mummy* films, in Dan Simmons' best-selling novel *Drood*; in Christian Jacq's thriller *Tutankhamun: The Last Secret*; as the villainous King Tut in the 1960s *Batman* television series; as the evil character Mumm-Ra (who even had a magical potion called Tutantiny!) in the 1980s cartoon *ThunderCats*; and, most recently, in James Patterson's true-crime tale *The Murder of King Tut* – Tutankhamun has become an institution. The oldest fantastical writing linked to the mummy's curse was published in 1699 in the *Traité des embaumements selon les anciens et les modernes* (*Treatise on Embalming According to the Ancient and Modern Ways*) by Louis Pichier, and texts on this subject have been published regularly ever since. It is therefore all the more important to retrace the true story of the curse of King Tut and quite how it came to envelop London's West End like a dark veil.

For twelve years, between 1923 and 1935, London was gripped by the supposed curse of Tutankhamun, whose tomb was opened in the Valley of the Kings in February 1923 by the British archaeologist Howard Carter. For some strange and unsettling reason, those who had provoked the indignation of King Tut found London's West End a particularly perilous place to inhabit, and this book will chronicle the bizarre sequence of deaths and peculiar happenings (all of which can be directly attributed to the curse) that occurred in this vicinity throughout this disturbingly brief and turbulent epoch.

I stumbled upon this peculiar story purely by chance. Having read Ed Glinert's superb *London's Dead*, I came across a half-page he devoted to the Tutankhamun curse and its impact upon London's post-war West End. Having piqued my curiosity, and with a particular interest in the gregarious and decadent period that was 1920s London, I felt compelled to further investigate this singular tale in the hope that it would make a convincing tome. My preliminary research wasn't directed towards finding a credible cause or an architect behind these deaths (apart from the one provided by King Tut himself) as any plausible perpetrator with a motive would surely seem too unbelievable. Instead, it was merely directed towards presenting the facts of the case as candidly as possible. Initially concerned that this approach wouldn't provide me with enough material, my fears were soon allayed when I discovered, to my genuine surprise, further significant (and in some cases more fantastical) connections between the curse of Tutankhamun and the baffling series of deaths that took place in the close proximity of London's West End – including damning links to a notorious occultist. From this moment on the book became much more than just a profile of a sequence of sinister, if somewhat coincidental, deaths with a solitary connection running through them. Moreover, it has since become a posthumous murder investigation, acting as the case for the prosecution.

As previously stated, I have held a long-standing interest in the social climate of 1920s London. I find it fascinating how the city, famous for its glamour before its many neon lights were dimmed by the Zeppelin raids of the First World War, was able to transform itself back into the most ostentatious and celestial city in the world in spite of the many wartime regulations still imposed upon it. Yet what is more intriguing is that just as Londoners dared to continue their lives without the fear of threat and reprisal, the mystifying legacy of a 3,000-year-old pharaoh, whipped up by a frenzied newspaper campaign, had many of them scared of their own shadow and looking over their shoulders once more. To begin with, however, I had to research the events that took place in a country that was a far cry from this and where this extraordinary story had its origins in one of the most legendary archaeological discoveries of all time – 1920s Egypt.

Howard Carter, a prominent Egyptologist and archaeologist, had been handed one final season of funding by his sponsor, George Edward Stanhope Molyneux Herbert, Lord Carnarvon, with which to discover the tomb of Tutankhamun that had so famously eluded archaeologists for years. It was 1922 and the wealthy Carnarvon was becoming increasingly despondent at the lack of return from his considerable financial investment. After his initial success in excavating Beni Hasan in 1891, the grave site of the princes of Middle Egypt, and discovering the tomb of Queen Hatshepsut in Deir el-Bahri in 1903, Carter fell on several hard and uncompromising years, especially when he was forced to resign from the Egyptian Antiquities Service following a dispute between Egyptian site guards and a group of raucous French tourists.

Lord Carnarvon had met Carter in 1907 when, after a serious road accident, he travelled to balmy Egypt for periods of convalescence throughout the winter months when he was susceptible to illness in the damp English weather. At the time Carter was an antiquities dealer and an artist, although he had gained valuable experience as an archaeologist in the employment of the prosperous American businessman Theodore Davis. It was Davis who held the enviable permit to dig on the west bank of the River Nile in the Valley of the Kings – a permit that Carter had long coveted. Carnarvon, who crucially had a keen interest in antiquity and Egyptology himself, was on the lookout for his own archaeologist to dig at nearby Thebes (modern Luxor), and was strongly recommended to employ Carter, who had a fine, if a somewhat cantankerous, reputation. It was to be the beginning of a fruitful partnership. In their first season together, Carter excavated the tomb of a late sixteenth-century BC mayor and a written tablet which chronicled the expulsion from Egypt of the Hyksos. In the years following, Carter and Carnarvon made further remarkable discoveries, including the temples of Hatshepsut and Ramesses IV (*c.* 1154–48 BC) as well as a number of important tombs belonging to nobles dating from 2000–1500 BC. But it was the tomb of the boy-king Tutankhamun that was the prize they most desired; the tomb that was surely buried somewhere in the land inaccessible to them: the Valley of the Kings, the legendary burial site for the kings and powerful nobles of the New Kingdom (the Eighteenth to the Twentieth Dynasties of Ancient Egypt).

Tutankhamun was born in 1341 BC and was an Egyptian pharaoh of the New Kingdom. Already fabulously wealthy, he was 8 or 9 when he became pharaoh and was ruler for ten years before his untimely and mysterious death ended his short and eventful reign. In historical terms, Tutankhamun's legacy stems from his rejection of the radical religious policies introduced by his father and predecessor, Akhenaten (the heretic pharaoh), his restoration of the traditional deities, his abolishing of Tell el-Amarna, Akhenaten's short-lived capital, and returning the New Kingdom to order after chaos and heresy blighted the tumultuous previous reign. As a boy, Tutankhamun married his half-sister, Ankhesenamun (preserving a strong regal kinship that was paramount to the Ancient Egyptians), with whom he had two daughters; it is assumed they both died premature and stillborn as their minuscule mummies were discovered alongside Tutankhamun in his tomb.

The cause of Tutankhamun's death is still uncertain and has been the subject of much debate; the most recent studies on the mummy have pointed to malaria and a rare bone disorder as being responsible, yet numerous X-rays had previously revealed a dense spot at the lower back of his skull that indicated he suffered a subdural haematoma. It is fair to assume that such a significant injury would almost certainly have led to Tutankhamun's demise, but whether or not the wound was the result of an accident or something more sinister is harder to ascertain. Experts have stated that the injury could not have been attributed to natural causes and that the blow was to a protected area of the head that is not easily injured by accident. Upon the release of this captivating information, inevitable theories soon circulated as to who, or what, was responsible for the death of King Tut: the suspects have included his immediate successor, Ay, his wife and even his chariot driver, whom many suspect of throwing Tutankhamun from his hunting chariot. Whatever the cause and whoever the perpetrator, it is certainly more fascinating, in relation to the context of this book, if one buys into the theory that Tutankhamun was murdered in cold blood.

Theodore Davis, who had already searched long and hard for the elusive tomb of King Tut, had become elderly and ailing, and in 1914 he finally gave up his concession to excavate the Valley of the Kings. Unsurprisingly the permit was swiftly acquired by Carter and Carnarvon, sensing they had at last an opportunity to discover what no other archaeologist could. Although the outbreak of the First World War put work in the valley on hold, Carter was still able to excavate the tomb of Amenhotep III (*c.* 1390–52 BC) and a cliff tomb of Hatshepsut dug for her before she became pharaoh. However, once the war came to an end and digging resumed in the valley, Carter's luck turned for the worse. Between 1918 and 1922, Carter and Carnarvon dug with limited success, and by September 1922 Carnarvon firmly believed that the entire network and labyrinth of tombs had been found. It was only after Carter proposed to finance the remainder of the excavation himself that Carnarvon was shamed into offering one final season of funding, handing Carter just one more month to locate the tomb of Tutankhamun.

Having spent the best part of a decade searching for King Tut, and with time running agonisingly short, the excavation's water-carrier fortuitously stumbled on the corner of a door on a barren hillside. Carter and his workers hastily unearthed twelve steps that led down to a tomb entrance; the location miraculously overlaid by the already discovered tomb of Ramesses VI and a mere 6ft from where Davis and his archaeologist Harry Burton had already dug. On the threshold of a remarkable discovery, and with the seal impressions unclear as to whose tomb it was, Carter was understandably anxious to continue with the excavation. He wrote in his book, *The Tomb of Tutankhamun*: 'Anything, literally anything might lie beyond that passage, and it needed all my self-control to keep from breaking down the doorway and investigating then and there.'

Instead, Carter composed himself and telegraphed the news to Carnarvon in England. After twenty long days of patient waiting, Carnarvon, accompanied by his glamorously blithe 22-year-old daughter, Lady Evelyn Herbert, at last arrived in Egypt. They were immediately taken to the burial site in the Valley of the Kings and the entire stairway was excavated, this time revealing the sacred seal impressions of Tutankhamun and of the necropolis authorities amidst the dusty debris. The sealed door was eventually prised open, exposing the rubble-filled passageway within. With evidence of tomb robbers having disturbed it in the reign of the pharaoh Horemheb, Carter was desperate to find the entrance to the burial chamber, hoping and praying that the same rogues had left it uncompromised. The following afternoon, 30ft down from the outer door, Carter discovered the doorway to the antechamber, the large room adjoining the burial chamber, and he later remarked in his book:

> The decisive moment arrived. With trembling hands I made a tiny breach … At first I could see nothing … but presently, as my eyes grew accustomed to the light, details of the room within emerged slowly from the mist, strange animals, statues, and gold – everywhere the glint of gold. For the moment – an eternity it must have seemed to the others standing by – I was struck dumb with amazement, and when Lord Carnarvon, unable to stand the suspense any longer, enquired anxiously, 'Can you see anything?' it was all I could do to get out the words, 'Yes, wonderful things.'

Among these 700 'wonderful things', together with the artefacts Carter could see through the plunderer's hole he had made in the doorway to the adjacent annexe, were gold-covered couches in the shape of grotesque animals, statues, mannequins and effigies of Tutankhamun, items for hunting, caskets, chariots, an elaborate headrest made of elephant ivory, vases, jars, pots, a boat carved from alabaster, black shrines, one with a golden snake peeking out, bouquets of flowers, beds, chairs, painted chests, a golden throne, and more humble objects such as intricate ivory gaming boards, boxes and firelighters – everything the Egyptians believed Tutankhamun would require in his infinite journey through the afterlife. However, there was still no sign of the mummy.

Demanding yet more patience from Carter and Carnarvon, the two men returned to the site weeks later (once a thick steel gate from Cairo had been put in place for security), this time to remove carefully and photograph every item in the antechamber (the many items in the annexe weren't cleared until the rest of the tomb had been emptied due to its haphazard layout – the legacy of the tomb robbers). In clearing the antechamber, Carter had finally discovered the doorway to the burial chamber, and the end of his arduous hunt was at last in sight.

Against the protocol laid out by the Egyptian government and the regulations of the permit itself, Carter, along with his assistant, Arthur 'Pecky' Callender, Carnarvon and Lady Evelyn, compelled by the thought of what was lurking just beyond the door, couldn't wait for the official opening of the burial chamber and broke in through a small hole one night in late November 1922. Although an act of illegal entry that would have seen his concession revoked, Carter's description of what he saw that night provides an incredibly atmospheric account of the most crucial part of the excavation, as well as displaying his own adroit ability with prose:

I suppose most excavators would confess to a feeling of awe – embarrassment almost – when they break into a chamber closed and sealed by pious hands so many centuries ago. For the moment, time as a factor in human life has lost its meaning. Three thousand, four thousand years maybe, have passed and gone since human feet last trod the floor on which you stand, and yet, as you note the signs of recent life around you – the half-filled bowl of mortar for the door, the blackened lamp, the finger-mark upon the freshly painted surface, the farewell garland dropped upon the threshold – you feel it might have been but yesterday. The very air you breathe, unchanged throughout centuries, you share with those who laid the mummy to its rest. Time is annihilated by little intimate details such as these, and you feel an intruder. That is perhaps the first and dominant sensation, but others follow thick and fast – the exhilaration of discovery, the fever of suspense, the almost over-mastering impulse, born of curiosity, to break down seals and lift the lids of boxes, the thought – pure joy to the investigator – that you are about to add a page to history, or solve some problem of research, the strained expectancy – why not confess it? – of the treasure seeker.

On 16 February 1923, and with twenty guests eagerly looking on, the day had finally arrived for Howard Carter and Lord Carnarvon. Personally taking the task of removing the entire sealed doorway at the far end of the antechamber, Carter had to manipulate it so as not to damage the treasure that lay behind. When he shone a lamp into the dark abyss, a solid wall of gold, a huge shrine built to protect Tutankhamun's sarcophagus, reflected and shimmered in the lamplight. There were loud gasps from the convened crowd as Carter opened the doors of the shrine and within it discovered a second shrine – the seal of which was miraculously still intact. The official excavation newspaper, *The Times* of London, reported the dramatic event as follows:

> This has perhaps been the most extraordinary day in the whole history of Egyptian excavation. Whatever anyone may have guessed or imagined of the secret of Tutankhamun's tomb, they surely cannot have dreamed the truth as now revealed. Entrance today was made into the sealed chamber, and yet another door opened beyond that. No eyes have yet seen the King, but to a practical certainty, we now know that he lies there, close at hand, in all his original state undisturbed.
>
> Moreover, in addition to the great store of treasures, which the tomb has already yielded, today has brought to light a new wealth of objects of artistic, historical, and even intrinsic value which is bewildering. It is such a hoard as

the most sanguine excavator can hardly have pictured even in visions in his sleep, and puts Lord Carnarvon's and Mr Carter's discovery in a class by itself above all previous finds.

The process of opening the doorway bearing the Royal insignia and guarded by protective statues of the King had taken several hours of careful manipulation under the intense heat. It finally ended in wonderful revelation, for before the spectators was the resplendent mausoleum of the King, a spacious beautiful, decorated chamber, completely occupied by an immense shrine covered with gold inlaid with brilliant blue faience.

This beautiful wooden construction towers nearly to the ceiling and fills the great sepulchral hall within a short span of its four walls. Its sides are adorned with magnificent religious text and fearful symbols of the dead, and it is capped with a superb cornice and torus moulding.

The foregoing narrative is necessarily hasty, and may be subject to correction in details as the result of future investigation.

Much to Carter's relief, the tomb robbers had not breached Tutankhamun's sarcophagus, leaving behind them the most complete Ancient Egyptian tomb ever found; this included an elaborate gold death mask that at last gave the pharaoh a face. Perhaps one of the reasons for the robbers vacating the chamber without plundering its many treasures was an ominous clay tablet above Tutankhamun's tomb which bore a menacing hieroglyphic inscription that was similar to the one previously discovered in the tomb of Ursa, who lived a century before King Tut:

As to anyone who violates my body which is in the tomb and who shall remove my image from my tomb, he shall be hateful to the gods, and he shall not receive water on the altar of Osiris, neither shall he bequeath his property to his children, for ever and ever.

Typically, this inscription was amended by the newspapers to make it both spectacular and manageable for their readership unfamiliar with Ancient Egyptian mythology. Rewritten as a famous theatrical curse, it appeared in print form as: 'Death shall come on swift wings to him that toucheth the tomb of the pharaoh.' Indeed, it wasn't uncommon for magic spells and curses to adorn the walls of Ancient Egyptian tombs, and the inscriptions of these were frequently placed upon ritualistic objects found in royal burial chambers; these objects included amulets, statues and magic bricks. Similar foreboding inscriptions were found on the four magic bricks carefully placed at the principal positions in the walls and niches of Tutankhamun's tomb – the four cardinal compass points of north, south, east and west. According to Egyptian legend, each of these cardinal points was associated with one of the four sons of Horus, the god of Ancient Egyptian religion, who offered protection to the dead pharaoh by ascribing spells taken from chapter 151 of the Egyptian *Book of the Dead*. The most significant of the magic brick inscriptions found in Tutankhamun's tomb was on a black and gold Anubis shrine; this inscription was deemed of particular interest and importance as Anubis was the Ancient Egyptian god of the dead. The spells inscribed on the four magic bricks were mixed together and reported in the newspapers, alongside the inscription on the clay tablet, as the following:

> It is I who hinder the sand from choking the secret chamber, and who repel that one who would repel him with the desert-flame. I have set aflame the desert. I have caused the path to be mistaken. I am for the protection of the Osiris. This is to repel the enemy of Osiris, in whatever form he may come.

As Carter and Carnarvon lapped up the praise and admiration from their peers and the public the world over, little did the two men realise that this bleak proclamation would be proved correct in a disastrously short space of time, receiving swift and terrible fulfilment, and that Lord Carnarvon would never get to see the mummy of Tutankhamun.

1

Of Curses, Newspapers, Writers and Books

In Cairo, in the Continental Hotel, a sick man, early in the morning, breathed his last. At the same moment, across the city, all the lights flickered and then at once went out. A darkness veiled Cairo, as heavy as that of an unopened tomb. At the same moment, in the Valley of the Kings, a guard by the tomb of Tutankhamun was disturbed. In the rocks above his head he heard a sudden noise, and as he rose from his chair he saw a scattering of dust, descending in a rivulet of dislodged pebbles. When he went, however, to investigate the cause, he could find nothing, nor hear anything save a gusting of wind.

Tom Holland, *The Sleeper in the Sands*

Legend has it that just as Howard Carter crossed the threshold of Tutankhamun's burial chamber his beloved pet canary was killed by a cobra. The canary, which Carter had bought in Cairo in an attempt to liven up his humble lodgings, was kept in a gilded cage outside his house near the entrance to the Valley of the Kings. Many people believed the bird would bring good fortune to the excavation, and even the *fellahs* (Egyptian workmen) at the site had adopted the canary as a lucky charm, naming Carter's great discovery as the 'Tomb of the Bird'. But not long after Carter and Carnarvon had entered Tutankhamun's burial chamber, the incident occurred and was noted by the visiting American Egyptologist James Henry Breasted. Carter had sent his trusted assistant archaeologist Arthur Callender on an errand to his house, but on nearing it Callender thought he heard a faint, almost human cry. He immediately looked up at the cage hanging near the doorway; to his abhorrence a cobra was coiled up within it devouring the small songbird. An extremely rare sight in the Valley of the Kings, the cobra was the Ancient Egyptian symbol of royal power and a symbolic serpent was often carved on the brows of pharaohs' headdresses to ward off their enemies. Across the Valley of the Kings many people justifiably took this as a sign of the pharaoh's fury.

Herbert Winlock, another esteemed American Egyptologist who was employed by the Metropolitan Museum of Art, described and summarised in a letter the effect the incident had on Carter's workmen:

When Carter came out last October, alone, he got a canary bird, in Cairo, in a gilded cage to cheer up what he figured was going to be a lonely and deserted house. Carter, coming over to his house with his servant, Abdul Ali, carrying the canary behind him and guards and the foremen greeting him and right off, when they see a golden bird they say: '*Malbrook* – it's a bird of gold that will bring luck. This year we will find *inshallah* [God willing] a tomb of gold.' Within a week they had made the most fabulous find of all time and at first the tomb was called 'the tomb of the Golden Bird' by the natives. The Canary almost had a halo around its cage ... Callender was living alone in Carter's house with the bird in his special care. Suddenly, one afternoon he heard a fluttering and squeaking and went into the next room and there in the cage with the bird was a cobra just in the act of gulping the canary down halo and all.

Now cobras had never been known around there before, and cobras, as every native knew, grow on the heads of Old Kings. The conclusion was obvious. The King's serpent had struck at the mascot who had given away the secret of the tomb. And the sequel was equally obvious – at least to them, though I admit to have lost some links in the chain of argument – that before the winter was out someone would die. It was all very dismal.

As dawn broke on the morning of the tomb's opening, a majestic-looking hawk was seen flying above the sun-drenched excavation site before disappearing to the west. This sighting was considered a bad omen; a warning that left the *fellahs* frightened and whispering among themselves that before long the foreigners would find gold and death. As the excavating party descended the steps that led down to the sepulchre, a miniature sandstorm swept across the desert and circled over the tomb. Only days earlier Howard Carter had been bitten on the hand by a scorpion; although the wound wasn't infected, it would hamper him throughout the course of the excavation.

Although these stories have, in all probability, been embellished over the years, the dramatic events that were to follow the opening of the pharaoh's burial chamber have not. With the world's imagination gripped by the story of the excavation of King Tut's tomb, the tale of Carter's unfortunate canary was eagerly regurgitated by newspapers attempting to cash in on the alleged curse of Tutankhamun. The *New York Times*, a prime carrier of Tutankhamun news since the city's own museum was heavily involved in the excavation, reported that:

> Already in this land of superstition myths are beginning to grow up … out of [the canary's death] the most fantastic stories are being manufactured … so it has been easy to weave a legend that brought in the little bird, which in some ways symbolised the modern spirit of civilisation, and the cobra, which stood for the powers of old dynasties …

The delicate state of affairs with the press had already come to a head on 9 January 1923, when Lord Carnarvon signed a £5,000 exclusive contract with *The Times* of London to cover the excavation of the tomb of Tutankhamun. Throughout the 1920s, *The Times* was the leading newspaper in Britain, with a worldwide reputation and an influential readership that spanned the vast British Empire.

Angered by this deal and resentful of being shut out of the biggest story of the age, journalists and reporters of rival newspapers and magazines were subsequently forced to write more exciting, stimulating and, in some cases, deliberately frivolous stories in order to win their readership back; this in turn caused a huge amount of friction on Fleet Street with newspapers clamouring over who had the most scintillating scoop on the curse. Their over-zealous reporting endeavours soon got the better of Carter, and he remarked how he was 'weary of telegrams and sick to death of reporters … [he] wanted to avoid being followed by gentlemen of the press'. But Carnarvon had already made an enemy of the newspapers, and one journalist working for the *New York Times* wrote how he would 'Drive C and C out of their minds for having sold a piece of the world's ancient history to the London Times'.

Carter understandably found the story of the curse an unnecessary and ridiculous sideshow. Although rumours began to circulate that he had catalogued the warning inscription found upon the clay tablet before erasing it from written record and burying it in the sand, Carter indicated in his book just how disgusted he was with the reporters and their fabrications:

> It has been stated in various quarters that there are actual physical dangers hidden in Tutankhamun's tomb – mysterious forces, called into being by some malefic power, to take vengeance on whomsoever should dare to pass

its portals. There was perhaps no place in the world freer from risks than the tomb … Unpardonable and mendacious statements of this nature have been published and repeated in various quarters with a sort of malicious satisfaction. It is indeed difficult to speak of this form of 'ghostly' calumny with calm. If it be not actually libellous, it points in that spiteful direction, and all sane people should dismiss such interventions with contempt.

Carter supported this statement when he was quoted, on 4 October 1924, as saying: 'It is rather too much to ask me to believe that some spook is keeping watch and ward over the dead pharaoh, ready to wreak vengeance on anyone who goes too near.'

However, it is worth mentioning that when Carter, in the early years of his tenure in the Valley of the Kings, was working as an archaeologist in the employment of Theodore Davis, he was far more open to the possibility of curses. In his book *Howard Carter: The Path To Tutankhamun*, T.G.H. James recalls a young Carter, who was giving a female visitor a guided tour of the recently discovered tomb of Amenophis II, saying: 'The pharaoh's mummy was probably protected … by a curse pronounced in the band of hieroglyphics around the top of the sarcophagus upon any marauding hands.' Also, Sir Thomas Cecil Rapp, the British vice-consul to Cairo at the time of the excavation, supported this claim when he wrote in his unpublished memoirs how '[Carter] was suffering too from a superstitious feeling that Lord Carnarvon's death was possible nemesis for disturbing the sleep of the dead, a nemesis that might extend to him'.

Yet the initial notion or mention of the curse of Tutankhamun (before the press got hold of it), coinciding with the swell of Egyptian national pride that seemed to follow the end of the First World War, must have originated with the native Egyptians who were appalled by the colonial and increasingly imperialistic British invading, monopolising and tampering with their ancient artefacts for their own ends (Carter had already found himself cast in the role of the jingoistic villain, for example). Perhaps more importantly, the hieroglyphic caveats in the pharaoh's tomb, as well as the pharaoh himself, were yet to be discovered, and Carter's canary had yet to meet the dreaded cobra. However, whispers of curses weren't uncommon in Egypt as magic brick inscriptions issuing warnings to trespassers had already been discovered in other tombs in the Valley of the Kings; the natives quite rightly believed that Tutankhamun's tomb would yield similar threats. For example, the tomb of the Priestess of Hathor, Lady of the Sycamore, Nesysokar, from Giza, bore a curse that stated: 'O anyone who enters this tomb, who will make evil against this tomb: may the crocodile be against him on water and the snake against him on land. May the hippopotamus be against him on water, the scorpion against him on land.' Her husband, Pettety, had a similar curse inscribed in his tomb, except he calls upon the crocodile, lion and hippopotamus to aid in his protection. The tomb of Harkhuf at Aswan, which dates from the Sixth Dynasty, *c.* 2340 BC, was also found to display the warning: 'As for any man who shall enter into this tomb … I will pounce upon him as on a bird; he shall be judged for it by the great god.'

With the British public initially incredulous to such outwardly fanciful stories, in March 1923, just weeks after the opening of Tutankhamun's tomb, their scepticism had all but disappeared. Lord Carnarvon had been bitten on the cheek by a mosquito, and, although the scar was innocuous-looking, the bite soon became infected when he cut it with his shaving razor; within two months of the discovery of King Tut's sarcophagus, Carnarvon succumbed to septicaemia and pneumonia in his suite at the Continental-Savoy Hotel in Cairo. It was believed he uttered the words 'I heard his call and I will follow him. Pharaoh, I am returning to you' just prior to his passing. Shortly before he died, Carnarvon began to suffer from a raging fever during a film screening at an Egyptian cinema, and even in his delirious state he could be heard muttering, 'A bird is scratching on my face'. It was another Egyptian belief that the Nekhabet bird would scratch the face of anybody who dared to disturb the peace and sanctity of the pharaoh's tomb. To many, it seemed uncanny that the benefactor of the excavation, the leader of the dig, should be the first victim of the newly proclaimed 'Curse of the Pharaohs'.

In the weeks preceding his death, Carnarvon's relationship with Carter had become increasingly strained and had turned sour. Although the two men were the complete opposite in every way – Carnarvon was a nonchalant aristocrat and dilettante with vast sums of money – they had enjoyed a healthy and amicable friendship. However, the discovery of Tutankhamun's tomb, which propelled both men to international superstardom, inevitably led to disagreements. Arguments over the distribution of the finds (Carter had urged Carnarvon to renounce any rights to the contents of the tomb in fear of further inflaming Egyptian national feeling) and Carter's brusque handling of the pushy reporters merely aggravated the situation, but it wasn't until Carnarvon's daughter Lady Evelyn arrived on the scene that things took a turn for the worse. She was the apple of her father's eye and he naturally disapproved of Carter's growing affection for her. Carnarvon could see that Carter was an outwardly gauche figure, seemingly without feelings and rather lacking in diplomacy; yet Carnarvon still cared enough for Carter to write him the following note shortly before his death – a clear indication that Carnarvon was willing to make amends: 'I have done many foolish things and I am very sorry. But there is only one thing I want to say to you which I hope you will always remember – whatever your feelings are or will be for me in the future my affection for you will never change.'

Perhaps a note in Carter's diary which read 'Poor Ld. C died during the early hours of the morning' indicates that the two men were able to bury the hatchet before Carnarvon's untimely demise. Either way, his death provided the catalyst for the hysterical reporting in the more sensationalist newspapers that followed. Reporters happily embellished the discovery of the inscription upon the magic brick of the Anubis shrine and the strange coincidence that the mummy of Tutankhamun was found to have a wound on the left cheek. The wound was in the exact same position as the mosquito bite that had led to the death of Lord Carnarvon.

The seeds of the curse of Tutankhamun had been sown. It was even reported that Carnarvon's dog – a three-legged fox terrier named Susie at his family estate at Highclere Castle howled inconsolably and died at the same instant as her master, and that Cairo was simultaneously plunged into darkness following a power cut; its complete electricity supply, four entire grids, failed for a full five minutes at 1.40 a.m., precisely five minutes before Carnarvon passed away. Nobody at the power station knew how to explain the return of electricity after the short breakdown as no one had time to fix the fault; its cause was also unknown and remains so today. As Lord Carnarvon, who was being watched over by his wife, Lady Almina, his daughter and his son, Lord Porchester, breathed his last, the *Daily Express* reported on the incident as follows: 'Suddenly all the lights in Cairo went out leaving them all in complete darkness. After a lapse of a few minutes the lights came back on again, only to go out abruptly. This curious occurrence was interpreted by those anxiously awaiting news as an omen of evil.'

Although power cuts were by no means a rarity throughout Cairo at the time, it is unsurprising that the public began to feel perturbed by the curse, as the relish with which the newspapers reported these coincidental, if somewhat unnerving, events would have led even the most disbelieving to question the very nature of Lord Carnarvon's demise. However, amidst the speculative hearsay, idle conjecture and vengeful reporting that seemed to swamp the front pages, there was some corroboration for the curse from respected and valued sources.

Arthur Weigall, an esteemed reporter and Egyptologist working as a correspondent for the *Daily Mail* (who would himself later become part of curse folklore), wrote of 'the malevolence of Ancient Egyptian spirits' and how he felt 'pity' for the 'ordeal' the mummy faced. He also wrote, in response to dismissive claims about the curse, that '... I must admit that some very strange things – call them coincidences if you will – have happened in connection with the Luxor excavations'. However, on Thursday 25 January 1923, Weigall wrote to Carter from the Winter Palace Hotel in Luxor 'in an attempt to persuade him to defuse the mounting resentment being hurled against him and Lord Carnarvon in the international press. At one point in the lengthy letter – sent with genuine concern from one Egyptologist to another – Weigall stated, quite bluntly':

> The situation is this. You and Lord Carnarvon made the initial error when you discovered the tomb of thinking that the old British prestige in this country is still maintained and that you could do more or less what you liked, just as we all used to in the old days. You have found this tomb, however, at a moment when the least spark may send the whole magazine sky-high, when the utmost diplomacy is needed, when Egyptians have to be considered in a way in which you and I are not accustomed, and when the slightest false step may do the utmost disservice to our own enemy. You opened the tomb before you notified the Government representative, and the natives all say that you may therefore have had the opportunity of stealing some of the millions of pounds' worth of gold of which you talked. (I give this as an instance of native gossip about you.)

Although it should be mentioned that Weigall, who had previously worked as an archaeologist for Theodore Davis, had fallen out with both Carnarvon and Carter over *The Times* deal and, years earlier, over Carnarvon's decision to employ Carter ahead of him, he was too much of a professional to let a personal vendetta tarnish his journalism. Yet there is little doubt that this letter would have exacerbated the already growing resentment between Weigall and Carter. Whatever his true motive for writing it, Carter would have likely dismissed the letter as mere envy, a reaction that may well have contributed towards Weigall's subsequent conduct. 'Much to his own chagrin that he was not allowed into the tomb except with the public', and observing Carnarvon's good humour at the opening of the burial chamber doorway, Weigall was reputed to have commented, 'If he goes down in that spirit, I give him six weeks to live'. Just over six weeks later, Carnarvon was dead. But this was neither Weigall's nor Carnarvon's first brushes with Ancient Egyptian mysticism.

Indeed, there are two interesting vignettes that involved both Weigall and Carnarvon, firstly with their American artist friend, Joseph Lindon Smith, which occurred in 1909 on the west bank of the Valley of the Queens. Weigall and Lindon Smith, along with their wives, devised an ill-fated play that would portray the reincarnation of the heretical pharaoh, Akhenaten, Tutankhamun's father. Weigall, writing about Akhenaten's revolution, cast him as a visionary who had dared to challenge the ancient priesthood, and compared him to Moses.

Performing in a water-formed area of the Valley of the Queens that provided a natural amphitheatre and a suitable locale for the ghostly drama, Lindon Smith took the role of Horus and Hortense Weigall, Arthur's wife, took the role of Akhenaten in front of an invited group of distinguished Egyptologists, a veritable 'who's who' in the field of archaeology, that included Lord Carnarvon, Howard Carter, Theodore Davis and, 'The Father of Egyptology', Flinders Petrie (whose head has been preserved at the Royal College of Surgeons). A four-page invitation to the initial rehearsal had been sent out and cleverly contained supposed ancient documents all leading to one date – the day when the excommunication of Akhenaten would be over and when his ghost would appear for the last time. This fortunately conspired to occur 3,300 years to the day, on 26 January 1909, the date of the intended performance. 'The four pages of excellently worded information also helpfully added that food would be served and the audience could expect to return to their respective dwellings by 9 p.m.'

As they sat down to enjoy the evening's entertainment, with the stated aim of appeasing the ancient god of Amen-Ra and lifting the curse that had condemned Akhenaten to a ceaseless wandering after death, a violent storm suddenly blew up; an actress was blinded by a sudden attack of trachoma, while Weigall's own wife was struck down with a life-threatening stomach condition. Both women later recovered, but numerous others subsequently complained of flu-like illnesses (and even a broken leg) and the play itself had to be abandoned, never to be performed again. The audience prudently tore up their invitations and threw them on to the fire in the hope that they would escape the wrath of Amen-Ra. 'The story quickly became legend, for everyone leapt at the notion that the players had been cursed by the ancient priests of Amon. Soon Weigall found that complete strangers seemed to know all about it: on his way back to Egypt from his summer leave that year, for example, he told Hortense that he heard someone say to his wife, "That man Weigall is on board I see," and then he began to describe our play and how you and Corinna [Lindon Smith's wife] got ill etc etc.'

Not long before this unsettling event took place, Carter and Carnarvon had made a discovery in the Valley of the Kings of a mummified cat, painted black with yellow eyes:

> This was carried to the dig-house and accidentally placed in the bedroom of Arthur Weigall ... When he returned, late at night, the cat's coffin was in the middle of the room; Weigall fell over it, bruising his shin. At the same time,

the butler in the house was stung by a scorpion and, in his delirium, believed he was being pursued by a grey cat. Weigall went to bed, amid the butler's cries, but took some time to fall asleep. Just before he dropped off, he swore the mummified cat turned its head to look at him, with an expression of anger. All the while the butler was screaming about a cat. After Weigall had been asleep for an hour or so, he was awoken by a loud bang, like a gun-shot. As he woke, a grey cat jumped over his bed and out of the window. The cat coffin lay split in two, as if the cat had jumped from within. Weigall went to the window and saw the house's tabby cat on the garden path, glaring into the bushes with an arched back. Weigall – and others in the house with over-active imaginations – believed the grey cat to be a malevolent spirit which had caused him to hurt his shin and the butler to be stung by a scorpion.

Soon the world was, perhaps inevitably, as transfixed by the story of the curse of Tutankhamun as it was by the excavation of his tomb. The *Los Angeles Times* soon chimed in with its own theories on the curse: 'No matter how little superstitious a man may be, the act of breaking the rest so carefully guarded through the centuries must cause an emotion which time can never efface.' The *New York Times* reported: 'Carnarvon's death spreads theories about vengeance; in Egypt, England, France and here, occultists advance stories of angered gods.'

The occultists the paper referred to were none other than the celebrated authors Sir Arthur Conan Doyle and Marie Corelli, both of whom ensured that the story of the curse continued to dominate the front pages. Fanning the flames of public interest the world over, Conan Doyle repeated his opinions in the newspapers that Carnarvon's death could have been a result of 'elementals – not souls, not spirits – created by Tutankhamun's priests to guard the tomb'. Indeed, the story of the curse had all the hallmarks of one of Conan Doyle's classic Sherlock Holmes tales, and it is perhaps interesting to note that Conan Doyle had a proclivity for writing ghost stories which were largely based around Egyptology and Egyptian relics. In *The Ring of Thoth*, first published in the *Cornhill Magazine* in 1890, a young English Egyptologist visits the Louvre and accidentally witnesses a strange and eerie event, and in *Lot No 249*, first published in 1892, an Oxford University student, through the use of Egyptian magic, reanimates an Ancient Egyptian mummy to use as an instrument of revenge.

It is certainly worth mentioning the story of Bertram Fletcher Robinson, a close friend of the London literati, including Conan Doyle and P.G. Wodehouse, who had died mysteriously in 1907. It was widely held that Fletcher Robinson died of typhoid fever, but Conan Doyle never believed this, and in 1923 he began to give interviews to the newspapers declaring that Fletcher Robinson had succumbed to an Ancient Egyptian curse. Fletcher Robinson was an editor for the *Daily Express* and *Vanity Fair*, and, at the time of his death, was studying a coffin lid of a priestess of Amen-Ra at the British Museum in order to write some articles for the paper. In an interview about the cause of his friend's death, Conan Doyle stated:

> It is impossible to say with absolute certainty if this is true. If we had proper occult powers we could determine it, but I warned Fletcher Robinson against concerning himself with the mummy at the British Museum ... I told him he was tempting fate by pursuing his inquiries, but he was fascinated and would not desist. Then he was overtaken by illness. The immediate cause of his death was typhoid fever, but that is the way in which the elementals guarding the mummy might act. They could have guided Mr Robinson into a series of such circumstances as would lead him to contract the disease, and thus cause his death – just as in Lord Carnarvon's case, human illness was the primary cause of death ...

Recent theories have suggested that Fletcher Robinson, who was widely regarded to have inspired the storyline for *The Hound of the Baskervilles*, was poisoned by Conan Doyle who feared he would be exposed as a plagiarist and a fraud. Permission to have Fletcher Robinson's grave exhumed in order to prove this theory was subsequently denied. The case of Fletcher Robinson and the British Museum is discussed in depth in chapter five.

Eminent author Marie Corelli, who vehemently disapproved of the violation of King Tut's tomb, added further credence to the curse by writing the following, which was published in both the London and New York newspapers:

> I cannot but think some risks are run by breaking into the last rest of a king in Egypt whose tomb is specially and solemnly guarded, and robbing him of his possessions. According to a rare book I possess ... entitled The Egyptian History of the Pyramids [an ancient Arabic text] ... *the most dire punishment follows any rash intruder into a sealed tomb.* The book names '*secret poisons enclosed in boxes in such wise that those who touch them shall not know how they come to suffer*'. That is why I ask, was it a mosquito bite that has so seriously infected Lord Carnarvon?

On 24 March 1923, the *Daily Express* reprinted a letter to the *New York World* in which Corelli remarked that she had repeatedly warned Carnarvon of his fate. Under the dramatic headline 'Pharaoh's Guarded by Poisons? Lord Carnarvon Warned by Marie Corelli', she declared that even before his death she had seen the hand of the pharaoh in Carnarvon's illness rather than the mosquito bite, and had written to Carnarvon in an attempt to warn him of the perils he faced in Luxor.

Even the prominent clairvoyant Count Louis Hamon, more famously known as Cheiro (*Ki-ro*), wrote in his book *Real Life Stories* that an Ancient Egyptian sorceress, 'the seventh daughter of the King Akhenaten', Princess Mekitaten (Tutankhamun's sister), had apparently transmitted a warning to him. The warning stated: 'It was to the effect that on his arrival at the tomb of Tutankhamun, [Lord Carnarvon] was not to allow any of the relics found it in to be removed or taken away.' The message concluded by saying that if Carnarvon ignored the warning he would suffer an injury while in the tomb, a sickness from which he would never recover, and that 'death would claim him in Egypt'. It is a point of interest that throughout his vocation as a clairvoyant:

> from the 1890s onwards, [Cheiro] attracted an elite clientele both at his Indian-style salon in London's trendy Bond Street, and while on his travels abroad. The list is mind-boggling, and apparently included, among others, Mark Twain, Sarah Bernhardt, the British statesman Sir Austin Chamberlain, the writer Oscar Wilde and the Dutch dancer and spy Mata Hari, with whom he became a close acquaintance. Sir Ernest Shackleton, the explorer of the Antarctic, went in disguise to his Bond Street address in order to test him, but was told, correctly, that he would not return home from a second expedition. When Field Marshal Horatio, Lord Kitchener, the hero of the Sudan, turned up to see [Cheiro] he was informed that his death would come at sea … As [Cheiro's] reputation as a fortune-teller grew, he was introduced to more and more clients of distinction … Most famous of all his clients was Edward VII, for whom he predicted the exact date of his coronation in August 1902 and subsequent death in 1909.

'The society palmist and "seer" Velma also claimed (in a book published after the event) that Lord Carnarvon had been warned before returning to Luxor for the last time – on this occasion in a private consultation. In *My Mysteries and My Story* he wrote':

> Lord Carnarvon had more than an ordinary interest in the occult. He was keen that I should keep nothing back … 'I see great peril for you,' I told him

[after the consultation]. 'Most probably – as the indications of occult interest are so strong in your hand – it will arise from such a source.'

His interest aroused, he discussed the excavations in the Valley of the Kings. 'Whatever happens,' he said, 'I will see to it that my interest in things occult never gets so strong as to affect either my reason or my health ...'

Not so very long after asking Velma the very reasonable question 'Is it preposterous rot to think of the influence of all these old priests still surviving today?' Lord Carnarvon was dead. Armed with such sensational material, the newspapers continued their mission to spread unbridled rumours about the curse, and were happy to oblige their readership by featuring articles which included the following: 'Those most intimately connected with [the tomb] during the last few months suffered in some way or other. Even the journalists who covered the story have felt the reaction. Three of them have been ill ...'

The press influenced public opinion and how they viewed the Tutankhamun saga to such an extent that even American politicians went so far as to demand a study of mummies to determine whether or not they carried the same medical dangers as those thought to be present in the tomb itself. This brand of coverage was invaluable and gave drama and stimulation to what was once considered a scholar's work, bringing the high-culture event to a mass audience willing to accept what it read. One article from the *New York Times* famously stated:

All the district is [Tutankhamun's] court. There is only one topic of conversation ... One cannot escape the name of Tutankhamun anywhere. It is shouted in the streets, whispered in the hotels, while the local shops advertise Tutankhamun art, Tutankhamun hats, Tutankhamun curios, Tutankhamun photographs, and tomorrow probably genuine Tutankhamun antiquities. Every hotel in Luxor today had something a la Tutankhamun ... There is a Tutankhamun dance tonight at which the piece is to be a Tutankhamun rag.

'The public in the 1920s was fascinated by the mysterious East; it was the decade when Valentino was *The Sheik* and Fairbanks was *The Thief of Baghdad*; when Tutankhamun's tomb was opened and when, throughout the Western world, crop-haired jazz girls daubed their eyelids with Egyptian kohl.' Before long, by the spring of 1923, 'Tutankhamun Ltd' was well established, offering jewellery, skirts, three-piece suits, mummy wraps, gloves and even sandals to eager consumers the world over. It was all freely available, from the most upmarket of outlets, such as Cartier's, to the common street peddler:

Mass-produced accessories and ornaments made of Bakelite and plastic, with hieroglyphic, winged discs, scarab beetles, obelisks, nude goddesses and assorted stepped forms, appeared in the shops next to Tut-related tins, cigarette packets and other ephemera. In 1924 Huntley and Palmer issued a biscuit tin in the shape of a funeral urn, with Ancient Egyptians bearing gifts all around the sides; a rival firm, Dunmore & Sons, preferred a multi-faceted tin with a portrait of a 1920s-looking pharaoh on the lid, for containing mummy-col-oured confectionary. Luxor toilet requisites ('preferred by fastidious women') launched a new advertising slogan: 'Have you, *too*, discovered Luxor?'

On Bond Street and in the Burlington Arcade you could buy handbags covered with hieroglyphics. Meanwhile, the *Daily Express*, on 9 March 1923, excitedly announced 'The Tutankhamun hat has arrived'. It could be viewed at Liberty's off Regent Street, where 'old Egyptian patterns borrowed from the British Museum have been adapted to headgear'. Even the 'Tutankhamun Over-Blouse' was available from Jessette's on Sloane Street. The *New York Times* reported how *Vogue* had added 'Madame Tutankhamun's frocks' to its repertoire of dream and fantasy images, and a month earlier, on 7 February, the newspaper declared that 'businessmen all over the world are pleading for Tutankhamun designs for gloves, sandals and fabrics'. A fortnight later, their headline read 'Egypt Dominates Fashion Show Here – Designs Copied From Luxor – Pictures Decorate Many Suit Models – Prize Wrap Has Hathor – Tomb Vogue Will Prolong Bobbed Hair'. Shortly after this, on 25 February, under the headline 'Tutankhamun Art to Sweep New York – Much Traffic in Name – Trade-mark Is Sought for Hats, Dolls, Toys, Parasols, Jewelry and Cigarettes', 'there was a story about patent lawyers asking the $64,000 question of the moment: "Who owns the name of Tutankhamun?"' 'Apparently, claims for the exclusive commercial use of "Tut, Tut-tut and Two-Tank and other variations" had been filed all over the place.'

However, this zealous reporting by the press would only become more concentrated, especially when George Jay Gould, the illustrious American financier and friend of Lord Carnarvon's, died of pneumonia on 16 May 1923, on the French Riviera. It was widely reported that he had contracted a fever in Egypt following his visit to the tomb of Tutankhamun. Until that moment Gould had been a picture of health as well as a keen and competitive tennis player. Disregarding the diatribe from the press for a moment, it is certainly difficult to ignore the fact that something peculiar was going on in Luxor, and the tomb of King Tut seemed to be at the epicentre of all the singular happenings. Indeed, events would soon take an even stranger and darker turn.

In June 1923, Philip Livingstone Poe, kin of the great horror writer Edgar Allan Poe, died at home in Baltimore shortly after returning from King Tut's tomb and contracting pneumonia. The *New York Times* remarked: 'Ever since the Poes returned from their tour friends have been jokingly warning them of the "mummy's curse". The joking wore off, however, when Mr Poe became ill.' In November, British financier and racing owner Woolf Joel, who was one of the very first members of the public allowed into Tutankhamun's tomb, died mysteriously onboard a boat destined for Egypt after slipping into a coma. Joel, who was only 30 years old at the time of his death, was another seemingly fit and healthy man in the prime of life. In the same month, American society woman Evelyn Waddington Greely, upon her return from the tomb in Luxor, committed suicide at her home in Chicago. Shortly after the curse appeared in London's West End for the first time, renowned British radiologist Sir Archibald Reid, who was responsible for taking X-rays of Tutankhamun's mummy before it was transported to the museum in Cairo, suddenly became ill upon returning to his home in Chur, Switzerland. Another able-bodied man with a seemingly robust constitution, Reid died on 17 January 1924. Just under a month later, Professor Lafleur, a close friend of Howard Carter's and a Molson Professor of English at Montreal's McGill University, was yet another casualty of pneumonia when he succumbed to it in Luxor. It was reported that he had only recently visited the tomb of Tutankhamun himself.

Perhaps one of the most chilling deaths associated with the curse of Tutankhamun occurred just under eight months later when British Egyptologist and lecturer Hugh Evelyn-White, who, after Howard Carter, was one of the first archaeologists to enter Tutankhamun's burial chamber, shot himself in a taxicab in Leeds after being summoned to attend an inquest on the body of Mary Helen Nind. It was reported in the newspapers that Nind, a music teacher, was infatuated with Evelyn-White and took her own life when he rejected her numerous advances. In his suicide note, Evelyn-White wrote the following: 'I knew there was a curse on me, though I have leave to take those manuscripts to Cairo. The monks told me the curse would work all the same. Now it has done so.'

The nature of the manuscripts and the identity of the monks have remained a mystery to this day, although Evelyn-White's reference to Cairo leaves a chilling reminder that some kind of anxiety, no doubt forged in his frequent trips to Egypt, had compelled him to take his own life. It was also rumoured at the time that Evelyn-White had plundered fragments of Egyptian artefacts from a monastery in Egypt and subsequently lived in fear on account of his actions. Three months later, in November 1924, the Sirdar of the Egyptian Army, Sir Lee

Stack, was assassinated in Cairo by a local fanatic shortly after his own visit to Tutankhamun's tomb.

In March 1926, two distinguished French Egyptologists, both of whom examined tombs in the Valley of the Kings, died within a few days of one another. Georges Benedite, a curator at the Louvre, died shortly after visiting the tomb of King Tut in Luxor and was reported to have succumbed to heat stroke in Egypt. His death closely followed that of another great authority on Ancient Egypt, Professor M. Casanova of the College de France. Unsurprisingly, the *New York Times* waded in with its usual grace and gusto when it reported 'Sixth Tomb Hunter Succumbs in Egypt; Dr Mardrus Advances Theory of Strange Force'.

However, amidst the fervent reporting of 'Tutmania', 'the black-bearded, sinister' Dr Joseph-Charles Mardrus, translator of *The Arabian Nights* and erudite scholar and doctor, who pointed out that 'he was neither an occultist nor a spiritualist and made no claims to prophetic gifts', offered further corroboration plus lengthy and significant credibility to the curse when he was quoted in the article:

I am, unfortunately, not at all surprised at the sad death of Professor Benedite. About the same time as he there died another no less prominent savant, M. Casanova, who also occupied himself with excavations in the Valley of the Kings, passed away. They continue the list of which I wrote about two years ago. Since the opening of the tomb of Tutankhamun a number of dramatic events have occurred which I foresaw and announced one month previously in a newspaper.

The mysterious series of deaths commenced with that of Lord Carnarvon and was followed by those of George J. Gould, Woolf Joel and Sir Archibald Douglas Reid, all of whom succumbed to an inexplicable malady. This is no childish superstition which can be dismissed with a shrug of the shoulder. We must remember that the Egyptians during a period of 7,000 years in order to assure the calm of subterranean existence which was supposed to delight their mummies and prevent all attempts to disturb their rest, practiced magic rites the power of which held no doubts for them. I am absolutely convinced that they knew how to concentrate upon and around a mummy certain dynamic powers of which we possess very incomplete notions.

Remember the ark which the Jews dragged along on their flight from Egypt? They had stolen it from an Egyptian temple and it was no other than the ark of the god Amon. Now, according to the Bible's own version, that ark struck down hundreds of priests and Levites who dared to approach it too closely. It must surely have been charged with an accumulation of forces unknown to us today.

It is a deep mystery, which it is all too easy to dismiss by skepticism.

Further intrigue was aroused when the English archaeologist Arthur Mace, who had greatly assisted in the opening of Tutankhamun's tomb and in removing the last stone blocking the entrance to the burial chamber, began to complain of persistent tiredness and fatigue. Shortly after leaving Egypt and returning to his home in Haywards Heath, Mace became bedridden before falling seriously ill; he died in July 1928. It should be mentioned that although Mace, who co-wrote *The Tomb of Tutankhamun* with Howard Carter in 1923, had been suffering from deteriorating health since his departure from Egypt, his death struck a chord with those seeking to substantiate the gravity of the curse as he was an integral member of Carter's team, as well as the Metropolitan Museum's conservationist. Though not as unsettling or perhaps as baffling as the earlier cases, to this day Mace's death is still considered to be an important part of the curse folklore.

As an introduction to the curse, these mystifying cases, which took place indiscriminately across the globe over a period of several years, provide one with a fascinating preface and a link to a more chilling and astonishing story. However, this story would be inexplicably confined to a single district within a city – a city that had embarked on an incredible social resurgence; a city that had only just woken from a previous nightmare: London, and its West End.

2

Golden Twenties and Bright Young Things

The Bright Young People came popping all together, out of someone's electric brougham like a litter of pigs, and ran squealing up the steps. Some 'gatecrashers' who had made the mistake of coming in Victorian fancy dress were detected and repulsed. They hurried home to change for a second assault. No one wanted to miss Mrs Ape's début.

Evelyn Waugh, *Vile Bodies*

The 1920s – or the 'Golden Twenties' as they are now more famously known – marked a renaissance for London and Londoners. Once the country had come to terms with the tragic loss of a young generation through bitter conflict, London, much like the proverbial phoenix rising from the ashes, emerged from the First World War greater, stronger, brighter and more willing to face the prospect of the future. Perhaps born of the relief of peacetime, there seemed an atmosphere of tolerance which initially encouraged a period of social, artistic and cultural vigour. As a direct result of the war, there was also a renewed interest in both spiritualism and occultism: both movements offered channels through which the bereaved might communicate with their loved ones in the afterlife. Around this same time, an intense appetite for news about the latest archaeological discoveries that were being made in Egypt was similarly widespread.

Although the legacy of war had bestowed social upheaval and record-breaking levels of inflation upon the city, once London had re-lit its many neon lights it fully embraced the new inventions and discoveries of huge importance, the radical changes in lifestyle, the unparalleled industrial growth and the accelerated consumer demand and aspirations that had arisen. From a social perspective, the extravagant 1920s club scene that evolved from its comparatively rigid Edwardian predecessor is perhaps one of the most endearing and legendary legacies of this bygone age. Indeed, it was truly a worthy stage for the dramas that would soon unfold upon it.

In 1914, Chancellor of the Exchequer David Lloyd George, alarmed that civilian drunkenness was hampering the war effort on the Home Front, famously stated that Britain was 'fighting the Germans, Austrians and drink, and as far as I can see the greatest of these foes is drink'. The House of Commons soon passed, without debate, the Defence of the Realm Act (DORA) in an effort to curtail the escalating problem of alcoholism – a problem that interestingly mirrors a more contemporary social scene. In broader terms, DORA proved to be an opportunistic piece of legislation as it allowed the police the freedom to stop and search suspect individuals (indicative of the rampant spy peril within the British Isles at the time) or to imprison them if they refused; it also permitted press censorship and milk price control, and handed out the death penalty to both service personnel and civilians who were caught fraternising or colluding with the enemy. In social terms, it was the pub drinkers who were the hardest hit by the new legislation, which limited pub opening times and, perhaps more heinously, ordered beer to be watered down. DORA was designed to make the pub-going experience as insipid as possible, and before long it had achieved its desired effect. By the time 'treating' (buying a drink at the bar for someone else) became a criminal offence, the stifling effect of DORA on the city's nightlife was in full force.

Although DORA survived the war and the Edwardian era, many nightclub owners, shrewdly observing that a hardcore drinking culture was re-emerging and being driven 'underground', were tempted to break the inflexible and tyrannical regulations that were still imposed upon the city's young party-goers. While the United States was in the grip of prohibition, in 1921 an opportunity arose when the British government passed a negligible Licensing Act that merely extended pub opening times to eight or nine hours on weekdays and Saturdays, depending on location, and five hours on Sundays. With the new legislation principally retaining the strict and dogmatic nature of DORA, the club owners made a move to exploit the government's slender amendment to the drinking laws and the brazen fact that there was plenty of money to be made from a new generation of revellers. Many of these revellers were young, rich and aristocratic socialites, desperate to break the oppressive shackles imposed upon them by a government they felt was running the country as if it were still fighting a war. Nineteen million young men had died in a seemingly pointless conflict and, when the war ended, there was a desire to see the bringing down of the old order that had created such misery and destruction. Inevitably, drugs, alcohol, clubs, sex and vice became foremost themes throughout the 1920s, and they soon found a comfortable and familiar home in London's West End.

As Howard Carter was busy pillaging the tombs in the Valley of the Kings, the Soho nightclub scene began to flourish, and with it London's nightlife started to transform. As improved transport links from the growing number of suburbs drew vast crowds of pleasure seekers of both sexes to central London, the frenetic West End soon became thronged by fun lovers. The eclectic decors and interiors of the new clubs were more than matched by their eccentric staff, their bohemian clientele and a diverse new music scene that thrived in the cosmopolitan climate. This was to the despair of many who believed England's capital city should retain a display of regularity and restraint – but they were in the overwhelming minority.

Dalton Murray's the Morgue in Ham Yard had a receptionist dressed up as a nun, doormen and waiters dressed as devils complete with elaborate make-up, coffins as tables and skeleton lamps hanging from the ceiling; the Blue Peter in Great Windmill Street was decked out like a battleship; the Riviera Club, 'Venetian in its beauty', overlooked the Thames from its elegant rooms in Grosvenor Road; the Bull Frog Club had electric lighting that shone through oiled silk and waiters dressed up as Mexican bandits; the Cave of Harmony in Gower Street, opened by the actress Elsa Lanchester, was a lavishly bohemian affair; the Gargoyle in an alley off Dean Street had a roof-top dance floor that was garlanded by Christmas trees in pots, neighbouring chimneys painted in red and tables with frosted-glass tops lit from underneath; Ciro's had a luxurious glass dance floor; the Lambs Club had a dance floor above Leicester Square tube station; the Kit-Cat Club, 'the very stadium of nightclubs', in the Haymarket had the largest dance floor (for 400 people) and the most expensive cabaret shows: 'Everything is on the big scale. It is the dance club most favoured by Americans visiting London'; the Hell Club in Gerrard Street had a unique and novel lighting system that changed colour slowly; Scottish entrepreneur Tom Gordon's London Club off Baker Street had over 10,000 members and forty tables inside; and Irish businesswoman Kate Meyrick's Silver Slipper in Regent Street had a famous glass dance floor, copied from clubs in Paris and Rotterdam, that was illuminated by hundreds of different coloured rippling lights which gave the effect of sea waves.

With beautiful and beguiling dance hostesses always the main attractions, these clubs, many of them art deco or neo-byzantine, 'were grand affairs, afforded only by the middle and upper classes'. Often frequented by the rich and famous, their guest lists included the likes of HRH the Prince of Wales – before he became the ill-fated Edward VIII – who was known to visit the Café de Paris in Coventry Street at least three times a week and the Embassy Club in Old

Bond Street on Thursdays (where he would recline on his own sofa); Edwina and Dickie Mountbatten, who spent most evenings at a nightclub, revue, play or dinner, often a combination of the four; the Duke of Kent, Noël Coward, Arnold Bennett, Billy Leeds, Sophie Tucker, Rudolph Valentino, Lady Diana Manners, Georges Carpentier and Hermione Baddeley. Before long there were clubs that catered for all walks of life: the Caravan Club, run by Jack 'Ironfoot' Neave, and the 50/50 club, run by gay matinee idol Ivor Novello, were for homosexuals; Café de Madrid, the Trident Club, Sovrani's Club, Florida Club off Brook Street, Cosmo Club in Wardour Street and the Ambassador Club in Conduit Street were for music lovers; and the Big Apple in Gerrard Street, Grafton Galleries and a notorious den known, rather perceptibly, as Black Man's Place near Tottenham Court Road were clubs for black men.

Prominent bands from across the globe, including acclaimed American jazz bands such as the world-famous Paul Whiteman's, Paul Specht's and Hal Kemp's, attracted by London's ever-increasing glitz and glamour, soon arrived in their droves; many of the musicians were black Americans who brought with them across the Atlantic the chic jazz music scene that had so famously made its mark upon New York's 'Roaring Twenties'. However, an undercurrent of racism arrived with them and the references to 'black' people in the British press make dismal reading today. 'BLACK DEVILS AND WHITE GIRLS', headlined *John Bull* magazine in the autumn of 1923, alleging that 'coloured men are still lurking in our cities, living depraved lives on the immoral earnings of the white girls they have lured to their betrayal'. Another police raid was reported as 'COLOURED MAN'S CLUB … Black men and white girls mingling in a bacchanalian setting'. In London, these 'degenerate negroes' lived in the streets off Tottenham Court Road and the eastern end of Shaftesbury Avenue, areas 'honeycombed with black men's nightclubs and thieving lodging houses … They run gambling houses, they trade in dope, they spread disease …'

Sadly, this vulgar display of racism was by no means confined to *John Bull*. Many other newspapers carried regular features which told of 'Negro haunts of crime … hotbeds of evil' and 'Negro orgies', usually linked with drug-taking and prostitution, sometimes adding, for good measure, that an accused black man was 'a member of a jazz band'. Reports of 'flashily-dressed, bejewelled negroes', the men, who, as a shocked *Daily Mail* correspondent reported in September, were found to be provocatively dancing with white women at nightclubs, fanned the flames of racial unrest within the city.

Indeed, the same sour attitudes prevailed in America, and an article in the American magazine *Tatler* described the atmosphere in New York before it descended upon London:

It's women, women everywhere; and, as Mr George Robey would say, ber-lieve me – berlieve me not, but it's mighty few of them are looking very war-torn. On the contrary, as everyone who runs has read, never have there been such weeks as these of Armistice for the doing of all those things it is pre-eminently feminine to do – dancing, shopping, love-making, marrying, sight-seeing, theatring, and the rest.

They say the night clubs are opening up in rows, and dressmakers say they're dizzy with the orders for dance frocks that keep on pourin' in. And they just can't have enough niggers to play jazz music, and I hear are thinkin' of hiring out squads of 'loonies' to make the mad jazz noises till there are more ships 'vailable to bring the best New York black jazz 'musicians' over.

Stirring up the craze for 'jazz-ragging' and 'dinner-dancing', these musicians found regular success in many of London's clubs and venues, most notably at the Nest in Kingley Street, where one could see 'all the famous coloured stars', and Rectors in Tottenham Court Road. But it was not to everyone's liking, as the following article in *The Observer* famously demonstrated: 'Crude and vulgar, it is performed by niggers to the accompaniment of two or three banjoists and a drummer, whose chief business is to make noises. In fact, the dance has been defined as "a number of niggers surrounded by noise."'

Meanwhile, apart from reputable places like the Embassy and the Kit-Kat, there was a rash of dubious clubs and later bottle parties which particularly attracted the younger set despite their exorbitant prices for liquor and 'cover-charges'. Mrs Kate 'Ma' Meyrick, always dressed in demure black – 'I'm the mother-in-law of two peers, dear' – was driven time and again in her limousine from her notorious 43 Club in Gerrard Street to the dock at Marlborough Street.

Indeed, the haughty Meyrick's iniquitous 43 Club, previously known as Proctors, whose early patrons included the ill-fated Lord Loughborough and 'Dandy' Beauchamps, Prince Christopher of Greece, J.B. Priestley, Augustus John, Jacob Epstein, Joseph Conrad and the novelist Evelyn Waugh, was another club that embraced such 'noise'. Although it was Waugh who immortalised Meyrick as the character of Ma Mayfield in *Brideshead Revisited*, it was his book *Vile Bodies* that provided *the* biography of the age, and he accurately dramatised the hedonistic antics and lifestyles of the Bright Young Things – an extraordinary band of pleasure-seeking bohemian party-goers and blue-blooded socialites – who romped their way through the newspaper gossip columns of the 1920s. His work is fairly typical of his class and era, portraying a way of life and ethos of clubland snobbery that gives an insight into the values of the time, good and bad. Thus the Bright Young Things Waugh drew inspiration from 'drank far more than was good for them, tore about town in bright-coloured sports cars and even brighter-coloured clothes, played absurd and sometimes unkind practical jokes, indulged in riotous parties, as well as in promiscuous sex, and generally made nuisances of themselves'.

> Waugh's novels evoked the zeitgeist of the 1920s and 30s. The outrageous behaviour of his 'Bright Young Things', their endless parties, the fast cars, the outlandish absinthe cocktails – all of these point to an absolute determination to put the misery of the war behind them and to make up for lost time. Hence the almost hysterical gaiety, fuelled by desperation and cynicism. In the frantic desire to forget death and celebrate life, the cocktail played an important role. The cocktail was new and everything new from the Picasso to the automobile was embraced with enthusiasm. The cocktail celebrated the modern and the urbane. It was sophisticated and fun: to drink it was to identify with the young and the fashionable, an image that the cocktail has retained to this day.

The Bright Young Things included Oxford alumni Anthony Powell, Robert Byron, Henry Green and John Betjeman, who, much like Waugh, would achieve great success as writers themselves, and precocious young society women such as Elizabeth Ponsonby, Barbara Ker-Seymer and the morphine-addicted actress Brenda Dean Paul.

Alongside the London nightclubs, many of the West End's hotels and restaurants, still renowned for their pre-war decadence and their house bands and lively music, also provided the milieu for this generation and the darlings of the stage as they were discreet venues in which the fly-by-nighters could partake in their frivolous activities and debaucheries. Furthermore, hotels and restaurants were allowed the 'theatre-supper clause', a piece of legislation that provided the 'Supper Hour Certificate', whereby the well-to-do were granted an hour's extra drinking time by paying for the meal that was a legally required accompaniment to the liquor; as was so often the case in England at the time, a class distinction had crept into law-making and 'the patronage of wealthy and fashionable people helped to deter efforts by those in authority to suppress them'. The Metropole had been one of the first hotels to take advantage of this new clause, but, inevitably, others soon followed suit, and by 1923 a majority of the great hotels and restaurants provided dinner-dance facilities that competed for business with the neighbouring nightclubs.

In Mayfair was Claridge's and the Cavendish Hotel (Shepheard's Hotel in *Vile Bodies*); in the Strand was the Savoy (where one could sample a famous Harry

Craddock cocktail in the American Bar), the Strand Palace Hotel (which included the renowned Winter Garden) and the Hotel Cecil and Simpson's and Romano's restaurants; in Aldwych was the Waldorf Hotel; in Piccadilly was the Ritz, the Piccadilly, Prince's and the Berkeley hotels and the Criterion, the Trocadero and the Monico restaurants; in the newly designed and sumptuous Regent Street (which largely symbolised the West End's transformation with its influx of department stores such as Liberty's) was the Café Royal – 'London's Fairyland' according to John Betjeman – and Verrey's Restaurant; and in Soho was the opulent Kettner's, made famous for being Oscar Wilde's old stomping ground.

As the technological wonder of the moving picture grew in popularity in the 1920s, London soon began to embrace the transition from stage to screen when several West End theatres were transformed into cinemas complete with resplendent neon glow. Making their own mark upon London's nightlife, these venues provided unlikely settings for further gaiety.

Interwar cinemas were typically called Odeon, Gaumont and Astoria, though some proprietors, hoping to foster a feeling of opulence, favoured Ritz, Regal, Rex, Paramount, Essoldo, Embassy and Ambassador. Inside the decor was carefully calculated to suggest a smart, modernist ambience by means of the art-deco style, or to create an exotic illusion by using Mexican motifs, the Spanish hacienda style or, more suitably, Egyptian temple decoration.

Indeed, while the *Daily Mail* was busy exclaiming 'The 1923 Season has begun!', it was Carter and Carnarvon's famous discovery in the Valley of the Kings in the same year that largely inspired the latter, and pictures of their famous discovery would frequently appear in the newsreel footage at the cinemas they had directly inspired the design of:

Cinemas, such as, in the London area alone, the Kensington Cinema (1926), the Carlton, Upton Park (1929), the Luxor, Twickenham (1929), the Astoria, Streatham (1930), and the Carlton, Essex Road (1930), were built with temple façades or 'daring Egyptian decorative schemes' within. A hastily concocted film (now lost) called *Tutankhamun's Eighth Wife* was released, and, in the *Sketch Magazine*, the irrepressible cartoon dog Bonzo appeared in a special coloured portrait by George E. Studdy showing his surprised reaction to a row of mummified cats in a glass case (actually the British Museum's collection).

The Tivoli cinema on the Strand, which was previously a theatre, was one cinema of choice for hoi polloi, and the old Empire Music Hall in Leicester

Square, which was acquired by MGM in the 1920s, became another when it was reopened in 1928 as the largest cinema in London with over 3,000 seats complete with a lavish interior on a High Renaissance theme. American comedies and 'atmospherics' arrived along with their actor stars. Tallulah Bankhead, Elsa Lanchester and Fred and Adele Astaire all added their celebrity to the West End's glittering appeal. Unlike theatres, purpose-built cinemas could flourish in the suburbs, and audiences could also be attracted into the West End by the thought of the luxurious 'super-cinema' which put everything else in the shade for exuberant extravagance. The 2,400-seater at Marble Arch, for example, was opened in November 1928 to amazement at its 'fairyland interiors with glades of autumnal trees, Roman temples and starlit skies, and Europe's largest theatre organ and a carillon of bells'. By 1928, there were 250 cinemas in London, twenty-five of which were within a mile of Charing Cross, and fourteen within a quarter of a mile of Leicester Square. A poster for the London Underground famously claimed that: 'The Cinema is the Londoner's most accessible form of entertainment. Yet, to be in the swim and greet the latest films, the enthusiast must visit the central cinemas.'

The 1920s West End was also famous for the café culture that originated in Soho and soon engulfed the entire district. A radical departure from the lavish cinemas, hotels, restaurants and clubs, the London cafés were comparatively modest, and it was these more intimate versions that began to make an impact on London culture. The predominantly young clientele were fiercely loyal to their own cafés, spawning an atmosphere within them akin to that belonging to a members-only club. Much of London's fashion seemed to stem from the cafés rather than the pubs, especially when they were taken over by the smart and exotic Italian and Cypriot families in the 1920s. The penny-in-the-slot gramophones and the 'mahogany-coloured horseshoe or lemon-shaped bar' behind which coffee, tea and cake were dispensed provided further elegance for the faithful customers. The cafés would often close late, around 2 a.m., and disregarding the priggish licensing laws was easier for the smaller premises; this presented further attraction to the young as it provided them with somewhere to visit after the cinemas had closed for the evening.

However, it was Kate Meyrick's flotilla of clubs – which also encompassed the Cat Burglar's, the Bunch of Keys and the Manhattan (opened in Denman Street in 1925) – that were arguably the most infamous venues in 1920s London and hold lasting notoriety. Meyrick, who was something of a celebrity herself for her ingenuity in evading the licensing laws, was an unlikely nightclub entrepreneur who had entered the business when her husband left her with two sons at Harrow and four daughters at Roedean to support. The self-proclaimed

'Queen of Clubland', Meyrick's nightclubs famously attracted infamous gang-sters and criminals from around the world; in the 43 Club, for example, 'the underworld and the aristocracy met on equal terms, free-spending burglars like "Ruby" Sparks mingling with the owners of the jewels and furs from whom they stole'. 'This was the crossroads of London society where the rich and feckless met the criminal and reckless, a place of seamy, raucous glamour.' The 43 Club famously included a secret exit at the back of the premises through a courtyard which led to a shop, and was kept unlocked at all times as an escape route from police raids. 'This may have saved the faces of some of London's politicians and aristocracy who loved to mix with the underworld.'

> [Meyrick] was by no means a conventional Irish beauty. A stern rather dumpy little woman, Kate Meyrick is said to have run her flagship the 43 Club in Gerrard Street (where centuries earlier Dryden had lived) with a rod of iron, expelling Darby Sabini's men, Billy Kimber's Elephant Boys (from the Elephant and Castle) and rowdy Oxbridge undergraduates with the same aplomb.

Confidante to millionaire playboys, showgirls, sportsmen, exiled kings and notorious murderers, all of whom frequently passed through the doors of her clubs, Meyrick would soon become hounded by the police and pilloried by the press and public when a young dance hostess at the 43 Club, Freda Kempton, died of a drug overdose in 1923. Displaying the darker and seedier side of the 1920s West End, as well as the stark vulnerability that lurked beneath the glit-tering surface of the high life, the deeds of the shadowy figures that graced the 43 Club remind one of the often tragic costs of hedonism. Around them, in the streets off Shaftesbury Avenue, the Strand and in Leicester Square, swirled a raffish group of seedy and rebellious profligates seeking the ultimate high. Thus the drug problem was born, amid a surge of extravagant tabloid detail.

Indeed, Kempton's death recalled the tragic and scandalous case of the tal-ented young actress Billie Carleton, who, only five years earlier, was the first woman to expose the lurid and problematic relationship between high soci-ety and rampant drug use in London's West End. Described as being 'a young girl of flower-like beauty, delicate charm and great intelligence' and 'the very essence of girlhood', Carleton died of a drug overdose in her apartment at Savoy Court Mansions, an annexe of self-contained apartments behind the Savoy Hotel. Lauded for her beautiful looks, Carleton worked her way up from unknown chorus girl to illustrious leading lady, and her rise to fame and for-tune was meteoric at a time when many other performers' careers took severe downturns in the aftermath of the war.

However, there was a darker side to her new lifestyle that became increasingly evident as her career progressed. Coinciding with her falling in with the notorious bohemian crowd, frequent rumours of Carleton's drug use began to damage both her personal and professional reputations. Chief among the bad influences was Raoul Reginald (Reggie) de Veulle, a member of the bohemian set in London and New York and a hardened cocaine user. De Veulle first met Carleton when he was working at Hockley's, a Bond Street costumier with a theatrical clientele, where he was designing and making flamboyant dresses that required a model to show them off. With Carleton, who was an unknown chorus girl at the time, desperate to be noticed among the hordes of attractive young actresses vying for the same parts, it made perfect sense for her to model de Veulle's extravagant and eye-catching designs. Before long, and owing in no small part to de Veulle's impact upon her career, Carleton became the youngest leading lady in the West End. Friendship inevitably developed between the two of them, although the theatre and lavish costumes were not their only common interests.

Carleton was introduced to opium in 1915, and to have started on such a potent drug placed her firmly and favourably in the eyes of the drug underworld. Her initial success on stage was as a comedy actress, and a critic at the *Tatler* observed: 'She has cleverness, temperament and charm.' At first her raging drug habit didn't appear to affect her performances; however, by the time Carleton became addicted to cocaine as well as opium there was a marked deterioration in her appearance. Between *The Boy*, based on a Pinero farce, and *Freedom of the Seas*, a play by Walter Hackett, the photographs seem to show her changing from one woman into another, and by 1918 her life had become a bottomless pit of darkness, despair and depression. Failed relationships, 'disgusting orgies', frequent opium parties and worsening reviews set in train Billie Carleton's final drama. On 27 November 1918, Carleton travelled the short distance from her apartment to the Haymarket theatre off Piccadilly, where she was appearing in the evening performance of *Freedom of the Seas*. Shortly after the show had finished, she travelled with friends to the Victory Ball at the Royal Albert Hall, having already commissioned de Veulle to create her a 'wonderful frock' for the occasion. Knowing that there would be a dearth of alcohol at the Ball, de Veulle and Carleton had made preparations to purchase cocaine in advance, and by the time she had returned home from the Ball in the early hours of the morning, Carleton was very much the worse for wear. Her maid, May Booker, arrived to begin work at half past eleven. Hearing loud snoring emanating from Carleton's room, Booker, fully aware of Carleton's nocturnal habits, deemed it best to let her sleep. When the snoring stopped at half past three, Booker entered Carleton's bedroom to try to wake her. But she was already dead.

The parallels between Billie Carleton's death and Freda Kempton's were strikingly similar. In Kempton's case, the exotic, foreign drug-pusher exerting his bad influence on a glittering career was a Chinese businessman and restaurant proprietor known, rather eccentrically, as Brilliant (Billy) Chang. Operating out of bases in both his disreputable Regent Street restaurant and the Limehouse opium dens, Chang, who had initially met Kempton at Meyrick's 43 Club, was a unique figure in the underworld of London's West End, and was often referred to as 'The Dope King'. In her book *Secrets of the 43 Club*, Meyrick described Chang thus: 'One of the most unscrupulous characters of post-war London. His snake like eyes and powerful personality used to fascinate nearly all of the women he met – and all too often led to their downfall.' Her dislike for the glib and gruesome Chang was no doubt born of his decision to sell his restaurant and become a partner in the Palm Court Club on Gerrard Street. Much to Meyrick's fear, it was a move that would prove to intensify the unwanted attentions of the police on her neighbouring 43 Club.

Similar to aspiring actresses, Meyrick's dance hostesses' fortunes largely depended on their attractiveness, charisma and fortitude. It was a prerequisite to dance all night and attract male attention, and be charming as long as they were awake. Kempton had her own unique way of getting noticed – her unusual, eccentric dancing style. Following her death, a correspondent for the *Evening News* remarked: 'Freda was a clever dancer, though personally I used to think her steps of an exaggerated type. She was always full of energy, even at four or five in the morning she would still be dancing and showing very few signs of fatigue.'

It was entirely obvious what fuelled her remarkable stamina. Cocaine was integral to the lifestyle of an energetic and enigmatic dance hostess, much in the same way it provided actresses and prostitutes with similar endurance. Fulfilling the necessary requirements of a Meyrick foot soldier, Kempton 'used to chew gum to mask the involuntary tooth-grinding the drug induced'. Unlucky in love, despite her engagement to a successful Mancunian businessman, and suffering from depression following her witnessing a suicide (which would have no doubt been exacerbated by the frequent cocaine come-downs), Kempton's life would take a fateful turn for the worse the moment she became acquainted with Brilliant Chang. At his Chinese restaurant at 107 Regent Street, Chang plied Kempton with port and cocaine. A few nights later, on 5 March 1922, and after a wanton day of drinking and dining at the 43 Club, Kempton, Chang and friends finished their evening with whiskies at the Regent Street restaurant. Here, according to witnesses, Chang gave Kempton a little blue bottle of powder. 'Can you die while sniffing powder?' Kempton asked. 'No, the only way you can kill yourself is by putting cocaine in water,' Chang replied. It was in the taxi on the way back to her apartment that Kempton threatened to drink the cocaine. She was dead the following morning.

With the tragic Carleton case still fresh in the public's imagination, Chang and Meyrick were subsequently vilified by the press, the public and the politicians. During the inquest into Kempton's death, Chang was portrayed as a man with a magnetic attraction to white women, one newspaper writing: 'Some of the girls rushed to Chang, patted his back, and one, more daring than the rest, fondled the Chinaman's black, smooth hair and passed her fingers slowly through it.' While Chang was eventually convicted of drug trafficking and was deported in 1924, police raids on Meyrick's clubs increased in frequency, and the New Follies (previously Folies Bergère) came under particular scrutiny from the police in the wake of Kempton's death. Indeed, *The People* newspaper branded Meyrick as 'one of the most dangerous women in London'.

By 1925, London boasted 11,000 nightclubs, and it wasn't until the reign of the puritanical Home Secretary Sir William Joynson-Hicks (known dismissively as 'Jix' to the Bright Young Things), when he vowed to take things in hand by denouncing the clubs as 'a blot on the life of London', that the tide of fortune began to turn against the shrewd nightclub owners. This sudden and unwanted public and police scrutiny would last for the rest of Meyrick's career, the downturn of which occurred in 1927 when the Silver Slipper Club was raided by the police on Christmas Eve whilst the patrons were performing a Cossack dance. The following March the Silver Slipper closed its doors for the final time, and in May the Manhattan suffered a similar fate after yet another police raid – leaving Meyrick with only her original 43 Club to show for her empire. Before long, and despite previously being in collusion with high-ranking officers in the Metropolitan Police, the 'Queen of Clubland' had been dethroned, and with her the seemingly indestructible 'Golden Twenties' made way for another decade of decadence, this time featuring different characters and different venues.

It is perhaps interesting to note that the New Follies was often frequented by Woolf Joel, victim number three of the Tutankhamun curse, when he was staying in London. Meyrick described him in her book, *Secrets of the 43 Club*, as 'a curiously unromantic little fellow'. Indeed, in the same book, Meyrick details a fascinating conversation she had in the 43 Club with King Fuad of Egypt about the recent excavation of Tutankhamun's tomb in Luxor: 'Ah yes,' he said solemnly, 'it is all very wonderful of course, but I tell you it is ill work. The dead must not be disturbed. Only evil can come of it. Those who desecrate the resting-places of the ancient dead do so at their own great peril. You will see.'

Within weeks of this grim prophecy, Lord Carnarvon had died in Cairo and the great storm had descended upon London.

3

Prince of Darkness

The Savoy really is history and we have come to feel this as an asset, not
something to be discarded.

Sir Hugh Wontner

On Tuesday 10 July 1923, the *Daily Telegraph* reported on one of the worst storms
that London – and in particular its West End – had endured for many years:

The outbreak appeared to travel from the direction of Kingston and
Richmond. Soon afterwards the storm reached London itself, and broke with
all its fury at a time when, luckily, most of the theatre-goers had been able to
reach their homes in safety. The lightening was vivid to a degree. For over two
hours the sky was illuminated by brilliant, continuous flashes that gave the
buildings an eerie appearance, and at least once what seemed to be a gigantic
fireball broke into a million fragments of dazzling fiery sparks. Equally dramatic were the heavy crashes of thunder which grew in a mighty crescendo,
intense and majestic, and then into a diminuendo as the storm swept irresistibly over the city. The storm followed a day of almost tropical heat.

Moreover, *The Times* remarked that the storm was 'one of the most remarkable
and spectacular [thunderstorms] seen in London for many years … a journey through the streets of London between 1.00 and 5.00 a.m. was a thrilling
experience'; to the *Daily Mail* it was 'the greatest thunderstorm by far in this
country that living man can remember'. And at the Star and Garter Home in

Richmond, many of the resident ex-servicemen, 'still traumatised by the horror of the trenches, were reported to have been severely disturbed by the noise of thunder and the brilliant flashes of lightning, a cruel reminder of the Great War'.

Unbeknown to the writers of these articles, the raging storm would provide a suitably fitting and foreboding milieu to the shocking events that were about to take place within the Savoy Hotel on the Strand – the second hotel in the international Savoy chain to play host to a death attributed to the curse of Tutankhamun after Lord Carnarvon died in the Continental-Savoy in Cairo. For the Savoy, 1923 had already been something of a marquee year; the hotel had already welcomed the likes of Fred and Adele Astaire, who famously danced on its roof, the golfer Walter Hagen, who struck golf balls from the roof into the Thames, and the opera singer Luisa Tetrazzini. And, most dramatically, it would soon host 23-year-old Ali Kamel Fahmy Bey, a wealthy Egyptian prince (having bought his title) and a leading society figure in the Egyptian court of King Fuad, along with his French wife, Marie-Marguerite, who had recently arrived in London. Having travelled the relatively short distance from Paris, the newlyweds had earlier visited the tomb of Tutankhamun in Luxor not once but twice during their honeymoon. At 32 years of age, Marie-Marguerite was markedly older than her husband and had a young daughter, Raymonde, from a previous marriage, who was being educated in London. Understandably eager to provide for her daughter, Marie-Marguerite reluctantly agreed to become a Muslim so that her husband could claim his considerable inheritance. With the lure of Fahmy Bey's fortune too great for Marie-Marguerite to resist, the couple were married on 26 December 1922. Sadly and tragically, it was to be an unhappy marriage fraught with violence and abuse.

To begin with, however, their relationship had been one of happiness, excitement and spontaneity. Having met in Egypt while on holiday with friends, Marie-Marguerite was introduced to Fahmy Bey, and, although he was nine years her junior, he was instantly captivated by her sophistication and dignified carriage. 'Tell her,' he announced to one particular party host, 'that I will arrange a *fête Vénitienne* on my yacht in her honour.' As a spectacularly wealthy and highly presentable young bachelor, Fahmy Bey was every inch the international playboy. 'So it was with a mixture of piqued vanity and puzzlement that he learned that Marie-Marguerite had declined his offer of a party in her honour.' Refusing to take no for an answer, Fahmy Bey decided to travel to Paris – where Marie-Marguerite worked as an escort for rich European and American dignitaries – where he sought, unsuccessfully at first, to be introduced again. Eventually Fahmy Bey managed to get a message to her, and a rendezvous was arranged for tea in the lounge of the Majestic Hotel on 30 July 1922. This time Fahmy Bey would sweep Marie-Marguerite off her feet and a fairytale courtship ensued. In September, Marie-Marguerite agreed to spend a week with Fahmy Bey in Biarritz. 'For eight days in that wonderful resort he was so affectionate that I felt my whole being suffused with a sort of radiant sympathy towards him … Nothing was too good, too beautiful, or too dear for me. Cartier's was ransacked for the latest creation in jewellery, and [Fahmy Bey] chose and gave me a really beautiful bracelet of corals and emeralds.'

In November, Marie-Marguerite finally yielded to Fahmy Bey's pleas and agreed to join him in Egypt, where, on 26 December, the couple were married in Cairo. Among those at their wedding was Lord Carnarvon, a close friend of the Fahmy family. However, the wedding wrought a transformation in the young prince. The ardent, doting – almost reverential – suitor became an abusive, domineering tyrant, who seemed to take pleasure from publically degrading his new bride in front of his retinue of aides and servants. In mid-January, Fahmy Bey wrote a taunting missive to Marie-Marguerite's sister, Yvonne Alibert, announcing that he was 'training her … ha, ha, ha … Yesterday, to begin with, I did not come in to lunch or to dinner, and I also left her at the theatre. This will teach her, I hope, to respect my wishes. With women one must act with energy to be severe – no bad habits.' Of course, Fahmy Bey knew that their marriage was bound by the Muslim faith, and under the Islamic marriage contract Marie-Marguerite could not divorce her husband – something she regretted almost immediately.

Fahmy Bey, who was known to enjoy a vibrant and a somewhat diverse social life, sought the finest clubs in the West End to frequent throughout his stays in London. Kate Meyrick's New Follies club in nearby Newman Street provided a perfectly discreet venue for someone who attracted the unwanted attention of Britain's persistent tabloids. Meyrick recalled her impressions of Fahmy Bey in *Secrets of the 43 Club*:

> The young Egyptian prince was handsome and fabulously rich, but his best friends could not have credited him with intellectual brilliancy. Yet he never failed to attract universal attention by reason of his graceful, dignified carriage, good looks and the vague air of mystery that seemed to brood over him. He used to come in fairly frequently at about midnight, generally accompanied by some beautiful and exquisitely gowned woman. But somewhere in the background, as a rule, would hover his 'shadow', a wiry Egyptian detailed to act as his special bodyguard.
>
> From one of our dance hostesses I learned that Fahmy Bey had not long been married to a Frenchwoman, and that his wife was staying with him at

the Savoy Hotel. Later on, when I got to know him fairly intimately, he began to talk to me about this wife of his, and eventually confided to me that he was unable to find real happiness in his married life.

On Monday 9 July 1923, only hours before the famous storm unleashed its fury upon an unsuspecting London, the elegantly dressed and beautiful Madame Marie-Marguerite Fahmy was asked by the orchestra leader of the resident Savoy Havana Band if she would care for a special piece of music. 'I don't want any music,' she replied in a hushed, almost anxious voice. 'My husband has threatened to kill me tonight and I am in no mood for music.' Unperturbed, the maestro bowed and backed away, murmuring as he did so: 'I hope you will still be here tomorrow, Madame' – a model of hotel diplomacy. The other diners ignored Marie-Marguerite's bizarre declaration. By this stage, the Fahmys had already been staying at the Savoy for over a week, having booked into the hotel on 1 July, and their tempestuous appearances in the public rooms had become commonplace. Few of the guests knew who they were; fewer still cared. However, a mere metre away from Marie-Marguerite, sat at his usual table, was Sir Edward Marshall Hall, KC, unaware that the strikingly attractive Parisienne brunette would soon be his client.

As his wife drank alone in contemplative silence at the Savoy Grill, the swarthy Fahmy Bey, who was described by one commentator as 'the wastrel heir to a great industrialist who had no need to work at anything but pleasure', was drinking at the New Follies. His great fortune – an estimated annual income of £3 million inherited from his tycoon father upon his death, a palace on the Nile, two yachts, a racing car and four Rolls-Royce automobiles – would have been of great interest to the money-loving dance hostesses at Meyrick's clubs. Meyrick herself enjoyed frequent conversations with the prosperous prince, the most significant of which was recollected in *Secrets of the 43 Club*:

'You see, Mrs Meyrick,' he said on one occasion, 'I am passionately in love with my wife, and I am – jealous. She fascinates me, but sometimes I don't seem to understand her as I ought. I feel that she possesses a stronger personality than mine. I'm almost frightened of her beauty and her brilliant intellect; I'm so afraid that some more brilliant man than myself may attract her. When I'm with her I have a feeling of intellectual inferiority.'

Shortly after that infamous conversation took place, the fearsome thunderstorm broke with all its ferocity. Despite the bright lights and lively music inside the New Follies, the heavy atmosphere outside had left the dancers in the club subdued and apprehensive. Meyrick's attention was drawn in particular to a dark-eyed girl sat alone at a table. She was conspicuously restless, making repeated visits to the telephone, from which she returned each time with obvious anxiety and disappointment. At about half past two in the morning, a particularly terrifying clap of thunder tore through the building. The girl gave a low cry and sprang to her feet, before hastily crossing the floor to where Meyrick sat:

'Madame Meyrick, Madame Meyrick,' she burst out, 'what has happened to him.' I asked what she meant. 'To ze prince – Fahmy Bey.' 'Oh, so that's what has been worrying you so much all evening,' I answered. 'Surely this storm is enough to keep anyone away. He's certain to come back when it's over.' 'No, no,' the girl declared vehemently, almost in tears. 'He promised to meet me here at midnight. He always keeps his promises. Even a storm like zis would never keep him away.'

At that instant there was a clap of thunder that sounded like 'the very crack of doom'. For a moment or two the girl stood staring at Meyrick with a blanched face, and then she said, almost in a whisper, 'It has happened; something has come to him', and dashed out of the club without another word. Meyrick never saw her again. The incident made a most uncomfortable impression on Meyrick, and it became a hundred-fold more peculiar when she discovered the next morning how, at the very same time the stupendous thunder clap tore through the club, Fahmy Bey had been discovered lying dead outside his suite at the Savoy, while his wife stood over his body with a pistol still grasped in her hand and three empty cartridge shells at her feet.

Earlier in the evening, before the storm had descended upon London, Fahmy Bey, his secretary, Said Enani, and Marie-Marguerite had been to the theatre. 'On an oddly still, humid evening, they were chauffeured to Daly's Theatre, which then stood in Coventry Street, just off the north-east corner of Leicester Square. At 8.15, the curtain rose on a musical comedy which turned out, with grim hindsight, to have been a blackly humorous choice. It was *The Merry Widow*.'

On returning to the Savoy for a late dinner, Fahmy Bey and Marie-Marguerite continued to quarrel and, at one stage, he was heard to have threatened to smash her head in with a bottle of champagne. 'I will disfigure you and after that you can go to the devil,' one witness claimed was said. 'No doubt to the relief of the restaurant staff, the Fahmys and the ubiquitous Said Enani then went down to the ballroom, where the band was entertaining guests on a 2.00 a.m. extension. The tense and gloomy threesome sat on their white and gold lyre-backed chairs at one of the numerous tables in the ballroom.

Fahmy Bey tried to defuse the situation by asking Marie-Marguerite to dance, expressing the vain hope that they could make things up, but she curtly refused.'

Shortly after one o'clock in the morning, Marie-Marguerite went to bed alone. Said Enani escorted her to the lift before returning to Fahmy Bey for a brief heart-to-heart.

> The two men then went back to the foyer, from where it was evident that the thunderstorm was raging outside. When it rains in London, taxis become a rarity and almost an extinct species during a thunderstorm, but the Savoy is a powerful magnet and, even on this wild night, there were one or two cabs hopefully waiting under the entrance canopy. Said Enani went to bed immediately after his chat with Fahmy Bey, but his young master had other ideas. He was seen by hotel staff, still wearing formal evening dress, standing for a short time in the entrance lobby at 1.00, before the Savoy's doorman ushered him into a cab, whose driver was instructed to take Fahmy Bey in the direction of Piccadilly.

At 2.30, while the storm continued to batter the neon lights of the West End outside and while Kate Meyrick was conversing with the mysterious woman at the New Follies club, John Paul Beattie, a night porter at the Savoy Hotel, was wheeling a luggage trolley along a fourth floor-corridor of thick dove-grey carpet of the Savoy Court (the hotel's block of luxurious service flats where, coincidentally, Billie Carleton had died of a drug overdose only five years earlier). Fahmy Bey, dressed sophistically in his mauve silk pyjamas and green velvet backless slippers, leapt out of the entrance to Suite 41 and approached a startled Beattie, saying, 'Look at my face! Look what she has done!' Beattie did as instructed and noted a slight pink mark upon Fahmy Bey's left cheek. It was at that moment that the other door to the suite was thrown open and Marie-Marguerite emerged in the doorway wearing a low-cut evening gown, fashioned out of shimmering white beads. She began to shout at her husband in French, and Beattie, concerned that the argument would wake the guests occupying the nearby rooms, politely and diplomatically asked the couple to return to their suite rather than create a furore in the corridor.

As Beattie began to push the trolley back along the hallway, he heard a shrill whistle come from behind him. Naturally believing he was being summoned, Beattie turned around and saw Fahmy Bey snapping his fingers at a small dog that had seemingly ventured out of the suite. Continuing on his journey, Beattie got as far as the next corner towards the front of the hotel when he heard a loud bang, then another and then a third. Beattie, leaving the luggage trolley in the corridor, instinctively ran back towards the Fahmys' suite, and, upon reaching it, was confronted by a terrifying tableau outside Suite 42, next to the Fahmys' apartment. He found Marie-Marguerite throwing down a pistol and falling to her knees, crying, 'Sweetheart, speak to me!'

'The tidiness of the woman was contrasted with the mess her pistol pointed at. A spilled bundle of mauve and green materials, dusky skin, black hair; all splashed, and splashed round about on the dove-grey carpet with blood.' Fahmy Bey was lying motionless on the floor, bleeding profusely from a head wound. His wife, who had noticeable bruises around her neck and whose dress was flecked with blood, had fired three shots from a .25 Browning semi-automatic pistol, one of a matching pair that the mistrustful couple kept by their bedsides to protect their jewels and other valuable belongings. Beattie picked up the pistol and put it safely in his pocket before kneeling down beside the stricken prince. The porter looked up at Marie-Marguerite, who was, by now, weeping and trembling. 'What have I done?' she implored in French.

The noise of the gunshots had brought the startled guests into the corridor. Using the house phone, Beattie summoned the Savoy's assistant managers, Clement Bich and Michael Dreyfus, and the night manager, Arthur Marini, all of whom spoke fluent French. 'What shall I do? I've shot him,' wailed Marie-Marguerite to Marini. She was also heard to say, 'I have been married six months and I have suffered terribly', followed by '*J'avis perdu la tête*', the translation of which was later disputed. Literally this means 'I lost my head', but Marie-Marguerite's defence counsel argued that it was meant idiomatically, and was intended to mean 'I was scared out of my wits'.

Fahmy Bey was stretchered into the luggage lift and rushed to Charing Cross Hospital. He was pronounced dead within the hour. Meanwhile, Marie-Marguerite was using the house phone to make a frantic call to Said Enani, who was in a 'very bad state of nerves'. 'Come quickly, come quickly!' she pleaded. 'I have shot Ali.' Said Enani, whose room was on a different floor, pulled on his dressing gown and rushed to the Fahmys' suite. There he was greeted by the sight of his mistress talking excitedly to her physician, a Dr Edward Gordon, who had been summoned to tend to the dying man. Another arrival at the crime scene was Detective Inspector Albert Grosse. He ordered Marie-Marguerite to change out of her blood-stained evening wear, before receiving from Beattie three cartridge cases, a spent bullet and the gun that Marie-Marguerite had used to shoot her husband. 'Grosse was just the sort of detective that the Savoy might have ordered: smart but not dandy, taciturn, and quiet when he did speak; clearly not a paying guest at the hotel but possibly a paying guest's valet. Nice and unobtrusive.'

Marie-Marguerite, now dressed for the street in a black satin coat and a black mushroom-shaped hat, was driven the short distance to Bow Street police station, along with Dr Gordon, who insisted on accompanying her. By 9 a.m., Grosse had returned to the police station to charge Marie-Marguerite with the murder of her husband. She was now quite calm. An interpreter relayed her reply: 'I have told the police I did it. I told the truth. It does not matter. My husband has assaulted me in front of many people since we have been married. He has told me many times, "kill me", and many people have heard him say so. I lost my head.'

The link between the Fahmy Bey murder and the curse of Tutankhamun was an obvious one. The peculiar and brutal demise of an Egyptian prince, who not only 'claimed descent from the Pharaohs' but who had also recently visited the tomb of King Tut, was surely another in the growing number of deaths directly attributed to the curse; this would later include his advisor, Hallah Ben, who committed suicide after visiting the tomb at Luxor with the Fahmys. Yet the West End had its own ties to the 'Curse of the Pharaohs' that were forged long before Fahmy Bey met his grisly end within the Savoy Hotel. The Egyptologist Dominic Montserrat believed that the tale of the mummy's curse actually originated during the 1820s with an English author and a bizarre theatrical striptease act during which state mummies were unwrapped by the eminent archaeologist Giovanni Belzoni. The show, which took place in the very heart of the West End near Piccadilly Circus in 1821, seemed to have inspired a little-known novelist called Jane Loudon Webb to write a fantasy book entitled *The Mummy!: A Tale of the 22nd Century*. In the book, published in 1827, the mummy comes back to life to strangle the hero. The book follows the style of Mary Shelley's *Frankenstein*, with a man-made monster as its central character.

Of course Fahmy Bey's death could have simply been the result of a tempestuous and tragic relationship. At the subsequent trial of Marie-Marguerite – which received such feverish interest from the public and press that a queue for the public gallery at the Old Bailey stretched halfway down Fleet Street – she revealed the extent of the abuse she suffered at the hands of her domineering, tyrannical husband. As well as often physically beating her, Fahmy Bey, who was reputed to have been involved in a clandestine homosexual affair with Said Enani, six years his elder, repeatedly forced Marie-Marguerite into 'unnatural sexual acts which caused her to have distressing ailments in an embarrassing place'. It had been Marie-Marguerite's wish that during their stay in Europe she would be allowed to return home to Paris in order to receive the appropriate surgery for her injuries. When Fahmy Bey denied Marie-Marguerite her wish, this culminated in an argument that led to the tragic events of 10 July.

The formidable Sir Edward Marshall Hall, who was sufficiently moved by Marie-Marguerite's plight, and who, at the tender age of 64, was at the height of his legendary powers, agreed to represent her in the ensuing trial that would last for just six days.

> Marshall Hall was the most sought-after defending barrister of his day (his nickname was 'the Great Defender') … [his] career was built on theatricality, and it helped … that he was tall and exceptionally handsome. Everyone remarked on it. One friend, the playwright Arthur Pinero, thought him, 'a revelation of manly beauty'. Another, Edward Marjoribanks, said he was 'endowed with pre-eminent personal beauty of the most virile type'. In the opinion of the politician F.E. Smith: 'He was a man of remarkable appearance. Very greatly above the average height, admirably proportioned, exceptionally handsome, he radiated vigour, courage and personality.'

The *Murder Casebook* described him thus:

> His silver hair curled at the temples, and his penetrating eyes and aquiline features gave an impression of vitality and power. To his clients he exuded an air of enthusiasm and zest … But Marshall Hall also possessed an explosive temper and an uncertainty of judgement that verged on recklessness. These defects brought about several notable reverses in his 44-year career at the Bar. His passionate belief in his cases propelled him into several well-documented clashes with the Bench.

Throughout Marie-Marguerite's trial, Marshall Hall painted a vivid picture of a woman who was frequently tormented and abused by her oppressive husband. 'Fahmy Bey, shortly before he was shot, attacked his wife like a ravaging lustful beast because she would not agree to an outrageous suggestion he made – a suggestion which would fill every decent-minded person with utter revulsion,' declared Marshall Hall, standing proudly in front of the jury. 'Almost throughout their miserably tragic life of six months, this treacherous Egyptian beast pursued his wife with this unspeakable request, and because she – immoral as she may have been – resisted him, he heaped cruelty and brutality on her until she was changed, by fear, from a charming, attractive woman to a poor quaking creature hovering on the brink of nervous ruin.'

However, Marshall Hall saved his finest rhetoric for his closing speech, a flowery piece of oratory, which was undoubtedly one of his most memorable and has since been described as one of the best pieces of dramatic acting ever seen in a court of law. He painted an eloquent picture of Marie-Marguerite's turbulent married life, described the thunderstorm and the supercharged atmosphere it had created, and then the woman's terror as her husband seized her viciously by the throat. Marshall Hall folded back his barrister's robes and crouched like a tiger ready to spring:

> She made one great mistake, possibly the greatest mistake a woman of the West can make. She married an Oriental. I dare say the Egyptian civilization is, and may be, one of the oldest and most wonderful civilizations in the world. But if you strip off the external civilization of the Oriental, you get the real Oriental underneath. It is common knowledge that the Oriental's treatment of women does not fit in with the way the Western woman considers she should be treated by her husband … The curse of this case is the atmosphere which we cannot understand – the Turk in his harem, this man who was entitled to have four wives if he liked for chattels, which to us Western people with our ideas of women is almost unintelligible, something we cannot deal with. Was that deliberate murder? Would she choose the Savoy Hotel for such an act? To use the words of my learned friend's great father in the [Adelaide] Bartlett case: 'I don't ask you for a verdict – I demand a verdict at your hands.' You will remember the final scene, where this woman goes out of the gates of the garden into the dark night of the desert. Members of the jury, I want you to open the gates where this Western woman can go out – not into the dark night of the desert but back to her friends, who love her in spite of her weaknesses; back to her friends who will be glad to receive her – back to her child who will be waiting for her with open arms. I ask you to open the gate and let this Western woman go back into the light of God's great Western Sun.

Marshall Hall looked up and pointed to the skylight, where the bright English September sun was streaming in, bathing the court with warmth and brightness. With this final dramatic gesture, he sat down. It is interesting to note the use of the word 'curse' in this statement – a word that had become increasingly used by the mid-1920s. Indeed, Marshall Hall's flamboyant speech would have been largely based on the facts supplied by Marie-Marguerite's own testimony in which she stated that Fahmy Bey retained the right to divorce her without giving her a penny and be able to take four wives if he so wished. Marshall Hall also asked the jury to consider the effect the violent storm would have had upon a woman with a nervous temperament and the many previous threats Fahmy Bey had made, including threatening to throw his wife into the Thames in front of the revellers at London's Riviera Club. Yet it was the 'Secret Document', a letter that Marie-Marguerite wrote on her honeymoon – a cruise along the River Nile on

Fahmy Bey's largest yacht – which provided the defence counsel with their most compelling evidence:

> I, Marie Marguerite Alibert, of full age, of sound mind and body, formally accuse, in the case of my death, violent or otherwise, Ali Fahmy Bey, of having contributed in my disappearance. Yesterday, 21 January 1923, at three o'clock in the afternoon, he took his Bible or Koran – I do not know what it is called – kissed it, put his hand on it, and swore to avenge himself on me tomorrow, in eight days, a month, or three months, but I must disappear by his hand. This oath was taken without any reason, neither jealousy, bad conduct, nor a scene on my part. I desire and demand justice for my daughter and for my family. Done at Zamalik, at about eleven o'clock in the morning, 22 January 1923.
>
> Signed: M. MARGUERITE ALIBERT
>
> P.S. Today he wanted to take my jewellery from me. I refused, hence a fresh scene.

As the jury retired to consider their verdict, Mr Justice Rigby Swift's concise precis was still ringing in their ears: 'You have heard about the character of the dead man, but it is no excuse for homicide that the person killed was a depraved and despicable person.' 'One needs to remember how he [Mr Justice Swift] looked as he sat on the Bench; the round, rubicund face under the bob wig, the glowing cheeks, the nose like a button, the amiable lift of the mouth, the bright, observant eyes, the endearing air of bonhomie.'

Swift was the youngest judge on the High Court Bench, having been only 46 at the time of his appointment three years previously, but he had already made his mark by his effective handling of jury cases. However, his demeanour was far from genial that last day of the trial. He vehemently declared that he was 'shocked, sickened and disgusted' by some of the evidence presented to him. The jury seemingly agreed. The damning corroboration of the 'Secret Document', along with the lurid details of the physical and mental scars Marie-Marguerite bore as a result of her marriage, substantiated by her chauffeur, her physician, Dr Gordon, and her sister (who had witnessed Fahmy Bey threaten Marie-Marguerite with a horse whip), convinced the spellbound jury to acquit her in less than an hour. They believed that Marie-Marguerite had acted in self-defence and had not intended to shoot her husband, merely threaten him with what she thought was an unloaded pistol.

Indeed, the most dramatic moment of the trial came when Marshall Hall, who had already described his client as being 'terrified, outraged, abused, beaten and degraded', asked for a pistol like her own to be handed up to her in the witness box. Her small, black-gloved hand reached over the edge to collect it, but then suddenly recoiled as if stunned by an electric current. Marie-Marguerite buried her face in her hands and sobbed. The pistol clattered loudly on to the ledge of the witness box. 'Come, Madame Fahmy,' said Marshall Hall gently. 'Take hold of the pistol. It is harmless now.' She took the weapon in her hands and seemed unable to pull back the breach cover. The pistol was passed around among the jury for the same purpose and most experienced difficulty with the mechanism, a fact that substantiated Marie-Marguerite's account.

The *Sunday Morning Star*, on 16 September 1923, offered a considerable description of the end of the trial, including Marie-Marguerite's collapse after the verdict was read out. Under the headline 'JURY FREES PRINCESS WHO KILLED "SHEIK"', the paper reported:

> The collapse of the Princess in the Old Bailey just after she shook hands with the jury which freed her, came as a sensational end to the dramatic trial which has gripped the attention of all London for three days. She had been comparatively composed while the jury was out for more than an hour, sitting in the prisoner's dock clad in sombre black, with a black crepe veil accentuating her deathly paleness. The jury filed in and the Princess buried her face in her hands as if to shut out a possible unfavorable verdict.

After the verdict was announced:

> The Princess seemed almost stunned as the purport of the words which meant life and freedom were borne home to her. She convulsively removed her hands from her face, and clasped them nervously over her breast. Then her face broke into a smile of thankful relief as she was escorted from the box.

After her acquittal, Marie-Marguerite said in a statement:

> I never wanted to kill my husband. I only wanted to prevent him from killing me. I thought the sight of the pistol might frighten him. But I never wanted to do him any harm. I never did ... I never noticed that I had pressed upon the trigger ... I saw my husband lying on the ground before I could think or see what had happened. It is terrible to have killed Ali, but I spoke the truth.

As an aside, just under three years later, Marshall Hall would be involved in another high-profile murder case that brought echoes of the mysterious East to the British courtrooms; this time he represented the Cantonese Lock Ah Tam who had shot his wife and two daughters near Liverpool and had telephoned the police to tell them to come and arrest him. Marshall Hall offered a plea of insanity and suggested that the man was in a state of automatism at the time of the killing, induced by an epileptic fit caused by a previous head injury. This did not impress the jury and they took only twelve minutes to find him guilty. He was duly hanged at Walton gaol on 23 March 1926.

On the surface, there is seemingly little evidence of any mysterious Ancient Egyptian malediction in the Fahmy Bey case, and the brutal manner of his death is hardly in keeping with the inexplicable maladies that struck down the other victims of the curse. However, when examined in more detail, there are perhaps several aspects of this case that raise interesting questions and existential dilemmas that could possibly have forced Marie-Marguerite into firing the pistol. Firstly, the fierce, abnormal storm that appeared over London at the exact same moment of Fahmy Bey's death, including the dramatic thunder clap confirmed by Kate Meyrick, is more than a little coincidental; secondly, Lord Carnarvon was a close friend of the Fahmy family in Luxor and was present at Fahmy Bey's and Marie-Marguerite's wedding in Cairo and at their parties in Luxor; thirdly, and certainly most intriguingly, is the location of the Fahmys' suite within the Savoy Hotel. Situated at the rear of the hotel, the Savoy Court is behind the famous restaurant Simpsons-in-the-Strand, overlooking the River Thames and, more mysteriously, the Ancient Egyptian obelisk Cleopatra's Needle. This would have been clearly visible from their bedroom window.

Erected on the Victoria Embankment on 12 September 1878, Cleopatra's Needle has had its own chequered and tumultuous history that is all the more fascinating when evoked in relation to the Fahmy Bey murder. Presented to the United Kingdom in 1819 by Mehemet Ali, the Albanian-born Viceroy of Egypt, in commemoration of the victories of Lord Nelson at the Battle of the Nile and Sir Ralph Abercromby at the Battle of Alexandria in 1801, it wasn't until 1877 that the obelisk was finally transferred from Alexandria to London. Sir William James Erasmus Wilson, a distinguished anatomist and dermatologist, sponsored its transportation to London at the huge cost of some £10,000. It was dug out of the sand in which it had been buried for nearly 2,000 years, encased in a great iron cylinder dubbed 'Cleopatra', and was to be towed to London by the ship *Olga*, commanded by a Captain Booth.

However, the voyage met with disaster on 14 October 1877, when the *Cleopatra* began to roll wildly in a storm off the Bay of Biscay. The *Olga* sent a small crew on a rescue boat to save the stricken obelisk, but they were all lost at sea when their vessel capsized in the storm. Captain Booth reported the *Cleopatra* 'abandoned and sinking', but instead she drifted in the Bay until discovered four days later by Spanish trawler boats before being rescued by the Glasgow steamer *Fitzmaurice*.

Cleopatra eventually reached the Thames Estuary on 21 January 1878, where she was greeted by hordes of onlookers, including a group of schoolchildren from Gravesend who had been given the day off for the occasion. When the obelisk was erected the following year, a time capsule was buried beneath it, within which was entombed that morning's newspapers, a box of pins, 1878's mintage of coins, four Bibles and photographs of the twelve most beautiful women of London at the time (one of whom was the 60-year-old Queen Victoria). Cleopatra's Needle is surrounded by Egyptian flourishes, such as buxom winged sphinxes on the armrests of benches, and is flanked by two faux-Egyptian sphinxes, cast from bronze, that bear the hieroglyphic inscriptions:

Netjer nefer men-kheper-re di ankh (the good god, Thuthmosis III given life)

It is worthwhile mentioning that Tutankhamun was a direct descendent of Thuthmosis III, with both pharaohs ruling in the Eighteenth Dynasty. Ever since its erection in London, there have been rumours of ghostly manifestations in the proximity of Cleopatra's Needle, most notably that of phantom laughter coming from the area and an apparition of a suicide in which a naked spectral figure leaps over the edge of the Embankment wall and into the Thames – but there is never the sound of an accompanying splash. Another ghost that has been witnessed here is that of a Victorian girl. In the 1920s, a policeman walking on the Embankment noticed a young lady in hysterics who was frantically pointing towards the Needle but was speechless with dread. On turning, the policeman saw another young girl preparing to jump. Instinctively, he turned back to the first girl, but she had disappeared. In bewilderment, he turned his attention back to the girl by the Needle only to find that she too had vanished.

Although there is fun to be had from these ghostly yarns and they contribute to the peculiar legend of Cleopatra's Needle, they bear little relevance to the Fahmy Bey murder and the curse of King Tut. What is more pertinent, however, is the positioning of the obelisk, next to the Savoy Hotel and clearly visible from the Fahmys' apartment, that it was constructed (along with another that currently stands in New York's Central Park) on the orders of Thuthmosis III, a genuine antecedent of Tutankhamun, in around 1450 BC, and the fact that the victim was an Egyptian prince who had recently visited the tomb of Tutankhamun. Indeed, the English journalist H.V. Morton recalled the Fahmys' initial visit to King Tut's tomb:

After an hour's ride between the baking-hot rock walls that lead into the famous valley, he saw a little way ahead of him a man and a woman mounted on donkeys. 'At first,' recalled Morton, with sly racism, 'I thought he was a European. He was wearing a grey sun helmet, a well-cut shooting jacket and a pair of Jodhpur riding breeches.'

An hour or so later, Morton, who was sat outside the entrance to Tutankhamun's tomb, noticed the young couple, who had left their mounts at the barrier and were walking towards the crowd. He heard them speaking French and asked an English friend if he knew who they were. 'The Fahmys,' came the reply, delivered patronisingly with the peculiar smile with which a white man in the East refers to a mixed marriage. Morton asked his friend if they were part of the Egyptian royal family. 'No,' he said. 'Just a bey. Pots of money … I'll introduce you.' Fahmy Bey discussed London and Paris with Morton. No, they were not staying at the Winter Palace [Hotel], declared Fahmy Bey with evident pride, as he swished the ever-present flies away with an ivory-handled whisk of white horsehair. 'I have a yacht.' Morton was very suspicious of this glib, disgustingly rich foreigner. 'All the time he talked, he smiled,' and, subtle Easterner that he was, 'had a trick of looking at your mouth when you were speaking to him'.

Marie-Marguerite was much quieter, possibly because the journey had tired her, but she was a practised rider and may just have been out of sorts, in no mood for polite chatter. Morton spoke to her in English, but in French she replied that she did not understand and, after a few commonplace remarks, settled down to watch the porters removing the artefacts from the great royal tomb.

Less than a week after Madame Marie-Marguerite Fahmy was acquitted by Mr Justice Swift for the murder of her husband, Lord Carnarvon's younger half-brother, Colonel Aubrey Herbert, died in London on 23 September 1923. Herbert, who was a decorated soldier, politician (an MP for the Yeovil division of Somerset from 1911 to his death), diplomat and linguist, and who was widely regarded to have been the inspiration for the character of Sandy Arbuthnot, a hero in a series of novels by John Buchan, was reputed to have told friends that he strongly objected to his half-brother's activities in Luxor, believing it unlucky to interfere with the tombs of the dead. When the burial chamber of Tutankhamun was laid bare, Herbert, who later visited the site himself, remarked, 'Something dreadful will surely happen in our family'. Indeed, in his last correspondence to his brother shortly before he died, Lord Carnarvon, known affectionately to Herbert as 'Porchy', commented that: 'I have had a somewhat unpleasant time out here. The papers have been quite poisonous but that I don't mind.' The *New York Times*, which had refrained from its fanatical Tutankhamun reporting for some time, soon returned to glorious form when it printed an article under the fervent headline 'Carnarvon's Brother Dies: Death of Aubrey Herbert Revives Superstition on Pharaoh's Tomb'.

Herbert, who had become a passionate advocate for the independence of Albania, and who was well known for his eccentric manner and kindness, had suffered from bad eyesight for much of his adult life and was badly injured in the First World War. His friend Sir Desmond MacCarthy, the eminent journalist and literary critic, described him thus:

> He was well over medium height and slimly built. His normal carriage was stooping, his gait buoyant and careless, and he was apt to fling himself into chairs in any attitude of comfortable collapse and then to leap up again in the excitement of talk. All his moves were expressive. His dress was never intentionally unconventional, but unless he had taken special pains with his get-up, which he could seldom be induced to do, its general effect was decidedly unusual. He was untidy, his shirts bugled and his tie was apt to rise and obscure his collar. He would clap on his head any hat to hand regardless of the rest of his costume. He did not notice when his clothes were shabby, and strangers must often have been surprised to discover, as they must have done after a moment's conversation, that such an unpretentious-looking person was so politically adroit and so completely at home in the world.

Full of mirth and bonhomie, and having sufficiently recovered from his war wound, he was posted to Egypt as a captain of the General Staff, and it was his ability to speak fluent Arabic that kept him in the region for much of the conflict. Upon his return home from the Great War, Herbert went into bankruptcy and was forced to move into a rented flat at Seaford House, Belgrave Square, with his wife, Mary. Having been obliged to move out of their grand residence in Bruton Street, Herbert became a familiar figure in the West End's nightlife as a member of Meard Street's Gargoyle Club – despite his dire financial circumstances: '... the club committee brought together Clive Bell, [Aubrey] Herbert and Arnold Bennett – the doyen of Bloomsbury critics, a journalising independent MP and one of the wealthiest novelists of the day.'

By the mid-1920s, the Gargoyle 'was the haunt of artists, writers and actors, the epitome of decadent glamour. It could be reached by a tiny, rickety lift, the dimensions of which "were such that strangers entering it left as intimate friends at the top". The interior was decorated in a Moorish style, the walls adorned with mirrored shards of eighteenth-century glass inspired by Henri Matisse, who was a member, as were Nöel Coward, Augustus John and Tallulah Bankhead. Spies, including Guy Burgess and Donald Maclean, were drawn to its dark corners and air of secret assignation. The Gargoyle was half-lit, avant-garde, and slightly louche. The film-maker Michael Luke described the atmosphere inside this den as "mystery suffused with tender eroticism".' It was once 'home to the Bright Young Things, young men in dinner jackets and flappers in cloche hats dancing the night away, champagne glasses in hand'.

Conceivably it was Herbert's enjoyment of the 1920s club scene that led him to believe a straightforward procedure to remove his teeth would in some way repair his damaged vision. Perhaps inevitably, he suffered blood-poisoning – a rare side effect of the operation – and died at the Harold Fink Memorial Hospital, 17 Park Lane (now part of the Hilton Hotel); a rather unfitting end for such a decorated and celebrated man. He was 43 years old. It is a point of interest that the private hospital caring for him, as well as being situated in the heart of the West End at Park Lane, was partially funded by a donation from George Jay Gould, an earlier victim of the Tutankhamun curse, who also convalesced there. The hospital was founded by a Mrs Fink, widow of the Victorian financier Benjamin Fink, who bought the property in 1911 and converted it into a nursing home for the eminent Australian surgeon Dr Shields, who had gallantly attempted to save the life of her gravely ill son.

Septicaemia, before the days of antibiotics, was usually fatal. This was exacerbated by a duodenal ulcer, unknown to Herbert, that went undetected by his doctor, and when this burst during the night of his death, a dash to the private hospital was to prove, sadly, yet predictably, in vain. His family, which included his son-in-law, the novelist and Bright Young Thing Evelyn Waugh, were initially incredulous at the notion of the 'Curse of the Pharaohs'. Indeed, after Carnarvon's death in Luxor, it was Waugh who remarked: '… after the discovery came the death of Lord Carnarvon, and the public imagination wallowed in superstitious deaths.' In 1929, in one of his travel essays called 'Labels', compiled after visits to Bodell's Hotel in Port Said and the Mena House Hotel in Cairo, Waugh 'wrote so dismissively of the whole phenomenon of Tutmania':

> The romantic circumstances of the Tutankhamun discovery were so vulgarized in the popular press that one unconsciously came to regard it less as an artistic event than some deed of national prowess – a speed record broken, or a birth in the Royal Family … The fact that a rich and beautiful woman, even though living very long ago, should still require the toilet requisites of a normal modern dressing table was greeted with the revelations of surprise

and delight and keenly debated controversies in the press about the variable standards of female beauty. The fact that idle men, very long ago, passed their time in gambling and games of skill was a revelation. Everything of 'human' interest was extensively advertised, while the central fact, that the sum of the world's beautiful things had suddenly been enormously enriched, passed unemphasized and practically unnoticed.

However, with the Fahmy Bey murder still fresh in the public's mind, the West End would come under particular scrutiny from those seeking to validate Tutankhamun's retribution, especially when Herbert's memorial service was held at the church where the nonconformist artist and poet William Blake was baptised – St James', Piccadilly. It would be the St James' district that later featured heavily in the West End's ties with Tutankhamun. Much like the Fahmy Bey murder, the death of Aubrey Herbert is ostensibly an open and shut case; here was a man with a history of ill health who died as a result of a standard operation. When scrutinised, however, this story also throws open some interesting theories in relation to the curse of King Tut and its seemingly growing hold over London's West End.

Herbert, who spoke fluent Arabic and had ties to north Africa, spent time in Egypt. It is impossible to ignore that his half-brother was Lord Carnarvon, the very first and arguably the most infamous victim of the curse, and that Herbert succumbed to his illness in the same district and within the same year as Ali Kamel Fahmy Bey. It was even reported that the nurse who cared for Herbert died shortly after her patient. These facts were not overlooked, and the *New York Times*, among others, ensured that this would remain the case. In the penultimate entry in his diary, dated 4 September, Herbert wrote the following poem that came to him in a dream:

> I had a dream last night and went into Mary's room this morning to repeat it to her and make her remember it. The first lines were simply my dream, without any correction. The third I wrote when I was awake.

> Ambition was amusement, but now ambition's dead,
> So take, my pretty fellow, a little dose of lead
> Then you and your ambition will once again be wed.

It is the first two lines of the poem that are the most intriguing – the lines that came to Herbert in his sleep. Could 'a little dose of lead' be a reference to poison – the same poison that guarded the pharaoh's tomb?

4

1929–30:
The Second Coming

And he removed from thence unto a mountain on the east of Bethel, and pitched his tent, having Bethel on the west, and Hai on the east: and there he builded an altar unto the LORD, and called upon the name of the LORD.

Genesis 12:8

For six long years, the curse of Tutankhamun appeared to have vanished. The West End's vibrant nightlife continued to thrive, and as the agonising memory of the First World War began to slowly dissipate, Londoners dared to forget the zealous reporting of the curse of King Tut that had threatened to cause widespread panic. In 1928, London was agog with news of the 'Croydon Poisonings', or the 'Birdhurst Rise Murders', in which three members of the same upper-middle-class family were found to have been killed by arsenic poisoning. This salacious suburban murder mystery dominated the headlines for much of the year, somewhat aided by the fact that the killer or killers remained at large. However, that all changed the following year when Mervyn Herbert, brother of Lord Carnarvon and Aubrey Herbert, died in Rome in May 1929.

The youngest son of the fourth Lord Carnarvon, Herbert, who was an avid sportsman and ostensibly fit and salubrious, was reportedly travelling through Rome on his way home from Albania when he was taken ill with malaria. This soon developed into pneumonia, and Herbert eventually yielded to the illness at the British Embassy within the city. Coincidentally suffering from the same affliction that had claimed his brother in Luxor, it is interesting to note that

Herbert, who not only spent time in Egypt when he served in the Diplomatic Service in Cairo, was present at the official opening of Tutankhamun's tomb.

With yet another member of the Herbert dynasty with ties to Egypt having passed away in a relatively short passage of time, the interest in King Tut's curse awoke with startling ferocity. Unbelievably, the press coverage became even more concentrated when Captain Richard Bethell, an amateur Egyptologist, son and heir of Lord Westbury and personal secretary to Howard Carter and Lord Carnarvon in Luxor, died mysteriously in his sleep at Mayfair's exquisite Bath Club at 34 Dover Street on 15 November 1929.

One of the noted Dover Street gentlemen's clubs of the 1920s and '30s, the Bath Club, located merely streets away from the Harold Fink Memorial Hospital on Park Lane where Aubrey Herbert had met his grisly end, was a sports-themed club complete with squash courts, a Turkish bath, a card room, well known to serious bridge players, and a basement swimming pool. The pool, its most celebrated feature, was believed to have inspired the swimming pool within the fictional Drones Club – the club made famous by P.G. Wodehouse's *Jeeves and Wooster* stories. Moreover, it was in the Bath Club's pool where the young princesses Elizabeth and Margaret learnt to swim, and where their mother, Queen Elizabeth, was a patroness. The club, which was founded by one of Wodehouse's many uncles, was severely damaged during a fire in 1941 in which the lives of a guest and a fire watcher were lost, and was consequently forced to move premises. Its affluent members (who included Rudyard Kipling, Mark Twain and Sir Henry 'Chips' Channon), clearly unaccustomed to suspicious and irregular deaths – particularly in the club itself – became wary of what was to follow, and feared their relationship with Bethell would in some way make them susceptible to the curse.

On 16 November, the *New York Times*, true to form, ran an article on the front page that carried the headline 'Tutankhamun "Curse" Recalled by Death; Richard Bethell, Once Howard Carter's Secretary, Latest of 10 Excavators to Die'. Indeed, the death of Richard Bethell would initiate one of the most disturbing chains in this whole bizarre saga – leading many to surmise that a separate curse had been placed upon the Bethell family and the Westbury barony. As personal secretary to Howard Carter in Luxor and a close friend and confidant of Lord Carnarvon's, Bethell would have been one of the very first people allowed into the tomb of Tutankhamun. As a member of the Scots Guards, he had no previous health complications and was very much the dedicated family man, with a wife, two sons and a daughter. His daughter was named Nefertari after Tutankhamun's queen, and his eldest son, Richard Morland Tollemache Bethell, born in 1914, was heir to the barony and became the next Lord Westbury when he succeeded his grandfather in 1930. (It is a point of interest that when he died suddenly and mysteriously in Geneva in June 1961, Richard Morland Tollemache Bethell was 46, the same age his father was when he was found prostrate in his bed within Mayfair's Bath Club. His death, the papers declared, was another 'of the British family said to be marked by the legendary curse of the pharaohs.')

On Richard Bethell's death certificate, the official cause of death was listed as 'a coronary thrombosis'. However, what caused this has remained a mystery to this day. It is certainly important to remember that Bethell was mentioned by the notorious clairvoyant Cheiro in his book *Real Life Stories*. After sending a warning note to Lord Carnarvon detailing the dangers he faced in Luxor, Carnarvon allegedly disregarded the warning after showing the note to Bethell, his travelling companion in Cairo. Cheiro:

> an astute, intelligent and extremely charismatic man with a deep interest in spir-
> ituality and the occult, was very well connected in society circles, and it is clear
> that he not only knew Lord Carnarvon, but also his private secretary, the Hon.
> Richard Bethell, and his father, the third Lord Westbury. Both of these men
> were eventually to die under somewhat unusual circumstances, yet [Cheiro]
> tells us that, shortly after the opening of the Burial Chamber in February 1923,
> Lord Westbury voiced his anxiety over the recent actions of his son. According
> to [Cheiro], the elderly peer revealed: 'My son Richard has brought back with
> him many relics and mementoes from Tutankhamun's tomb. He had them in
> his house. Do you think these things will bring him harm?'

Shortly before Bethell's death, Cheiro was invited to his home at Manchester Square in the fashionable West End where, he claimed, 'on nearly every wall were some of the relics of Tutankhamun's tomb just as Lord Westbury had described'.

> Apparently, a close friend of [Cheiro's] had rented Bethell's house, which was
> deemed one of the finest of its kind in the capital's aristocratic quarter. Yet
> in the months that followed this man suffered a series of disasters, which
> [Cheiro] obviously put down to the relics in the house. Upon Bethell and his
> wife's return we are told that a number of strange occurrences took place in
> his home, including knocks and bangs, and even strange fires. After these had
> persisted for a while, the arsonist was found to be a trusted servant, who was
> duly arrested. Bizarrely, he stated in his defence that the relics from the tomb
> had 'got on his nerves' and thus felt that he should 'burn down the place so
> as to get rid of them.' Reference is made to the mysterious fires and the fact

that Bethell's house 'was stocked with treasures brought from the Valley of the Kings' in an account of his death which appeared in the *Daily Mail* on 16 November 1929.

It was one of these treasures, an alabaster vase, which Bethell subsequently presented to his father.

Following his son's unexpected and tragic death, the wealthy and socially prominent Lord Westbury was catapulted into a world of deep depression, mania and seclusion. An amateur Egyptologist himself (much like many of the well-to-do of the day), Westbury, whose obituary was printed in *The Times* on 22 February 1930, was reported to have been a 'well-known racing owner and an excellent game shot'. As grandson to the famous Lord Chancellor Westbury, it was on the horse-racing circuit where Westbury made a name for himself and where he made the acquaintance of Lord Carnarvon, himself a devoted race horse owner. He soon became known as a fearless spectator, and on one occasion in Paris, when he saw the famous English filly Pretty Polly beaten in the Prix du Conseil Municipal, Westbury was said to have lost £6,000. Having seemingly caught the 'racing bug', Westbury soon owned horses himself, the most successful of which were Lantana, 'a very speedy filly', who won six of her eight races, and Dalkeith, who won the Newbury Spring Cup.

However, it was after his frenetic career in horse-racing that Westbury's life was turned upside down. As he was settling down to enjoy his retirement, Westbury's only son was found dead and the repercussions of this tragedy would darken the rest of his days. He was subsequently visited daily by a nurse, over a period of ten weeks, who prescribed him a strong cocktail of drugs for his insomnia and depression: a dram and a half of bromide mixed together with one-twenty-fourth of a grain of heroin. Such a drastic concoction points towards the gravity of Westbury's melancholy, and the shocking event that was to follow came as no surprise to many.

On 21 February 1930, Lord Westbury was reported to have killed himself by throwing himself from his seventh-floor courtyard flat at St James' Court – an upmarket square of apartments less than a mile away from where his son had died at Mayfair's Bath Club. He had moved to the area in order to be closer to his doctor, but his son's sudden death just over three months earlier had contributed towards a severe downturn in his mental health. Although at the inquest into Westbury's death the verdict of 'suicide while of unsound mind' was recorded, when examined in more detail, this case is far from straightforward and is without doubt one of the most appealing to those seeking to substantiate the curse of King Tut. Indeed, what was it that had contributed towards Westbury's 'unsound mind'?

Apart from the obvious causes – his son's tragic death, his radical prescription and his age (Westbury was 77 at the time of his death) – the two suicide notes which were discovered in Westbury's flat pointed towards a man who was troubled by something far greater than grief. Both were written on black-edged notepaper; one was addressed to 'Dearest George', the other to a Mrs White Forwood in an envelope addressed to his wife, Lady Agatha Westbury. At the inquest, the coroner read out one of the letters – the other was illegible, although he wrote something about a Sister Catherine having a hundred pounds and thanked his housekeeper for her overwhelming kindness. The letter simply finished with the words, 'I am off.' The legible letter read as follows:

> I really can't stand any more horrors and hardly see what good I am going to do here, so I am making my exit. As I am aware I hope to meet you again. Goodbye, and if you were right, all will be well. Will say no more. Au revoir. Affectionately yours, Westbury.

What 'horrors' was Westbury referring to? And what did he mean by 'if you were right, all will be well'? Family and friends of Lord Westbury couldn't help but refer to the vast number of Egyptian artefacts strewn about his flat at St James' Court, including the rare alabaster vase that was decorating his bedroom – the vase his son had pillaged from the tomb of Tutankhamun and had given to his parents as a gift. The *Daily Record*, on 21 February, confirmed this thus: 'In the very flat from which Lord Westbury presumably jumped were several important and exquisite works of Egyptian art from the Egyptian Valley of the Kings which Bethell, who was his heir, had given his parents.' Westbury's friends and family were also well aware of his obsession with the 'Curse of the Pharaohs' – an obsession that had plagued his life for the three months following his son's death: 'Lord Westbury for months has worried over the strange circumstances of the death of his son, Richard Bethell.' Thus, when the newspapers responded to Westbury's demise by printing stories with headlines such as 'A King's so-called "curse"; the Tutankhamun Legend Is Again Revived by Prophets of Evil', hysteria ensued.

On 22 February, *The Times* printed a column-long report of the coroner's inquest into Westbury's death in which Miss Mary Terras, Westbury's night nurse, Sergeant Nicholls, the coroner's officer, and a Mr Ernest Charles Daintrey, Westbury's solicitor, were the main witnesses. Taking place at Westminster Coroner's Court, Terras told the coroner, a Mr Ingleby Oddie, how at 8.30 p.m., the night before his death, she had administered Westbury's medicine as instructed by his doctor to assist him in sleeping. He slept until midnight, at which time he woke and had some barley water, remarking to her that it was too early for his Ovaltine. He went back to sleep until 2.30 a.m., before waking again to have his Ovaltine. She repeated the dose of bromide and heroin at 3 a.m., before settling him back to sleep. When he woke again at 7.00 a.m., Westbury appeared to the nurse to be comfortable and drowsy. He asked her for the time and had another glass of barley water.

Terras went on to tell the court how she shook Westbury's pillow, before he turned on his side, saying it was too early to wake up for the day and that she should go out of the room and not wake him again until eight. Terras then put coal on the fire at about 7.10 a.m., before going to the kitchen to put on Westbury's coffee and see to the milk for breakfast. As she was doing this, she heard a crash of breaking glass and instinctively ran back to her patient's room where she found the bed empty and the window, which had previously been closed, wide open. A washing stand, upon which the suicide notes were later discovered, had been moved from in front of the window and the curtain had been dislodged. Terras immediately ran downstairs, but, she said, 'They would not let me go further'. No one thought to question her as to who 'they' might be or why they would stop her going to the man she was supposed to be nursing, who was now obviously very badly injured.

'Did you know he was likely to commit suicide?' Oddie asked Terras. 'No,' she replied. 'He often thought he was ill and that he was going to die, but never anything like that.' It was Westbury's notorious fixation with the 'Curse of the Pharaohs' that was the overriding reason why he 'often thought he was going to die'.

Cyril Evans, a valet at King's House, two doors down from Westbury's flat, told Oddie that at around 7.25 a.m., as he was going to court, he saw a felt slipper fall into the courtyard by the staff entrance. When he looked up, he saw, coming through the air, the body of Lord Westbury, which turned a complete somersault before it crashed through the glass veranda below, severing his neck almost immediately. A woman just had time to throw herself clear of Westbury's prone form. Evans added that Lord Westbury, who was patently very badly injured and unconscious, 'gave a couple of groans and a slight spasmodic heave and was dead within a minute'.

In what was curiously known as 'the year of the leaping Peers', the previous August Lord Loughborough had leapt to his death from an upper-floor window in a house in Kensington. Loughborough had reportedly suffered from financial and marital trouble in the years preceding his death, and, despite receiving immediate medical treatment following his fall, he died in hospital shortly afterwards. While *The Times* respectfully limited its reporting to the facts of Lord Westbury's death, newspapers in America typically indulged in an orgy of speculation. On 22 February, the *New York Times* reported:

The superstition that a 'curse' follows all those connected with the opening of King Tutankhamun's tomb in Egypt was revived today when Lord Westbury, a 78-year-old peer, leaped from a seventh-story window near Buckingham Palace and plunged through a glass roof to his death. He had been grieving over the strange death of his son, the Hon. Richard Bethell, who was Howard Carter's secretary during the excavations in the Valley of the Kings and who was found dead in the [Bath] Club last year. Ever since Tutankhamun's tomb was opened Egyptians have been repeating the ancient malediction, 'Death shall come on swift wings to him that toucheth the tomb of the Pharaoh.'

In his book *The Tutankhamun Deception*, Gerald O'Farrell points to the peculiarities in this case. Firstly, Terras insisted that she didn't see the suicide notes on the washing stand when she initially went into Westbury's bedroom following the sound of the crashing glass. Secondly, and more intriguingly, the manner of Westbury's fall from his seventh-floor flat raises its own questions. O'Farrell questions these peculiarities in the following passage, worth quoting in length:

The fall from the seventh-floor window to the ground was about seventy-two feet. To get out of the window the elderly Lord Westbury would have had to have got over a sill which was two feet three inches wide. Then there was another sill of eight inches and a gutter of two and a half feet and a parapet of thirteen inches. A total width of six and a half feet. We are asked to believe that fifteen minutes after the nurse had left the room, having been told to come back in an hour, a drowsy Lord Westbury, who had just imbibed a barley water and asked to be allowed to sleep for another forty-five minutes or so, made up his mind to get out of bed, move a washstand and launch himself from the window, flying over a parapet six and a half feet.

And where did the letters come from? Did he write them the night before and only get them out after he had enjoyed his night's sleep and various drinks? Did he dash them off in that quarter of an hour? At what stage did he decide to use black-bordered notepaper for his suicide notes? Why would he go to so much trouble and then allow his writing to become indecipherable at certain stages of the letters? Is it not more likely that someone came in through the window from the wide ledge outside, moved the washstand, pulled back the curtains, threw the elderly lord out of the window (thereby causing the somersault motion that the valet described) and left the letters on the washstand before disappearing.

The unusual nature of the death of Westbury's son, Richard Bethell, is also scrutinised in O'Farrell's book. Having suffered a 'coronary thrombosis' at Mayfair's

Bath Club, O'Farrell believes that Bethell's death was 'consistent with a pillow being placed over his mouth, smothering him'. So, who was the perpetrator of these crimes and what was their motive? Indeed, can the 'Curse of the Pharaohs' and its singular grasp on London's West End be disregarded in this instance? O'Farrell questions the presence of the mysterious woman outside the quiet courtyard of flats early in the morning. It seems more than a little coincidental that she just happened to be almost directly underneath Westbury's falling body. And why was it that no one sought to locate and question her? What is certain, however, is that what happened next involved neither malice nor sinister practice.

On 25 February, under the headline 'Hearse With Westbury's Body Kills Boy; Museum Death Also Laid to Pharaoh's Curse', the *New York Times* ran the following article:

> London, Feb. 25. Two more deaths which the superstitious were inclined to associate with the opening of Tutankhamun's tomb were attracting attention here today. As a hearse was bearing the body of the late Lord Westbury to a crematorium today, it knocked down and killed an 8-year-old boy, Joseph Greer. Lord Westbury had committed suicide on Saturday and his act was ascribed by many to the alleged curse of the Pharaohs. His son, Richard Bethell, died last November after serving as secretary to Howard Carter, who opened the tomb.

Eight-year-old Joseph Greer was knocked down and killed by Westbury's hearse near his home in Battersea as it was carrying Westbury to the crematorium at Golders Green. Although the River Thames separates Battersea from the West End and the settings for the previous dramas, Westbury's presence in this case would appear to be hugely significant. Of the vast funeral cavalcade, it was Westbury's hearse that knocked down and killed Greer. For the first time since the opening of Tutankhamun's tomb, Howard Carter denounced the curse, claiming that it 'is nothing but a myth', and, in response to a cabled enquiry from the *Evening Standard*, he wired the following reply from Luxor: 'Rumours of a curse are a libellous invention.' But even he would have found the following events unnerving. In the same article that was printed on 25 February 1930 in the *New York Times*, the newspaper made reference to 'a museum death also laid to Pharaoh's Curse'. The rest of the article read as follows:

> The other death was that of Edgar Steele, 57, a worker in the British Museum who cared for some of the relics from the tombs of Luxor. He died after an operation for internal trouble. The Pharaoh's Curse, legend has it, doomed to a quick death any one molesting the tombs of the Ancient Egyptian rulers.

Following this unnerving chain of events, newspapers the world over sum-marised the sensational curse-related activity following the discovery of the tomb of Tutankhamun. The *Berkeley Daily Gazette* was one such paper when it reported the following on 21 March 1930:

> Others who have succumbed since that trip to the rocky valley are:
>
> **Col. Aubrey Herbert**, half brother of Lord Carnarvon who was present at the opening of the tomb.
>
> **Sir Archibald Douglas Reid** who X-rayed the mummy.
>
> **Professor Laffeur** [sic] of McGill University, Canada, who died in Luxor after visiting the tomb.
>
> **H.G. Evelyn White**, noted Egyptologist, who committed suicide in 1924 leaving a letter saying 'I knew there was a curse on me.'
>
> **M. Benedite**, and his colleague, **M. Casanova**, French archaeologists, who took part in the research work.
>
> **Jay Gould**, American railway magnate, who died after a visit at the tomb while Carter and Lord Carnarvon were at work.
>
> **Dr. Jonathan W. Carver**, assistant to Carter, who was killed in an automo-bile wreck in the United States.
>
> **Mrs. Evelyn Waddington Greely**, American society woman, committed suicide in Chicago, it is said, upon her return from a visit to the tomb.
>
> **Prince Ali Fahmy Bey**, mysteriously shot to death after visiting the tomb.
>
> **Hallah Ben**, private secretary to the Prince who accompanied him to the valley, died soon afterward.
>
> **Edgar Steele**, member of the staff of the British Museum engaged in lettering a Tutankhamun exhibition including various relics direct from the tomb at Luxor.
>
> **Joseph Greer**, eight years old, knocked over and killed by the hearse carry-ing Lord Westbury's body to a London crematorium.

So, on the very same day that Joseph Greer was killed by the hearse carrying Lord Westbury, Edgar Steele, a sign-writer at the British Museum in London's West End who was caring for the relics from Luxor, succumbed to an infec-tion at St Thomas' Hospital following an emergency stomach operation. What made matters more bizarre was that many of Steele's co-workers at the British Museum complained of persistent fevers and headaches ever since the arrival of the Egyptian artefacts at the museum. But this was merely the beginning of the museum's link to the 'Curse of the Pharaohs' – a link that stretched back to the late 1880s when the museum had its 'First Egyptian Room' in which the curse of the 'Unlucky Mummy' was said to strike fear into the hearts of all who crossed it.

5

Museum Macabre and the 'Unlucky Mummy'

The Vandeleurs found it convenient to change their name to Stapleton, and he brought the remains of his fortune, his schemes for the future, and his taste for entomology to the south of England. I learned at the British Museum that he was a recognised authority upon the subject, and that the name of Vandeleur has been permanently attached to a certain moth which he had, in his Yorkshire days, been the first to describe.

Sir Arthur Conan Doyle, *The Hound of the Baskervilles*

In 1889, a Mrs Warwick Hunt of Holland Park, London, on behalf of her brother, a Mr Arthur F. Wheeler, donated to the British Museum a gessoed and painted wooden 'mummy-board', or inner coffin lid, of a mummified woman discovered deep in a sepulchre at Luxor. Although the identity of the woman remains a mystery, the high quality of the relic indicates that the coffin lid belonged to a person of high rank or perhaps even royal blood. Upon the lid, the deceased wears a very large floral collar, through which her open hands protrude, and below this is a complex arrangement of images of deities associated with the afterlife: solar discs and falcons, the winged sky goddess Nuit, ba birds and emblems of Osiris. It was usual for such ladies to participate in the musical accompaniments to the rituals in the temple of Amen-Ra; hence early British Museum publications described the owner of the coffin lid as a 'priestess of Amen-Ra' – an Egyptian priestess who lived in 950–900 BC in the Twenty-First or early Twenty-Second Dynasty. Amen Ra, or Amun-Ra, was an Egyptian god, who, alongside Osiris, is the most widely recorded of the Egyptian gods. Whilst remaining hypostatic deities, Amun represented the essential and hidden, and in Ra he represented revealed divinity. As the creator deity par excellence, he was the champion of the poor and central to personal piety. Amun was self-created, without a mother or father, and during the New Kingdom he became the greatest expression of transcendental deity in Egyptian theology.

There is a particularly interesting link between Tutankhamun and Amen-Ra. During the latter part of the Eighteenth Dynasty, the heretic pharaoh Akhenaten disliked the power of the temple of Amun and advanced the worship of the Aten, a deity whose power was manifested in the sun, both literally and symbolically. He defaced the symbols of many of the old deities and based his religious practices upon the Aten. He moved his capital away from Thebes, but this abrupt change was very unpopular with the priests of Amun, who suddenly found themselves without any of their previous authority. The religion of Egypt was inexorably tied to the leadership of the country, the pharaoh being the leader of both. The pharaoh was the highest priest in the temple of the capital, and the next lower level of religious leaders were important advisors to the pharaoh, many being administrators of the bureaucracy that ran the country. When Akhenaten died, the priests of Amun reasserted themselves. His name was struck from Egyptian records, all of his religious and governmental changes were undone, and the capital was returned to Thebes. 'The return to the previous capital and its patron deity was accomplished so swiftly that it seemed as if this almost monotheistic cult and its governmental reforms had never existed.' Worship of the Aten ceased and worship of Amen-Ra was restored. The priests of Amun even persuaded Akhenaten's young son, Tutankhaten, whose name meant 'the living image of Aten' – and who would later become a pharaoh – to change his name to Tutankhamun, 'the living image of Amun'. Therefore, it is worth bearing in mind this connection between Amen-Ra and King Tut and the following story – a blend of eyewitness accounts and allegory that details another legendary death-curse that wreaked havoc and came to roost in London's West End decades earlier.

The journey of the unknown priestess' coffin lid to the British Museum in London was rumoured to be a perilous and terrifying one, fraught with peril and rife with intrigue and rumour. Subsequently, the priestess of Amen-Ra, whose resplendent coffin lid can still be heard sobbing late at night within Room 62 of the British Museum today, acquired the name the 'Unlucky Mummy' on account of the misfortune, injury, death and disaster that came to be associated with the artefact.

In the late 1880s, four rich young Englishmen, visiting the Ancient Egyptian tombs in Luxor, were invited to purchase an elegantly designed 'mummy-board' containing the remains of a priestess of Amen-Ra. After drawing lots, the man who won paid several thousand pounds for the coffin lid and had it taken to his hotel. A few hours later, as legend has it, witnesses saw the man walking out towards the desert. He never returned. The last entry in his diary read: 'If such a thing is possible, when I looked at the face drawn on the sarcophagus, its eyes seemed to come back to life and looked at me with such hatred that my blood ran cold.' The next day, one of the remaining three men was accidentally shot by his Egyptian servant during shooting practice on the Nile. His arm was so badly wounded that it had to be amputated in order to prevent gangrene. Upon his return home, the third man in the foursome found that the bank caring for his estate and life savings had gone into liquidation. The fourth suffered a severe illness, lost his job and was forced to become a street-seller peddling matches. Nevertheless, the coffin lid finally reached England (causing other misfortunes along the way), where a London businessman, disregarding the unfortunate tales connected to it, bought the rare *objet d'art*. However, after three of his family members were injured in a road accident and his house severely damaged by fire, the businessman prudently decided to donate it to the British Museum. The gentleman's name was Arthur F. Wheeler.

As the coffin was being unloaded from a truck in the museum courtyard, the truck suddenly went into reverse, trapping and injuring an innocent bystander. Then, as two workmen were lifting the casket up the stairs to the Egyptian Room, one fell and broke his leg. The other, apparently in perfect health, died mysteriously just two days later. However, it was after the priestess was installed in the Egyptian Room that the trouble really began in earnest. The museum's nightwatchmen frequently heard frantic hammering and sobbing emanating from the coffin, and, on one occasion, reported an apparition with a yellowish-green face sitting on the lower part of the sarcophagus, which then glided silently towards him. He fled, followed by the spectre, before it finally disappeared into thin air. Other exhibits in the room were often hurled about late at night. Another watchman died on duty and the museum cleaners refused to go near the priestess, too. When a visitor derisively flicked a dust cloth at the face painted on the coffin, his child died of measles soon afterwards. Deciding enough was enough, the museum hierarchy had the coffin lid moved to the basement, figuring it could not do any harm down there. However, within a week, one of the helpers fell seriously ill and the supervisor of the move was found dead at his desk within the museum.

It was around this time that Sir Arthur Conan Doyle's friend, the intrepid Bertram Fletcher Robinson, arrived at the British Museum for twelve weeks of research with the sole purpose of disproving the wild claims of the curse of the 'mummy-board' that were running rampant in the *Daily Express* (the newspaper for whom he was once the editor). However, on 21 January 1907, shortly after writing his report, Fletcher Robinson died at his home at 44 Eaton Terrace, Belgravia. At just 36 years of age, he was outwardly fit and healthy, and was an accomplished rugby union player. The official cause of his death was recorded as 'enteric fever and peritonitis'. During 1913, a London-born journalist and writer called Douglas Brooke Wheelton Sladen had an autobiography published by E.P. Dutton of New York. The following year, the book, entitled *Twenty Years of My Life*, was also published by Constable and Company Ltd of London. On page 275 of the American edition, Wheelton Sladen wrote the following:

> The popular account of [Bertram Fletcher Robinson's] death is that, not believing in the malignant powers of the celebrated mummy case in the British Museum, he was determined to make a slashing attack on the belief in the columns of The Daily Express, and went to the museum, and sent his photographer there, to collect materials for that purpose: that he was then, although in the most perfect health, struck down mysteriously by some malady of which he died.

This report reveals that there was both discussion and debate following the untimely death of Fletcher Robinson. It also suggests that eminent writers – most notably Conan Doyle and Wheelton Sladen – had already linked his death to the research he had undertaken into the 'mummy-board' at the British Museum. Although neither Conan Doyle nor Wheelton Sladen initially confirmed the identity of the artefact Fletcher Robinson was researching, two years later, on 30 July 1909, *The Times* published an article entitled 'The August Reviews' that included the following statement:

> In *Pearson's* the true story of the mysterious British Museum mummy, a picture of which adorns the cover, is the most piquant of the contents. Misfortune has pursued everyone who has in recent years been connected with this famous mummy cover, and B. Fletcher Robinson, who two or three years ago investigated the story, himself died shortly afterwards at an early age.

Indeed, the cover illustration in question featured a painting of a 'mummy-board' that depicted the coffin lid belonging to the priestess of Amen-Ra. It wasn't long before the other papers got wind of the unnerving story of the 'mummy-board'. One plucky journalist photographer from Baker Street took a photograph of the artefact and, having had it developed, discovered the painting on the coffin revealed a horrifying human face; the carved and painted visage is supposed to have been miraculously replaced by the features of 'a living Egyptian woman of malevolent aspect'. The photographer was said to have gone immediately home before locking his bedroom door and shooting himself. Soon afterwards, the museum sold the coffin lid to a private collector. After continual misfortune, the owner reputedly banished it to his attic. A well-known authority on the occult, Madame Helena Blavatsky, visited the premises. Upon entry, she was gripped by a shivering fit and searched the house for the source of an evil influence of incredible intensity; she finally came to the attic and found the coffin lid.

'Can you exorcise this evil spirit?' asked the owner. Blavatsky replied, 'There is no such thing as exorcism. Evil remains evil forever. Nothing can be done about it. I implore you to get rid of this evil as soon as possible.' But no museum in Britain would take the 'mummy-board'; the fact that in barely ten years almost twenty people had met with misfortune, disaster or death from handling the casket meant that the story of the coffin lid belonging to the priestess of Amen-Ra was now a well-known and infamous fable. Eventually, a shrewd American archaeologist, who dismissed the happenings as quirks of circumstance, paid a handsome price for the 'mummy-board' and arranged for its removal to New York. In April 1912, the new owner escorted the treasure aboard a sparkling new White Star liner about to make its maiden voyage across the Atlantic from Southampton to New York. On the night of 14 April, amid scenes of unprecedented horror, the priestess of Amen-Ra accompanied 1,500 passengers to their deaths at the bottom of the Atlantic. The name of the ship was, of course, the RMS *Titanic*.

Some accounts of the story go on to suggest that the American collector bribed the crew of the *Titanic* to put the coffin lid in a lifeboat and had it smuggled onboard the *Carpathia* when she picked up the survivors. Having safely arrived in New York, the coffin lid continued to bring tragedy to those who handled it and so it was shipped back to Europe onboard the *Empress of Ireland*, which then sank with the loss of 840 passengers on 29 May 1912. Somehow, the 'mummy-board' was salvaged again. The collector decided to send the coffin lid back to Egypt via England on a third ship – the RMS *Lusitania*. The ship met with tragedy when it was torpedoed by a German U-boat on 7 May 1915, during the First World War. This time 1,198 lives were lost.

In truth, despite its gripping narrative, this was largely a cock-and bull story, the creation of the journalist and spiritualist W.T. Stead, who concocted the outlandish tale of the 'curse of the mummy-board' after visiting his Egyptologist friend, Douglas Murray. Murray had recently acquired an

Egyptian Mummy and displayed it proudly in his drawing room, but the morning after setting it up all the breakable items in the room were found smashed to pieces. The second part of the story followed a visit to the British Museum. Stead (well known for exposing child abuse in the 1880s in the *Pall Mall Gazette*) saw the coffin lid of the priestess of Amen-Ra and imagined a coffin whose picture on the front was one of sheer terror and anguish in the face depicted on it. The coffin's original occupant was a tormented and maligned soul, and her evil spirit was loose in the world to bring misery to those who got in her way. Stead, along with Murray (who, as one of the four rich young Englishmen invited to purchase an elegantly designed 'mummy-board', was accidentally shot by his Egyptian servant during shooting practice on the Nile), sold this elaborate story to the press who were apathetic towards publishing the truth. However, Stead's story was given additional credibility by the fact that he was onboard the *Titanic* that fateful night, regaling the story of the 'Unlucky Mummy' to an enthralled audience. Stead, who just sat quietly reading a book in the First Class Smoking Room as the ocean liner sank, would later perish with the other 1,516 bodies in the bitter Atlantic water, and his death would be embellished by the newspapers to which he sold the story as a fitting conclusion to the bizarre tale.

Also, Arthur Weigall, the *Daily Mail* correspondent who covered the excavation of Tutankhamun's tomb for the newspaper, wrote in his diaries of:

> a Mrs Gordon – who was convinced that she had been cursed by a mummy in the British Museum. Apparently, she had suffered a string of calamities, among which was a shipwreck when she was said to have 'hung with her teeth in her nightie to some rocks all night': Last night Mr and Mrs Gordon introduced themselves … She is tall and thin, with … shaggy eyebrows which she darkens with soot, and rows and rows of teeth absolutely made for hanging on to rocks with.

Indeed, which of the shipwrecks was Mrs Gordon referring to? The story went that there was an inscription upon the coffin lid warning anyone who recited it would meet with a violent death. Supposedly seven of the eight men who heard Stead regaling the story, as well as Stead himself, went down with the ship.

Before the *Titanic* was sunk, the *New York Times* showed a glimmer of what was to come from them when they published the following article on 12 December 1909, under an extraordinary headline for the time – 'Curse of a Mummy; Occult Manifestations of a Priestess of Amen-Ra Again in London':

In the First Egyptian Room of the British Museum there is a mummy case numbered 22,542; it contains the mortal remains of a priestess of Amen-Ra. Recently a superstitious dread has seemed to surround the case, for it is asserted by certain London papers that all who have come in contact with it have either met with serious accidents or violent death.

On 28 March 1921, *The Times* published an article about the Unlucky Mummy with the headline 'Mummies at the Museum'; it was an article that recalled and poked fun at the peculiar and eccentric legend of the priestess of Amen-Ra:

> It may be noted in passing that a change has been made in the place assigned to the Lady of the College of Amen-Ra (No 22,542). This is the so called 'unlucky mummy', about whom many stories have been circulated without any foundation. It was said by all sorts of people that anyone who interfered with her would meet with calamity, and the late Mr Stead predicted that if any further attempt was made to move the lady it would probably result in the utter destruction of the whole room, such was the virulent nature of the priestess as revealed to him by her astral body. Although she has been moved to another place in the Wall-case none of the dire results so confidently foretold are yet known to have occurred.

The lasting legend of this story is perfectly exemplified by an article in the *Washington Post* that appeared on 17 August 1980, almost seventy years after the sinking of the *Titanic*. At the time, attempts to salvage the remains of the *Titanic* were being thwarted by frequent storms and terrible weather: 'Some hunters have spoken darkly of the famous mummy that was allegedly on board, saying it transferred the curse of all who disturbed its grave to the vessel's maiden voyage and to all search efforts.'

In actual fact, the mummy of the priestess of Amen-Ra was never discovered. All that is left to show for her is her intricate coffin lid that is safely housed in a British Museum display case under the number EA 22542; the coffin lid itself never left the British Museum after its initial installation in 1889, making it highly unlikely that it ever ventured on to the *Titanic*. Nevertheless, in 1921, the museum authorities still felt perturbed enough by the singular happenings within the museum to hire two mediums, named Wyeth and Neal, to carry out an exorcism on EA 22542. They claimed that the priestess was a 'clairvoyant' capable of reading omens in a silver cup and that she had lived in a dark time when embalmed corpses were used in black magic rites. To protect herself from desecration, the priestess of Amen-Ra had the sarcophagus guarded by the tortured spirit of a servant. For a while, the exorcism rite appeared to have worked, as no other disaster seemed to be provoked by the keeper. However, on 7 April 1923, under the headline 'Egyptian Collectors in a Panic – Sudden Rush to Hand over Their Treasures to Museums', the *Daily Express* reported that:

> The death of Lord Carnarvon has been followed by a panic among collectors of Egyptian antiquities. All over the country people are sending their treasures to the British Museum, anxious to get rid of them because of the superstition that Lord Carnarvon was killed by the 'ka' or double of the soul of Tutankhamun.

'Apparently, a small avalanche of parcels, containing the shrivelled hands, feet, ears and heads of mummies, as well as wooden, limestone and ceramic shabti figures and "other relics from the ancient tombs" had been arriving on the doorstep of the British Museum with every post:'

> Few of the parcels received at the museum bear the senders' names. The owners, in their eagerness to wash their hands of the accursed things, have tried to keep their identity secret. Statuettes that peer out of the corners of slanting eyes are responsible for many cases of 'nerves' and the Museum is richer by several gifts of this sort – not much richer, however, for few of the pieces are valuable.

'"The British Museum", continued the article, "was something of a godsend to people who interpreted Carnarvon's death as 'confirmation of their fears', for it offered an easy means of shifting the liability to expert shoulders". But these expert shoulders, or rather the curatorial staff in the Egyptian Department, were not too excited about this shower of unsolicited donations. Quite apart from the accessioning problem, they may perhaps have resented the fact that members of the public thought they were "shifting" the curse on to them – like a real-life version of M.R. James' ghost story *Casting the Runes*.'

> The Museum authorities are used to such liabilities, having harboured the coffin-lid of the powerful Priestess of Amen-Ra for years, but they are not at all grateful for the present flood of gifts. The museum weathered a similar storm years ago, when the story of the curse of the Priestess of Amen-Ra became public. Sufficient scare gifts were received to fill a large showcase.

The British public appeared to have an alarmingly short memory. Just over two months earlier, on 23 January 1923, at the height of 'Tutmania', *The Times* reported in an article about mid-season evening gowns on the new fashion accessory, the 'Mummy Wrap': 'There is also the draped frock which seems to presage a return to the tight waist. It is based on the swathing of the priestess mummy in the British Museum, and heralds what the treasures of Luxor might suggest for evening wear.'

However, by 1930, once the curse of King Tut was again making headlines across the globe and some of the newly found relics from his tomb in Luxor were being held in the British Museum, the morbid legacy of Amen-Ra seemed to stir with alarming intensity, perhaps aggravated by the new arrivals from Luxor. It is a point of interest that the museum, which today houses the largest collection of Egyptian antiquities outside of Cairo (which includes 140 mummies and coffins), was originally established in 1753 and was largely based on the collections of Sir Hans Sloane – many of these coming from Ancient Egypt.

Already at the British Museum, sign-writer Edgar Steele, who was caring for the relics from Luxor, had died unexpectedly and many of his colleagues had complained of illness and fatigue since the arrival of the artefacts. Soon after, Henry (Harry) Reginald Holland Hall, the Keeper of the Egyptian and Assyrian Antiquities at the British Museum, upon his return from an Egyptological seminar in Brussels, died at his London home after catching pneumonia – an illness that seemed to appear frequently alongside whispers of the curse. What makes this case interesting is that Hall not only backed a campaign to keep Lord Carnarvon's Egyptian antiquities in the British Museum (before they were subsequently moved to New York), but he was also regarded as one of the first Egyptologists to have dug in Luxor. In his book *Wonders of the Past*, Hall wrote: 'Two benevolent djinns in the persons of Lord Carnarvon and Mr Carter seem to have revealed to us, by a touch of their wands, the ancient Pharaoh … preserved as by magic with his royal state about him until these latter days for us to behold him and wonder.' Coincidentally, following his service at Primrose Hill, Hall was buried at the crematorium at Golders Green, only months after Lord Westbury was interred at the same location.

Before long, incredible stories soon began to emerge in the tabloids of a phantom figure stalking the platforms of the British Museum underground station. The figure was said to be the ghost of an Ancient Egyptian, a mummy who had fled from the nearby repository, that was dressed in a loincloth and headdress and would appear late at night, wailing so loudly that the screams could be heard at Holborn station, the next station along on the Central Line. The rumour grew to such an extent that even a tabloid newspaper offered a reward to anyone who would spend the night there – although no one ever dared. Many people surmised that the ghost was that of the priestess of Amen-Ra, seeing as though the story of her coffin lid in the museum above had sparked such incredible tales. Others concluded that the ghost was that of an Ancient Egyptian male who was searching for his lost princess.

The story takes a stranger turn following the closure of the station in 1933 – ten years after the original discovery of Tutankhamun's tomb. The film *Bulldog Jack*, a comedy thriller that 'spoofed 1933 press reports that the British Museum station was haunted by an Egyptian ghost', starred Fay Wray, Ralph Richardson, Atholl Fleming and Jack Hulbert. The film revolved around Bulldog Drummond (Fleming), who is injured when his sabotaged car crashes, and Jack Pennington (Hulbert), who then agrees to masquerade as Drummond. He is enlisted to help Ann Manders (Wray) find her grandfather who has been kidnapped by a gang of crooks who want him to copy a valuable necklace they plan to steal. The plan goes awry in the British Museum and the film climaxes in an exciting chase on a runaway train in the London Underground. The film included a secret (fictitious) tunnel from an underground station to a sarcophagus within the Egyptian Room at the British Museum. The station in the film was called 'Bloomsbury' and in all likelihood was a stage set, but it was based on the ghost story of the British Museum underground station.

On 5 April 1935, the same night that *Bulldog Jack* was released in UK cinemas, two women reputedly disappeared from a platform at Holborn – where the screams of the Ancient Egyptian ghost were said to echo. The women were never to be seen again, and strange, indecipherable sigils were later found on the tiled walls belonging to the disused British Museum station a mere stop away. 'This legend is echoed in the sarcophagus motif on the walls of the present Holborn platforms', as well as in a picture of the priestess of Amen-Ra that appropriately adorns the wall of the westbound Piccadilly line platform. Further sightings of the ghost were reported before the station's closure, along with a terrifying moaning that was said to originate from the walls of the tunnels deep within the dark, dank metropolitan mine. It is an interesting coincidence that the station was closed by the authorities during a period when it had attracted much negative attention from the press and public. Although the modernisation of nearby Holborn station (which provided new platforms and lifts) was the official reason for the British Museum station's closure, it is impossible not to consider other, more infamous, reasons for its demise.

Indeed, the station has achieved lasting notoriety, not only from the story of the resident Ancient Egyptian ghost, but also by appearing in two novels; firstly in Neil Gaiman's *Neverwhere*, in which the main character, Richard Mayhew, a Londoner, protests that there is no British Museum station, only to be proved wrong when the train he is travelling on stops there; and secondly in Keith Lowe's *Tunnel Vision*, in which the lead character, who has to travel to every tube station on the network in a single day after a drunken bet, tells his girl-friend that the sound of Egyptian voices can be heard floating down the tunnel. The station even makes an appearance in *Broken Sword: The Smoking Mirror*, a computer game in which the protagonist, Nico Collard, escapes from the British Museum and comes across the station.

Perhaps the station's most notable appearance is in the 1972 horror film *Death Line*, starring Donald Pleasance, Norman Rossington and Christopher Lee (who also starred as Kharis, the mummy, a character loosely based on the legend of Tutankhamun, in Hammer Horror's 1959 film *The Mummy*). In the film, the station is portrayed as being the home of a community of cannibals descended from Victorian railway workers (who had been buried alive follow-ing an accident decades earlier). The cannibals venture out at night to snatch travellers from the platforms of operating stations and take them back to their gruesome lair within the disused station. Donald Pleasance plays the investigat-ing police inspector, and when finally cornered, one of the cannibals screams a corrupted form of 'Mind the doors', obviously having picked it up parrot-fash-ion from the guards on the underground trains. The station in question is simply named 'Museum' and is clearly stated as being between the Holborn and Russell Square stations in a conversation between Pleasance's character and a colleague. It is a suitably grim storyline – a fitting tribute to the station's nefarious past.

On 2 January 1934, Arthur Weigall, the respected English Egyptologist with exten-sive links to the British Museum who reported on the opening of Tutankhamun's tomb in Luxor, died at the London Hospital (now the Royal London Hospital) in Whitechapel aged 53. 'Arthur Weigall who denied Tutankhamun's Curse, is Dead', said the *Daily Express* on 3 January 1934; the following day it ran an arti-cle entitled 'A Curse Killed Arthur Weigall'. On 3 January, the *Daily Mail* ran the headline 'Death of Mr. A. Weigall, Tutankhamun Curse Recalled'; the *Daily Mirror* had 'Egyptologist who told Story of King Tut; That "Curse"'; and the *New York Times*, not one to miss out, simply declared 'Alleged Curse of Tutankhamun Recalled, as in Earl of Carnarvon's Death'. On 7 January 1934, *The Referee* simply went with a concise banner that read 'Curse of Tutankhamun'. These hysterical headlines perfectly reflect how the country, and in particular London, was react-ing to stories of the curse of Tutankhamun at the time of Weigall's death.

Weigall, who had enjoyed a career working as the Inspector-General of Antiquities under the Egyptian government before the outbreak of the First

World War, enjoyed an association with both the stage and the screen through-out the conflict. In a radical departure from his previous work, Weigall became a successful stage designer for the London revue stage before the bright lights of the cinema lured him into the UK film industry. Once the hostilities in Europe had come to an end, in 1919 Weigall wrote the screenplay for *Her Heritage*, which starred Jack Buchanan and was directed by Bannister Merwin, before Lord Northcliffe appointed him as a film critic for the *Daily Mail* in the early 1920s. It was this association with the newspaper that was to entice Weigall back into the world of Egyptology, and he consequently worked for the *Daily Mail* as a special correspondent in Luxor throughout the excavation of the tomb of King Tut in 1923, writing 'three or four articles for them, and a particularly big one for the actual opening'.

During this time, Weigall, described by Arthur Mace as 'very fat and oily, and pretending to be a journalist only by accident, so to speak', also published a collection of extensive essays called *Tutankhamun and Other Essays*, which fea-tured one entitled 'The Malevolence of Ancient Egyptian Spirits'. In this essay, Weigall, much like many other Egyptologists at the time, denied that there was ever a curse written on the walls of Tutankhamun's tomb. He explained that such curses were very rare and that they were only intended to ward off the tomb robbers of their day who had designs on the treasure within the mauso-leums. Weigall wrote: 'Modern excavators whose "sole aim" is saving "the dead from native pillage and their identity from the obliterating hand of time", fall into quite a different category: "no harm has come to those who have entered these ancient tombs with reverence."'

This opinion was to be the only thing Weigall ever shared with Howard Carter during their awkward relationship in Luxor. Weigall, who had previ-ously enjoyed a successful career working as an archaeologist for Theodore Davis, was cast aside by Lord Carnarvon, who favoured Howard Carter as his lead excavator in Egypt. Weigall not only resented this, but also the fact that Carnarvon had greatly profited from the deal he brokered with *The Times* to report on the opening of Tutankhamun's tomb officially. By the time the tomb was opened in 1923, Weigall surprised many of his loyal readers – who believed him to be a man of sober disposition – when he wrote an article, not in the *Mail* but in a published essay, about Lord Carnarvon's imminent death. For a man ostensibly not given to the notion of curses, it initially seemed to smack of sour grapes. Weigall told how he stood with fellow correspondents as they watched the excavating party descend for the opening of the inner chamber; how there was laughter among the excavators when Lord Carnarvon joked about the chairs down there and giving a concert in the catacombs; and how he, Weigall, suddenly turned to his colleague and said, 'If he goes down there in that spirit, I give him six weeks to live'. Weigall wasn't to know at that precise moment how right he would be. In *A Passion for Egypt*, a biography of Arthur Weigall, Julie Hankey, Weigall's granddaughter, writes:

> He couldn't think for the life of him why he said it – 'one of those prophetic utterances which seem to issue, without definite intention, from the sub-conscious brain,' he suggested. Despite his certainty that there was no curse written on the walls of Tutankhamun's tomb, there was a curious ambivalence about Weigall's attitude to these things in general. He writes in one piece about hearing 'the most absurd nonsense talked in Egypt by those who believe in malevolence of the ancient dead'. At the same time, he describes various spooky experiences of his own with a certain relish. All coincidence, of course, – and yet, he concludes teasingly, he likes 'to keep an open mind on the subject'.

Indeed, after Carter's canary was devoured by the infamous cobra, Weigall boldly stated that the royal cobra 'killed the symbol of the excavator's happiness displayed by the bird'.

> Weigall is an oddity in the story of the curse; he was an Egyptologist turned journalist who, although claiming there were no curses associated with the tomb, conveniently recalled numerous deaths which helped to fuel such rumours and give them an element of authority [Weigall was quoted in numerous newspapers shortly after the death of Lord Westbury as admitting the curse was 'strange']. His death is also sometimes cited as a product of the curse, even though he was instrumental in its creation.

Let us also not forget his previous brushes with the 'Curse of the Pharaohs' when, in 1909, he devised an ill-fated play that would portray the reincarnation of the heretical pharaoh, Akhenaten. Shortly before this took place, Weigall even believed that he was attacked by the malevolent spirit of a mummified cat.

After his spell in Luxor, which included a role on the staff of the Egyptian Exploration Fund as an assistant to Professor Flinders Petrie, Weigall returned to London where he set up home with his second wife, Muriel, at 41 Oakley Street, Kensington. In December 1933, Weigall, who was already seriously ill, was moved to a private room within the London Hospital. He was never to leave: Weigall had been diagnosed with terminal cancer and his last illness was 'extraordinarily intense, and his end rapid'. Hankey writes in *A Passion for Egypt* that: 'It is fitting that he [Weigall] should have gone off abruptly then, and equally fitting that Egypt should have had the last word.'

On 4 January 1934, the *Daily Express* ran an article quoting the view of a 'famous Egyptologist' on the real cause of Weigall's death. The Egyptologist in question was Sir Ernest Wallis Budge, a former Keeper of the Egyptian and Assyrian Antiquities at the British Museum (he retired from the position in 1924, two years after the discovery of Tutankhamun's tomb). The article quoted Budge as saying:

> Arthur Weigall … was a disappointed man at the time of the Lord Carnarvon and Howard Carter excavations of the Tutankhamun tomb. He had tried to obtain employment under Lord Carnarvon which would permit him to conduct the excavations. His negotiations failed. Carter was chosen to conduct the work … difficulties and failures obstructed the path of Arthur Weigall ever since the Tutankhamun discovery. He seemed to be the victim of some queer fate that never left him alone … He died, I believe, the unfortunate victim of the curse of the failure and hardship which he himself had wished for others.

This was a damning verdict. Budge even went so far as to suggest that Weigall had 'died the unfortunate victim of a curse. It was not, perhaps, any royal curse, but one self-inflicted.' Budge was referring to Weigall's rumoured drug addiction. In the same article, the journalist Winifred Lorraine added the following statement: 'Mr Weigall, Inspector of Antiquities to the Egyptian Government when Lord Carnarvon discovered the tomb of Tutankhamun, died in penury in a London Hospital as a result of hashish-eating and addiction to other drugs.'

In many ways, Budge's outburst was unsurprising, seeing as the two men had clashed almost thirty years earlier in the British Museum over Budge's alleged mislabelling of objects. Budge, much like Howard Carter, carried the fearsome reputation of being an argumentative man with a short temper. He was 'a bold explorer, a cantankerous individual, and a creative author who quite literally devoted his life to writing about Ancient Egypt'. The feud between the rotund, hubristic Budge and Weigall's family escalated further when, two days later, the *Daily Express* followed their initial article by printing a long inside piece about superstition in which Budge's idea that Weigall was haunted by a private curse was developed. In the same article they even compared Weigall to the likes of Shakespeare and Hamlet. The journalist described how: 'All of these men were souls tortured by doubt, by conflict between the material and the spiritual world, and all suffered from paralysis of the will.'

It was tragically predictable then when only ten months later Budge himself became the next victim of the curse and 'Tutmania' was once again in full swing. The second Keeper of the Egyptian and Assyrian Antiquities at the British Museum to succumb to the supposed curse following the death of Henry (Harry) Reginald Holland Hall, Budge, who had spent over thirty years in his position at the museum, died at home on 23 November 1934. Indeed, as the Keeper of the Egyptian and Assyrian Antiquities at the British Museum throughout the year of the discovery of King Tut's tomb, Budge had been 'encouraged by Lord Carnarvon, in the wake of the discovery, to draw together everything that was known about Tutankhamun and his era for a book on the subject'.

Ten days after the initial entrance to the tomb, Budge gave his views in an article for *The Times* on '300 Years of Discovery'. It was a piece of editorial that encompassed a larger article about the newly discovered tomb. It was unsurprising that Budge's opinions in his subsequent book, *Tutankhamun: Amenism, Atenism and Egyptian Monotheism*, on the possible relationship between the Amarna period, the story of Moses and the Exodus from Egypt were not shared by Arthur Weigall. It was in the same book where Budge would reprint a letter he had received from Lord Carnarvon on 1 December 1922, shortly after the discovery of King Tut's tomb; a letter that highlighted the close relationship between the two men at the time:

> One line just to tell you that we have found the most remarkable 'find' that has ever been made, I expect, in Egypt or elsewhere. I have only so far got into two chambers, but there is enough in them to fill most of your rooms at the B.M. (upstairs); and there is a sealed door where goodness knows what there is. I have not opened the boxes, and don't know what is in them; but there are some papyrus letters, faience, jewellery, bouquets, candles on ankh candlesticks. All this is in [the] front chamber, besides lots of stuff you can't see.

Furthermore, throughout the course of 1934, Egyptology recorded a heavier loss of life among its leaders than had occurred in any other single year of the century, and five of the seven who died were Englishmen. Although Budge was 77 at the time of his passing (the same age Lord Westbury was when he fell to his death), the circumstances surrounding his death are worthy of analysis. At his home at 48 Bloomsbury Street, Bedford Square, a smart, Victorian, terraced residence adjacent to the British Museum and the only complete Georgian square in London, Budge, a prolific author, had just finished writing his last book, *From Fetish to God in Ancient Egypt*, and had decided that his next project would be to carry out an experiment on 'Mummy Wheat' – wheat that was said to exist within the ancient tombs of dead pharaohs.

Having retired from his position at the British Museum ten years earlier after forty-one years of service, Budge was evidently after a project that would occupy his time and satisfy his rampant quest for knowledge, for he had already written to the editor of *The Times* on no less than fourteen occasions on topics as diverse as London pigeons, fireplace inscriptions in Farnham, a fire at Lustleigh and fifth-century Bible manuscripts. He was of the opinion that ancient 'Mummy Wheat' of the Dynastic Period was unable to germinate and grow (despite claims to the contrary from certain botanists), and he was keen to prove this theory once and for all. At the time of his death, Budge had sent samples of the wheat to numerous scientific institutions across the country in order to test this theory. In a letter to *The Times*, dated 18 September 1934, just over two months prior to his death, Budge wrote the following:

> If you, Sir, will give the space, it will be seen by your readers all over the world, and some learned body or agricultural authority or private individual seeing it may be induced to try and grow dynastic wheat and record their results in The Times. Here, naturally, the question will be asked, 'Where is the supply of Egyptian dynastic wheat to be obtained?' – wheat about the source of which there is no room for fraud and jest. I am very glad to say that I can supply the wheat, and I am prepared to devote a generous handful for experiment by any responsible authority. I obtained wheat in this wise. I was working in the Sudan about 1906, and when passing through Upper Egypt I was present at the opening of a very pretty Eighteenth or Nineteenth Dynasty tomb in Western Thebes. Among the articles of funerary furniture was a well preserved, painted model of an Egyptian granary more than half full of wheat. I acquired the granary for the British Museum, where it is now, but the 'company' of these natives, who were paying for the excavation of the tomb, refused to sell the wheat, as they intended to sell it, a few grains at a time, to the tourists. In the end, after paying substantial baksheesh, I bought the wheat for my own use and brought it back to the Museum. I gave small packets of it to scores of visitors, many of whom tried to grow it and failed. I have still some of this wheat remaining, and I should be glad to see some of it used by responsible people with the view of settling for everybody once and for all the question, 'will mummy wheat grow?'

Shortly after the experiment began, Budge was found dead at his home within London's West End. It is perhaps no coincidence that Arthur Weigall, Budge's fierce rival and adversary, had died only months earlier at a time when the curse of Tutankhamun was believed to have been stalking the streets of London once more. Indeed, not only was Budge dabbling in experiments involving 'Mummy Wheat', but he was also quoted, regarding the coffin lid of the priestess of Amen-Ra, as saying, 'Never print what I say in my lifetime, but that mummy-case caused the war'. Budge had also spent much of his career writing books about Ancient Egyptian magic and translating the Egyptian *Book of the Dead* – a translation that was drawn upon for inspiration by many mystics, writers and poets of the day, including Madame Helena Blavatsky, James Joyce and W.B. Yeats. Sigmund Freud, who was attracted by the symbolic qualities of Ancient Egyptian art, his colleague Carl Jung, who was fascinated by Egyptian solar mythology, and Sir James Fraser, 'the Father of Anthropology', who devoted several chapters of his influential book *The Golden Bough* to the myths of Osiris and Isis, were other notable intellectuals dependent on Budge's work.

Undoubtedly, for scholars of Ancient Egypt, it was Budge's translation of the *Book of the Dead* that was truly indispensible and has since been described as the only book on Ancient Egypt 'to make a real impact on followers of the occult'. One of these scholars was none other than Aleister Crowley, the 'Great Beast of Fitzrovia'; a man who had only recently been dubbed by the British press as being the 'Wickedest Man in the World' and whose name frequently appeared in this author's research alongside those who fell victim to the curse of Tutankhamun. But was this merely a coincidence, or did Crowley have a larger, more devilish part to play in this bizarre saga that fully justified his outrageous pseudonym?

PART II: THE BEAST

Prologue

London, 5 April 1935

Although the fire was burning up briskly, she was surprised to see that her visitor still wore his hat and coat, standing with his back to her and staring out of the window at the falling snow in the yard. His gloved hands were clasped behind him, and he seemed to be lost in thought.

H.G. Wells, *The Invisible Man*

Holborn underground station was deserted. The warm breeze that blew along the tunnel took with it a modicum of dust and a discarded edition of *The Times*; its middle pages were in the process of detaching themselves from the main body of paper and were subsequently spewed intermittently on to the line.

Apart from the rogue newspaper that tumbled innocuously along the platform edge, the station was scrupulously clean; the elegant emerald-coloured tiles that clung to the walls and floor reflected bright orbs of light that were fixed into the ceiling. Numerous posters adorned the curvature of the polished tunnel – the Crazy Gang Show was smeared across a poster depicting the London Palladium; the obligatory message that Guinness was indeed 'good for you' was endorsed by the famous toucan; Daly's latest offering was emblazoned upon a huge sheet of poster paper; and *Bulldog Jack*, a new motion picture starring Fay Wray and Jack Hulbert, was advertised as showing at the resplendent West End cinemas on a similarly vast slip of paper. Indeed, the red, white and blue Holborn station sign was almost lost amidst the hordes of advertisements vying for space.

The clip-clop of high-heeled shoes resonated along the staircase that descended into the metropolitan mine. Two elegantly dressed brunette women, both in their thirties, slowly emerged by the entrance at the far end of the westbound Piccadilly line platform; the gentle breeze emitting from the tunnel rustled the silk of their skirts as they stepped carefully on to the tiled floor.

'Have we missed the last train?' asked the elder and the more refined of the two, her pea-green dress blending into the emerald tiles that circled her.

'I don't know. What's the time?' her friend replied, brushing an errant cobweb off her forearm.

The elder woman threw a cursory glance at her Swiss wristwatch; a gold rim encircled its enamel dial indicating its high value and the wealth and status of its owner. 'It's ten-thirty. I told you we should have waited for a taxi!'

'Yes, hindsight is a wonderful thing,' snapped the younger of the two, impatience and fatigue getting the better of her. 'I told Theodore I would meet him in the Criterion at ten.' Her thoughts immediately turned to her poor fiancé having to endure a night alone with her austere parents without her moral support.

'We weren't to know the blasted picture would be *that* long. Did you see a guard on duty?'

'No.' The younger woman let out a weary sigh. 'You win. Taxi it is.'

As the two women turned back towards the staircase, a tall, heavy-set gentleman emerged by the archway at the opposite end of the platform, immediately catching their attention. Squinting into the distance, they could just about make out a top hat, a dark cloak and a walking cane belonging to the phantom-like figure. His pallid countenance and ashen eyes, too, were just about visible, in stark contrast to his black ensemble.

'I do believe we've stumbled upon Jack the Ripper,' whispered the elder woman, struggling to suppress a smile while at the same time inching backwards towards the platform entrance.

'Shhh,' her friend replied. 'Look.'

As the elder woman looked up, she could see that the figure had removed some kind of writing contrivance from inside his dark cloak and had begun to scribble furiously upon the tiled wall, seemingly unaware of the brazen attention coming his way. 'What the deuce is he doing?'

'I have absolutely no idea. Shall I ask him?'

'Ask him what?' The elder woman was incredulous.

'When the next train is departing.'

'No. I daresay we leave him to it.' The elder woman grabbed hold of her friend's arm and shepherded her towards the staircase. 'They only come out at night.' She glanced back towards the man, praying he hadn't detected their presence on the unusually quiet platform. To her evident dismay, the figure suddenly turned sharply on his heels, threw the writing contrivance to the floor, and began to stride purposefully along the platform towards them – the tap of his ivory-handled walking cane becoming louder and more belligerent with every pace. 'Quickly, he's coming!'

The younger woman let out a giggle, the absurdity of the situation getting the better of her. 'I'm sure he's perfectly friendly. Was he writing on the wall?'

'Yes. God only knows what.'

'You're being ridiculous, Joan. You take these moving pictures far too seriously. Perhaps he works here? Besides, he looks more like Moriarty than Jack the Ripper.'

'Yes, but neither are renowned for their chivalry!'

The two women, one more reluctant to leave than the other, held each other by the arm as they skipped up the staircase and shuffled awkwardly along the adjoining corridor.

'Dash it, Joan! I must have dropped my handbag on the platform. I'll go back and get it,' gabbled the younger woman, fighting free from her friend's vice-like grip and turning anxiously back towards the staircase. As she skipped down the steps, almost losing her footing in the process, she could see that her handbag was sprawled across the platform, its contents having fallen out of its opening and scattering themselves over the cold tiles. Hastily kneeling down to gather them up, she threw a quick glance to her left to see if the peculiar gentleman was still on the platform. To her palpable relief, he had departed. She immediately felt ridiculous for having reacted in such a histrionic manner. 'It's alright, Joan,' she whispered up the nearby staircase. 'He's gone.' There was no answer. She continued to shovel her belongings into the handbag, paying no heed to order or tidiness.

A sudden gasp from the corridor above, somewhere between a cry and sharp intake of breath, broke her concentration. The woman rose slowly to her feet, placed her handbag tentatively over her shoulder and inched her way back up the staircase. Feeling her knees trembling ever so slightly, she placed a gloved hand on the smooth wooden rail that was fastened to the wall. 'Joan, is that you? Are you all right?'

There was no reply, only the whistling of the warm wind once again rolling its way down the underground tunnel. The woman paused on the staircase, contemplating her next move, her heart beating rapidly in her chest and sweat greasing her palms. Ever the sceptic, she eventually shook her head, smiled gingerly and marched her way up the remaining steps with purpose.

'You're being a blasted fool,' she muttered to herself as she reached the top of the staircase. As she looked up, she was confronted by an image that came from the very darkest of her nightmares. Immediately recoiling in horror, she could see that her friend's pea-green dress had been torn – revealing her bare ribs – and was saturated by the blood seeping from a deep wound across her throat. The unusually dark-coloured blood flowed in a thick rivulet across the tiles, until it came to a stop by the wall and formed an innocuous-looking puddle, and the stark whites of the woman's eyes were in contrast to the broken blood vessels that inhabited them.

The strange gentleman was knelt over the woman's body, drawing what looked like a pentagram in blood upon her exposed breasts. As he murmured some indecipherable words, he looked up at the younger woman stood before him, his dark eyes meeting hers. She wanted to scream for help, but found herself hypnotised by the phantom's rheumy pupils. And then, before she could take another faltering step forward, she fainted, her head bouncing off the cold, hard floor.

The Beast smiled. That had been far easier than he imagined. The two women looked like fighters, vivacious and full of life. He was a gnarled old man now, but the thrill of it all kept the blood coursing through his needle-damaged veins. As he completed the pentagram of blood with his forefinger, he reflected on what he had achieved. At last it was over, and the anniversary of Carnarvon's death had been suitably besmirched. *I am the disciple of Aiwass and I will do his bidding.*

6

The Golden Dawn and the 'Wickedest Man in the World'

Then, as he looked up he saw a bull neck bulging out of a loosely tied silk cravat. The head was bald but for a froth of oily hair garlanding the crown, the glabrous pate hinting at a tonsure, making him appear like a degenerate monk. The Beast was young, still in his twenties, but burdened with a corpulence that aged him. Heavy jowls made a once handsome face bestially sensual. His whole countenance was disturbingly naked.

Jake Arnott, *The Devil's Paintbrush*

In 1888, the Hermetic Order of the Golden Dawn, a magical order founded by the Freemasons and members of Societas Rosicruciana in Anglia, Dr William Wynn Westcott, William Robert Woodman and Samuel Liddell McGregor Mathers, began to operate from its temple base in London. Soon after, temples were erected in Edinburgh, Weston-super-Mare, Bradford, Bristol and later in Paris and Chicago, to cater for the growing number of Golden Dawn members.

Without doubt 1888 was London's darkest year since 1666, the year of the Great Fire of London. The Autumn of Terror saw five East End prostitutes savagely murdered in the Whitechapel district of London by Jack the Ripper – a killer or killers unknown. Many theories soon circulated as to the identity of the now infamous serial killer, and one of the more accepted schools of thought was that his victims were brutally murdered according to Masonic ritual. Indeed, among other customs, the Golden Dawn practised Freemasonry, theurgy and spiritual development, and it is widely regarded to have been one of the largest single influences on twentieth-century Western occultism. Much like the Masonic lodges, the order was based on hierarchy and initiation; however, women were admitted on an equal basis with men. By the end of 1888, the increasingly popular Golden Dawn had thirty-two members who were being schooled in alchemy, Christian mysticism, renaissance grimoires and, probably most significantly, the religion of Ancient Egypt and the Egyptian *Book of the Dead*. The temples of the Golden Dawn were named after the gods and goddesses of Ancient Egypt: the Isis-Urania Temple was founded in London, the Osiris Temple in Weston-super-Mare, the Horus Temple in Bradford, the Ahathoor Temple in Paris and, naturally, the Temple of Amen-Ra in Edinburgh. Within these temples, the rituals would begin with a recitation of the eleven magick commandments:

> Thee I invoke, O Bornless One.
> Thee, that didst create the Earth and the Heavens.
> Thee, that didst create the Night and the Day.
> Thee, that didst create the darkness and the Light.
> Thou art ASAR UN-NEFER ('Myself made Perfect'): Whom no man hath seen at any time.
> Thou art IA-BESZ ('the Truth in Matter').
> Thou art IA APOPI IRASZ ('the Truth in Motion').
> Thou hast distinguished between the Just and the Unjust.
> Thou didst make the Female and the Male.
> Thou didst produce the Seeds and the Fruit.
> Thou didst form Men to love one another, and to hate one another.

Before long, the relative harmony within the Golden Dawn was replaced by internal fighting and power struggles that eventually saw Mathers wrestle control from Westcott. He wanted a magical order in which the initiates would study his main interest – esoteric knowledge centred on the Kabbalist notion of how all things in the universe connect via the Tree of Life. In 1892, the Golden Dawn moved from the Isis-Urania Temple at 17 Fitzroy Street to a new headquarters in London's West End: 24–25 Clipstone Street, a few streets north of Oxford Circus. It was a building unworthy of any religious movement, and one member of the order noted how it was 'dirty, noisy, smelly and immoral'. The Golden Dawn shared the street with a hairdresser, a dairyman, a confectioner, two sculptors, cabinet-makers, French polishers, a piano tuner and, most peculiarly, the officials of the German Waiters' Society. It was not an area that encouraged free-thinking or religious liberation. 'In 1900, Mathers was exposed as a fraud and was duly expelled from the Order, however, by this time, the members of the Golden Dawn had already come under the spell of a more potent authority – that of Aleister Crowley.'

Crowley was the self-proclaimed 'Great Beast' (from the book of Revelation). He was born on 12 October 1875, at 30 Clarendon Square, Royal Leamington Spa, and grew up in the Plymouth Brethren fundamentalist Christian sect. Over time he developed and exhibited a taste for what he called 'sex-magick', as well as rampant drug use, remarkable hedonism and increasingly erratic antisocial behaviour; this included his claims to be the reincarnation of numerous historical figures, such as the inveterate Pope Alexander VI (a Borgia), Elizabethan alchemist Dr John Dee, the eighteenth-century Sicilian mystic Count Cagliostro, the Kabbalist writer Eliphas Levi and Akhenaten, the heretic pharaoh and Tutankhamun's father.

Crowley, who matured in the boarding houses and opium dens of Victorian London, grew up in a staunch Plymouth Brethren household and was only allowed to play with children whose families followed the same faith as his. He was very close to his father, a bombastic, fanatical lay preacher, who travelled the length and breadth of Britain producing religious pamphlets. Prior to this he was a brewer and the founder of Crowley's Ales, leading to a somewhat radical career change. It was his father's death from tongue cancer that was to be the turning point in the young Crowley's life. He subsequently rejected Christianity, and his mother's efforts at keeping her son in the 'pious' Christian faith only served to provoke his scepticism and hatred towards both the 'bigoted' Church and his authoritarian upbringing. Crowley would later write: 'I had arrived at the conclusion that the Plymouth Brethren were an exceptionally detestable crew. I wanted sin, a supreme spiritual sin, but hadn't the faintest idea how to go about it.' His happy tenure at Trinity College, Cambridge, which began in 1895, would bring him into contact with liberal free-thinkers and encouraged his path into occultism and mysticism. It was also during this period that the Beast, a burgeoning mountaineer and poet, was finally able to sever his ties with the Church of England.

Throughout 1895, Crowley allegedly maintained a vigorous sex life, which was largely conducted with prostitutes and girls he picked up at local pubs and cigar shops, but eventually he took part in same-sex activities in which he initially played the passive role. In 1898, the year after he left university, Crowley was introduced to Samuel Liddell McGregor Mathers and the Hermetic Order of the Golden Dawn. It was to be a meeting that would propel Crowley to international infamy, and he soon found himself rising quickly through the ranks of the order:

Crowley's initiation into the grade of Neophyte of the Golden Dawn took place in the [second] Mark Mason's Hall, Great Queen Street, on 26 November 1898. In a real sense, this was Crowley's first distant brush with Freemasonry, as the Golden Dawn was created and led by an interlocking directorate of esoterically inclined freemasons, with ritual and organizational structure closely modelled on the Craft and certain Appendant Bodies.

Perhaps in an effort to ingratiate himself with the order, Crowley began to partake in depraved acts, including some with other members of the Golden Dawn, and had developed a particular penchant for the 'Serpent's Kiss' – biting the wrists of women with canine teeth specially filed for that purpose. 'I was not content to believe in a personal devil and serve him, in the ordinary sense of the word,' Crowley said at the time. 'I wanted to get hold of him personally and become his chief of staff.' Moving from his comfortable rooms at the Hotel Cecil on the Strand to a luxurious flat in Chancery Lane, it was from here that the Beast would burst upon the London scene in the guise of 'Count Vladimir Svareff'. Sharing the flat with his friend and fellow occultist Allan Bennett, Crowley's declared aim was to father a 'monster baby' after the 'ultimate orgasm', to which end he created tablets that were made from his own semen. At E.P. Whineray's chemist's shop on Stafford Street, off Old Bond Street, he gathered up the ingredients required to aid his unbridled sex drive: the Egyptian incense kyfi; the perfume and oil of Abra-Melin; the unguentum Sabbati; and onycha, the powder from the horned shell of a mollusc found in the Red Sea. But this merely represented a fraction of Crowley's fascination with all things Ancient Egyptian and the beginning of his extensive ties with London's West End.

It was at this point that he began to clash with other members of the Golden Dawn. Even the poet W.B. Yeats, who had himself assumed the mantle *Demon est Deus Inversus* (D.E.D.I. – 'The Devil is God Inverted'), objected to Crowley's overtly perverse, pornographic and blasphemous writings, as well as his alleged immorality. Yeats ensured that when Crowley attempted to win further promotion within the order, he would be rejected out of hand. 'Crowley's behaviour ... was too outrageous for most of the London members, who disapproved of his blatant sexual activities. In January of 1900, the Isis-Urania Temple refused to obey an instruction from Mathers to initiate Crowley into the second order, the RR et AC.' The Beast would later refer to Yeats as 'a lank, dishevelled demonologist', and, according to the author and fellow Golden Dawn member Arthur Machen, Crowley never got over the fact that Yeats was a better poet than he, and jealousy was enough to incite Crowley to hire some thugs to kill his rival. Indeed, if Machen is to be believed, this emphasises Crowley's ambivalence to murder – a point that will become increasingly apparent. The Beast inevitably sued the order, which in turn sued him.

> The prolix, labyrinthine machinations [that followed in court] were enlivened by Crowley's habit of assuming full Highland dress, his face covered by the black mask of Osiris, an enormous gold cross around his neck and a dagger by his side while the case dragged on without solution or satisfaction to either Crowley or Mathers.

By this time, however, Crowley had attracted the attention of the press and public, who, unsurprisingly, reviled his outwardly abhorrent and unusual appearance.

Over the next few years Crowley travelled extensively, all the while immersing himself in the occult to such an extent that he eventually became disillusioned with the Golden Dawn and its members, who, he believed, were not taking the issue of magick seriously enough. Increasingly eager to perform an extreme ritual, Crowley decided to purchase Boleskine, a house by Loch Ness, and quickly set about his preparations to perform the Abra-Melin, a black magic ritual dating from the fourteenth century. The purpose of the ritual was to have a conversation with the 'higher-self', or Holy Guardian Angel, and such was its power that numerous people staying in the house with Crowley reported strange happenings and a sinister atmosphere. It took six months to complete, and such was the risk attached to it that nobody had attempted it for centuries. Indeed, if it went wrong, it was believed that evil spirits could be set loose to take possession of the magician. However, despite having terrorised the Loch Ness locals for days, halfway through the ritual Crowley, who was now going by the name of Aleister MacGregor, Laird of Boleskine Manor, met a young society lady named Rose Kelly, daughter of the vicar of Camberwell and sister of the former Royal Academy president Gerald Kelly, who immediately fell under his spell and married him a day later; the Abra-Melin was soon forgotten.

While he did not officially break with Mathers until 1904, Crowley had lost faith in his teacher's abilities soon after the 1900 schism in the Golden Dawn that culminated in April with the 'Battle of Blythe Road', in which Crowley was ejected by a police constable after he broke into the order's London quarters at 36 Blythe Road, Kensington, and angrily confronted its members. He had also portrayed Mathers as the primary villain in his book *Moonchild*, including him as a character named SRMD, using the abbreviation of Mathers' magical name. Furthermore, throughout this episode the Beast was reputed to have exchanged magickal 'curses' with Mathers, now his sworn adversary. Indeed, it was in 1904 that Crowley not only took the material he had been working on with Mathers to create his own magickal order and fiefdom, the Argentenum Astrum, or Order of the Silver Star, but he also forged his initial link with the gods of Ancient Egypt – a link that would shape the remainder of his days.

Arriving in Cairo with Rose on their 'world-spanning honeymoon', the now 28-year-old Crowley said that a mystical experience which occurred on 8, 9 and 10 April, with a being whom he sometimes described as a 'praeternatural' intelligence, led to his founding of the religious philosophy known as Thelema – 'a hotchpotch of all the established and defunct religions, cults, rites, and mythologies, couched in a wealth of Greek, Latin, Hebrew, Sanskrit, German, Chinese and Arabic doggerel'. In between extreme sex sessions with Rose, Crowley practised more black magic rituals in an attempt to impress her. Deep within the King's Chamber in the Great Pyramid he recited the preliminary invocation of the occult ritual called Goetia. It had unexpected consequences. Reading out hermetic incantations by candlelight, the Beast claimed that the walls began to glow, eventually enabling him to read without the candle. Rose, whom he had taken as his first 'Scarlet Woman' (named after Babalon, the Mother of Abominations, who is often described as being girt with a sword and riding the Beast, with whom Crowley personally identified), started to behave in an odd way and began to chant. In a trance, she repeated the words 'They are waiting for you' over and over again. This led Crowley to believe that some entity had made contact with her, and on 18 March, Rose was able to reveal to Crowley that the voice seeking through her to address him belonged to none other than the Ancient Egyptian god Horus. Crowley had apparently offended Horus by not finishing the Abra-Melin weeks earlier. He was understandably sceptical; by his own admission, Rose had no knowledge of or any interest in Egyptology and could scarcely have had a reason to speak the name of that particular god. Crowley now cross-examined her in detail as to the attributes of Horus. Unbelievably, Rose answered each question correctly.

On 19 March, Rose had transmitted to Crowley a ritual for the invocation of Horus. At her instructions, Crowley performed the invocation the following day with, he wrote, 'great success'. According to Crowley, the god told him that a new magical aeon had begun, and that he would serve as its prophet. Rose continued to provide information, telling Crowley in detailed terms to await a further revelation. According to Lawrence Sutin – who wrote the biography of Aleister Crowley, *Do What Thou Wilt* – Crowley had become suspicious of Rose:

How could his wife have suddenly become a medium? He decided upon a further test of her powers. Together, on March 21, they went to the Boulak

Museum, which neither of them had visited before. Here, with two floors of exhibits to wander through, Crowley instructed [Rose] to find the god Horus without any sort of assistance. Again, her involvement with the March 20 invocation could have been of assistance here, but this possibility is not discussed by Crowley. [Rose] passed by several representations of Horus, a fact he 'noted with silent glee.'

But then they went upstairs:

A glass case stood in the distance, too far off for its contents to be recognized. But [Rose] recognized it! 'There,' she cried. 'There he is!' [Crowley] advanced to the case. There was an image of Horus in the form of Ra Hoor Khuit painted upon a wooden stele of the 26th dynasty – and the exhibit bore the number 666!

From 23 March to 7 April, Crowley went through a period of uncertainty – he was unsure of what was to come of the promised 'new link'. Having arranged for the hieroglyphic text inscribed on the two sides of the stele number 666 to be translated, the Beast discovered that the text elaborated on the central image of the stele portraying what would become the divine triumvirate of Thelema: Nuit, Hadit and Ra-Hoor-Khuit. Framing the scene is the sky goddess Nuit, her arching body forming the heavens, while her hands and feet touch the earth. Below her is a winged globe – the solar Horus, or Horbehurst; Crowley called this god form Hadit. Beneath these two is an Egyptian priest, Ankh-af-na-khonsu (who Crowley would later claim to be a re-embodiment of the magickal current represented by the priesthood to which Ankh-af-na-khonsu belonged), addressing an enthroned Horus in the form of Ra-Hoor-Khuit – a hawk-headed king overcome by a cobra head-band and a solar disc. (It is interesting to note the presence of the hawk and the cobra here, remembering the majestic-looking hawk seen flying above the excavation site of King Tut's tomb before disappearing to the west and the significant appearance of the cobra when it ate Howard Carter's canary on the day the tomb was opened.)

It was during this period that Rose revealed to Crowley the source of knowledge she had been transmitting had come in the form of a messenger of Horus with the mysterious name of Aiwass. Rose could provide no further evidence as to the background of Aiwass, who only gave her information as and when he chose. On 7 April, a dramatic event occurred when certain definite orders were issued by Aiwass through Rose. He ordered that the drawing room of the honeymoon flat they had leased in Cairo was to serve as a 'temple', and Crowley was summoned to enter the 'temple' precisely at noon for the following three days and write down what he heard during one hour – no more no less. It was the moment the Beast had been waiting for his whole life. On the 8, 9 and 10 April, Crowley did as he was instructed. It was at this point that he allegedly heard the voice for himself, and it dictated the words of the 'blasphemous' text *Liber AL vel Legis*, or *The Book of the Law*, which he duly wrote down. The voice claimed to be that of Aiwass (or Aiwaz) 'the minister of Hoor-paar-kraat', or Horus, the god of air, child of Isis and Osiris and self-appointed conquering lord of the new aeon, announcing through his chosen scribe 'the prince-priest the Beast'.

The plan was as follows: Crowley would enter the 'temple' a minute early, so as to seat himself with a Swan fountain pen and an ample supply of typewriter paper. He was now alone as Rose no longer served a purpose in his communication with Aiwass. 'Crowley described the unearthly voice that appeared over his left shoulder as a "rich tenor or baritone" of "deep timbre" musical and expressive, its tones solemn, voluptuous, tender, fierce, or aught else as suited the moods of the message.' Aiwass spoke without accent – it sounded to Crowley like pure 'English-in-itself'. Crowley, who was seated at a writing table which faced a southern wall, never spoke aloud during the three days he spent in the 'temple' with Aiwass, nor did he see him. He heard a voice coming from behind him, seemingly from a corner of the room. Yet Crowley experienced during those three days a vivid 'visualisation' of Aiwass within his own 'imagination'. In this 'visualisation', Aiwass possessed a:

> body of fine matter, or astral matter, transparent as a veil of gauze or a cloud of incense-smoke. He seemed to be a tall, dark man in his thirties, well-knit, active and strong, with the face of a savage king, and eyes veiled lest their gaze should destroy what they saw. The dress was not Arab; it suggested Assyria or Persia, but very vaguely.

The Beast later claimed that one manifestation took the form of a pyramid of light. Indeed, had Crowley become possessed by some Ancient Egyptian spirit? What is certain, however, is that Aiwass spoke at length to Crowley, issuing him with a clear set of instructions. Believing he was to be the messiah of a new epoch, the Beast stated that he would regularly perform depraved acts and learn to love them. Christianity was dead, he declared. In its place, Crowley's new religion had one all-powerful doctrine, a philosophy of life he had adopted from François Rabelais' fictional abbey at Thélème (and also adopted by the Hellfire Club as their maxim): 'Do what thou wilt shall be the whole of the Law.' In other words, people have the right to determine exactly how to live their lives, regardless of moral and religious boundaries. 'Free will, denied to Crowley as a child, had now become all powerful.'

While in Egypt, Rose discovered that she was pregnant. She later gave birth to a daughter, Lola Zaza, and it was during a trek in Vietnam that Crowley suddenly decided to abandon them both and return to England. Crowley cited Rose's excessive drinking as the reason behind the breakdown of their marriage and the fact that he had become disillusioned by the thought of a future with Rose and Lola Zaza. By December 1906, Crowley returned to London where he began to live what was essentially a single life – an all-too-appealing notion to Crowley at this stage in his life. As a regular haunt in the new London incarnation of his, Crowley spent much of his time at a chemist's shop on Stafford Street – his 'favourite rendezvous' – run by a man named E. P. Whineray, 'one of the most remarkable and fascinating men that I have ever met'. It was at Whineray's humble premises that Crowley was able to feed his rampant drug habit and where he met the Earl of Tankerville (referred to by Crowley as the Earl of Coke and Crankum), a wealthy man in his early fifties, whom Crowley had taken as a student in the occult. Tankerville, a paranoid cocaine addict himself, had become convinced that his mother, who was allegedly in league with others, was out to kill him and harm his wife and son by using magick against them.

In April 1907, the outwardly nervous and eccentric Tankerville began his training with Crowley in an effort to become less devoted to his family and to harness his own magickal powers to counteract those his mother was using. As Tankerville was a dedicated family man, it was a relationship that was doomed to fail, especially when Crowley became more interested in the handsome fee he was receiving for his troubles. Thus Crowley spent many of the following weeks hopelessly searching for another project to occupy his now over-active and fertile imagination. For only three months earlier, he had read about a certain Bertram Fletcher Robinson's research into a supposedly cursed 'mummy-board' at the British Museum. It was an elaborate story that had driven Crowley to murder.

7

The Crowley Connection
Part I

The horoscopes of the murdered are almost identical with those of the assassins.

Aleister Crowley

True love with black inchauntments filled,
Its hellish rout of shrieks and groans,
Its vials of poison death-distilled,
Its rattling chains and skeletons.

Aleister Crowley

In January 1907, just as former *Daily Express* editor Bertram Fletcher Robinson was settling down to finish his report into the cursed 'mummy-board' at the British Museum, he allegedly contracted 'enteric fever and peritonitis' and died at his home at 44 Eaton Terrace, Belgravia, on the 21st. At just 36 years of age, Fletcher Robinson was outwardly fit and healthy. It is perhaps no coincidence that in December 1906, when the debonair Fletcher Robinson was believed to have contracted the illness, Aleister Crowley had arrived back in London and Surrey following his escape from the trappings of his monogamous marriage with Rose abroad. With his long sojourn in New York, Vancouver and Europe at an end, Crowley was now ensconced in the capital and would have been privy to every newsworthy story in the London press – taking a particular interest in those concerning the growing curiosity in the magical properties of all things Ancient Egyptian.

Although Crowley had shed some light on what Aiwass told him in Cairo during those three days in April 1904, perhaps the complete dialogue between the two of them will never be known. It is not inconceivable then to assume that some bond was forged in those three days between Crowley and Aiwass that may have roused the Beast into a murder spree to protect and defend, in his mind, the gods of Ancient Egypt and the desecration of its artefacts. Crowley confessed that Aiwass had told him to 'regularly perform depraved acts and learn to love them'. Was this a clue? Were these 'depraved acts' in actual fact a succession of murders? Indeed, there is plenty of evidence that substantiates this extraordinary belief, none more potent than the fact that Crowley was now mentally ill, his sickness aggravated by Rose's prophecy. (This was a claim corroborated by the occult author and friend of the Beast's, Dennis Wheatley, who stated in his introduction to Crowley's book *Moonchild* that the Beast had spent four months in a private asylum outside Paris after being found insane and gibbering following an invocation of the god Pan.)

In Crowley's eyes he was a magician and 'these magicians and magi and clairvoyants ("clair" is scarcely the word that springs to mind when examining their output) had developed a relationship to objects on display in the Egyptian galleries of museums similar to that of an acquaintance of Jean François Champollion in the 1820s who had found an easier way of deciphering the Rosetta Stone: he stared at the stone, waited for enlightenment to strike and then said whatever came into his head. Sometimes, the adepts didn't even have to visit museums; they simply had to look at their mantelpieces, on which were displayed the trophies of a visit to the Theban Necropolis.' Had Crowley, who already possessed an overactive and troubled mind, 'developed a relationship' with the cursed 'mummy-board'? And had murderous 'enlightenment' come in the form of Aiwass? It was, after all, Aiwass who had instructed Crowley that a new dawn was coming and that he was the one to initiate it.

Having spent several years away from London, Crowley just so happened to return at a time when a well-publicised report into the curse of the 'mummy-board' at the British Museum was being prepared. In 1933, Fletcher Robinson's acquaintance from Cambridge University, Arthur Hammond Marshall, stated in his anecdotal autobiography that 'the very last time I saw him he told me a wonderful tale about a mummy, which had caused the death of everybody who had had to do with it. He was collecting his material, already had enough for a sensational story, and was on the track of more.' The report was never published. Soon after, its author was found dead in suspicious circumstances within London's West End.

Enteric fever is more commonly known as typhoid fever and is usually transmitted by the ingestion of food or water contaminated with faeces from an infected person. None of Fletcher Robinson's friends or family had shown symptoms of the disease, and Sir Arthur Conan Doyle even believed that

Fletcher Robinson had been struck down by an Ancient Egyptian curse. Was it Crowley, having read of Fletcher Robinson's 'blasphemous' research, who concocted an elaborate plan to stop his meddling? Given the fact that Crowley's eldest daughter Lilith had only recently died of typhoid herself and that he would have been in contact with the disease, it is not implausible to suggest that he infected Fletcher Robinson in some way, at the same time maintaining the illusion that Fletcher Robinson had died of natural causes.

Furthermore, when Wyeth and Neal were hired to carry out the exorcism on the 'mummy-board', they had claimed, it may be recalled, that the priestess was a 'clairvoyant' capable of reading omens in a silver cup and that she had lived in a dark time when embalmed corpses were used in black magic rites. Perhaps Crowley was also aware of the priestess' link to these 'black magic rites', hence his fanatical connection with the artefact? It is also worth remembering that the Beast was a regular visitor to the British Museum when he was in London, and spent much of his time at the adjoining Museum Street where he would later frequent his publishers, Mandrake Press, the Atlantis Bookshop and the Plough public house (known affectionately by its regulars as 'the Baby's Bum' due to its flesh-pink exterior).

Recognising the suspicious nature of Fletcher Robinson's death, historian Rodger Garrick-Steele believes that it was Conan Doyle himself, who, in collusion with Fletcher Robinson's wife (with whom he was having an affair), poisoned his friend in order to steal the idea for his book, *An Adventure on Dartmoor*. The book would, of course, become better known as *The Hound of the Baskervilles* – a tale which interestingly features an alleged 'curse' on the Baskerville family in the form of a 'demonic hound'. This far-fetched theory has been branded 'ludicrous' by many Conan Doyle and Fletcher Robinson aficionados, but there is one particular aspect of Garrick-Steele's supposition that is intriguing, especially when considered alongside the case against Crowley. He believes that Conan Doyle, fearing he was about to be exposed by Fletcher Robinson as an adulterer and a plagiarist, poisoned his friend using excessive amounts of laudanum. He goes on to say how, for the reasons of sanitation, it would have been unusual for a typhoid victim to be buried (as Fletcher Robinson was) rather than cremated 100 years ago, due to the infected bodily fluids escaping from the coffin. Garrick-Steele also believes that there are symptoms of excessive laudanum ingestion that mimic those of typhoid; they induce both stupor and coma, for example. So, bearing this in mind, was it laudanum that Crowley – perhaps the more likely suspect – was using as a poison? It would certainly seem more probable as he kept vast quantities of the opiate for his own personal consumption.

'While his spiritual life soared with its victories, [Crowley's] personal life crumbled under the stress of its burdens ... On November 4 [1906, shortly before infecting Fletcher Robinson with laudanum] he wrote in his diary, "dog-faced demons all day. Descent into Hell."'

Crowley blamed Lilith's death on Rose and her increasing alcoholism. Left alone in grief, Rose descended into a world of madness and depression. She would not be the last of Crowley's lovers to do so. Throughout this time, the Beast penetrated deeper into the world of the occult and 'sex-magick', this time taking a male lover, the writer Victor Neuburg. By the middle of 1907 Crowley was in search of a following and, looking to Cambridge for potential recruits, simply turned up one day in Neuburg's room at Trinity College. Neuburg was already a published poet, and Crowley had been attracted by the mystical leanings in his work. Neuburg was then in his mid-twenties, not having gone up to Cambridge until 1906 when he was twenty-three, by which time his family had finally admitted that he was not cut out for a career in business. He came from a comfortable middle-class home in North London and had been raised by his mother following the departure of his father for his native Vienna. Together, Crowley and Neuburg travelled to France, Algeria and the Sahara to perform an Enochian ritual to summon up Choronzon, the demon of the abyss, seen in the occult world as the devil himself. This rite was said to open the gates of hell. Inevitably, like Rose before him, Neuburg was left mentally traumatised by his relationship with Crowley.

By 1909, Crowley had returned to London where he had taken residence at 124 Victoria Street. Now wishing to embark on a career in publishing, it was from this premises that Crowley began to print *The Equinox*, a series of publications in book form that served as the official periodical of the Argenteum Astrum, the magical order formed by Crowley after his break from the Hermetic Order of the Golden Dawn. The following year, Crowley appealed against an injunction banning him from divulging the secrets of the Golden Dawn and the Rosicrucian Order in his *Equinox* publication. His appeal was successful and the injunction was overturned. On 22 April, the *John Bull*, a dedicated critic of the Beast's, printed an open letter to him that underlined their contempt towards his practices:

To Aleister Crowley, Esq., Editor of 'The Equinox'
Dear Mr. Crowley,
Congratulations on the result of your appeal.

It is rather nice to have lawsuits about Rosicrucian mysteries in the prosaic twentieth century.

Incidentally, there is also a fine advertisement for your periodical.

Meanwhile, I wish you would teach me to become invisible, to turn my enemy into a black dog, and to discover the buried treasures of the Djinn.

John Bull

Throughout his occupancy at Victoria Street, as well as in the 'uncongenial surroundings' of the nearby Caxton Hall, Crowley would regularly perform rituals, which included 'The Lesser Banishing Ritual of the Pentagram' – a ritual designed to banish the four elements. Crowley unwittingly granted access to one of these rituals to an undercover journalist from *The Looking Glass*, a popular paper at the time, whose subsequent headline on 29 October read 'AN AMAZING SECT'. Indeed, their article paints a vivid picture of the eccentric methods that Crowley employed here:

We propose under the above heading to place on record an astounding experience which we have had lately in connection with a sect styled the Equinox, which has been formed under the auspices of one Aleister Crowley. The headquarters of the sect is at 12[4], Victoria Street, but the meeting or séance which we are about to describe, and to which after great trouble and expense we gained admittance under an assumed name, was held in private at Caxton Hall. We had previously heard a great many rumours about the practices of this sect, but we were determined not to rely on any hearsay evidence, and after a great deal of manoeuvring we managed to secure a card of admission, signed by the great Crowley himself. We arrived at Caxton Hall at a few minutes before eight in the evening – as the doors were to be closed at eight precisely – and after depositing our hat and coat with an attendant were conducted by our guide to the door, at which stood a rather dirty looking person attired in a sort of imitation Eastern robe, with a drawn sword in his hand, who, after inspecting our cards, admitted us to a dimly lighted room heavy with incense. Across the room low stools were placed in rows, and when we arrived a good many of these were already occupied by various men and women, for the most part in evening dress. We noticed that the majority of these appeared to be couples – male and female. At the extreme end of the room was a heavy curtain, and in front of this sat a huddled-up figure in draperies, beating a kind of monotonous tom-tom. When all the elect had been admitted the doors were shut, and the light, which had always been exceedingly dim, was completely exhausted except for a slight flicker on the 'altar'.

Then after a while more ghostly figures appeared on the stage, and a person in a red cloak, supported on each side by a blue-chinned gentleman in some sort of Turkish bath costume, commenced to read some gibberish, to which the attendants made responses at intervals. Our guide informed us that this was known as the 'banishing rite of the pentagram.'

More Turkish bath attendants then appeared, and executed a kind of Morris dance round the stage. Then the gentleman in the red cloak, supported by brothers Aquarius and Capricornus – the aforesaid blue-chinned gentlemen – made fervent appeals to Mother of Heaven to hear them, and after a little while a not unprepossessing lady appeared, informed them that she was the Mother of Heaven [Crowley's lover at the time, the Australian Leila Waddell], and asked if she could do anything for them. They beg her to summon the Master, as they wish to learn from him if there is any God, or if they are free to behave as they please. The Mother of Heaven thereupon takes up the violin and plays not unskilfully for about ten minutes, during which time the room is again plunged in complete darkness. The playing is succeeded by a loud hammering, in which all the robed figures on the stage join, and after a din sufficient to wake the Seven Sleepers the lights are turned up a little and a figure appears from the recess and asks what they want. They beseech him to let them know if there is really a God, as, if not, they will amuse themselves without any fear of the consequences. 'The Master' promises to give the matter his best attention, and, after producing a flame from the floor by the simple expedient of lifting a trap-door, he retires with the Mother of Heaven for 'meditation', during which time darkness again supervenes. After a considerable interval he returns, flings aside a curtain on the stage, and declares that there is no God. He then exhorts his followers to do as they like and make the most of life. There is no God, no hereafter, no punishment, and no reward. Dust we are, and to dust we will return. This is his doctrine, paraphrased. Following this there is another period of darkness, during which the 'Master' recites – very effectively, be it admitted – Swinburne's 'Garden of Proserpine.' After this there is more meditation, followed by an imitation Dervish dance by one of the company, who finally falls to the ground, whether in exhaustion or frenzy we are unable to say. There is also at intervals a species of Bacchie revel by the entire company on the stage, in which an apparently very young girl, who is known as the 'Daughter of the Gods,' takes part. On the particular occasion we refer to the lights were turned up at about 10:15, after a prolonged period of complete darkness, and the company dispersed.

Perhaps unsurprisingly, the Beast became embroiled in a bitter court battle with *The Looking Glass* over the publication of this fascinating article. It was also during this period that Theodor Reuss, the head of the O.T.O. (Ordo Templi Orientis), travelled to London from Germany to make Crowley's acquaintance, and, according to Crowley, to persuade him to join his fraternal religious organisation. The Beast accepted the offer after much persuasion, and, in 1925, would become its leader, reorganising the O.T.O. around the Law of Thelema as its central religious principle. On 24 October 1914, shortly after his tumultuous break-up with Neuburg and with the First World War already underway, Crowley left his beloved London, where his studio at Onslow Court had become besieged by spies, and travelled to New York where 'he would endure – for the first time in his life – the dark desperation of an impoverished exile'. Crowley had already offered his services to British government agencies on behalf of the war effort, but was rejected because of the negative rumours concerning his character. It is unclear as to whether his split with Neuburg motivated his desire to relocate, or whether it was merely the intrusions of war playing on his mind, but soon Crowley found himself crossing the Atlantic onboard the ill-fated *Lusitania* (previously mentioned in relation to the curse of the 'mummy-board') 'carrying some fifty pounds in cash and an eclectic baggage of magical texts and documents'.

Upon his arrival in New York in late October 1914, Crowley discovered, to his genuine surprise, that his ill-gotten reputation had preceded him. Owing in no small part to the lurid accounts of his behaviour in London, Crowley was already something of a celebrity. In one account, published in *The World Magazine*, a publication of the *New York World* newspaper, the American author Harry Kemp, who was a renowned bohemian and poet at the time, described the illicit practices at Crowley's Onslow Court studio:

> One by one the worshippers entered. They were mostly women of aristo-cratic type … It was whispered to me that not a few people of noble descent belonged to the Satanists … Then came the slow, monotonous chant of the high priest: 'There is no good. Evil is good. Blessed be the Principle of Evil. All hail, Prince of the World, to whom even God Himself has given dominion.' A sound as of evil bleating filled the pauses of these blasphemous utterances.

Although Crowley had found himself out of favour with the modernist movement in New York that he so desperately wished to forge social ties with, he nevertheless continued undeterred to devote himself to experimentation with high magick. On one occasion, when Crowley was walking down Broadway with the writer William Seabrook, the Beast was asked to prove his magickal powers. In Seabrook's subsequent book, *Witchcraft*, he recalled what happened next:

> The crowd looked thinner ahead of us in front of the public library, and as we crossed Forty-second street, A.C. touched me gently on the elbow and put his fingers to lips. Ahead of us was strolling a tall, prosperous-looking gentleman of leisure, and Crowley, silent as a cat, fell into step immediately behind him. Their footfalls began to synchronize, and then I observed that Crowley, who generally held himself pompously erect and had a tendency to strut, had dropped his shoulders, thrust his head forward a little, like the man's in front, had begun to swing his arms in perfect synchronization – now so perfect that he was like a moving shadow or astral ghost of the other. As we neared the end of the block, A.C., in taking a step forward, let both his knees buckle suddenly under him, so that he dropped, caught himself on his haunches, and was immediately erect again, strolling. The man in front of us fell as if his legs had been shot out from under him … and was sprawling. We helped him up, as a crowd gathered. He was unhurt. He thanked us, and looked for the banana peel. There was no banana peel. With his hand on somebody's shoulder, he looked at the soles of his shoes. They were dry. He brushed himself off, regained his hat, tried his legs tentatively, thanked us, and strolled on.

By now, Crowley firmly believed that the final secret of 'sex-magick' was within his reach, and he took numerous lovers, both male and female, in New York, including a flurry of 'Scarlet Women' with whom he fell in love and had children. In one ceremony, performed at his apartment in Greenwich Village, he dubbed two American women the theriomorphic names of The Cat and The Snake, drawn from the Egyptian gods Pasht and Apophis. 'These individuals were, by this stage in his life, always women – those who played the Scarlet Woman to his Beast. The Cat and The Snake were the first of these in America.' With his desire to act as a spy for the British Intelligence shattered by an agency that neither found him useful nor completely trusted him, Crowley offered his services to both Germany and then America, who, by 1915, were still neutral in the conflict. (It would take the sinking of the boat that had transported Crowley across the Atlantic to precipitate America's entry into the war on the side of the Allies.) In what he would later claim was an act of sabotage, Crowley wrote pro-German propaganda for a New York publisher which, he explained, was intended to hurt the Germans by making them look ridiculous for having such bad propaganda written for them. 'In one stroke he turned his bad prose and treasonous leanings into a victory for freedom and democracy.'

In *Secret Agent 666: Aleister Crowley, British Intelligence and the Occult*, author Richard Spence states his belief that Crowley's mission to America 'was to gather intelligence about the German intelligence network, the Irish independence activists and produce aberrant propaganda, aiming at compromising the German and Irish ideals. As an agent provocateur he played some role in provoking the sinking of the *Lusitania*, thereby bringing the United States closer to active involvement in the war alongside the Allies.' However, in 1917, Scotland Yard, learning of Crowley's plight in America, didn't buy into this theory and decided to ransack an office of Crowley's in Regent Street, hoping to intercept his pro-German papers. Crowley drolly remarked in his *Confessions*: 'So, at the zero hour, reckless of peril, a devoted band of detectives, with revolvers drawn, went over the top, cheering wildly, to the third floor of 93 Regent Street, broke down the door, which I think was unlocked, and found a dozen mild old people trying to browse on the lush grass of my poetry.'

Whatever his reason for being in America and whichever side he had aligned himself with during the hostilities, in 1919 Crowley had found his new muse, a new Scarlet Woman – a Swiss-American by the name of Leah Hirsig. Hirsig, who already had a keen and extensive interest in the occult, sought out Crowley during his tenure in America and she made an immediate impact upon his life, so much so that never again would a 'Scarlet Woman play as deeply fundamental a role in the life of the Beast'. After their third meeting, Crowley had already painted the Mark of the Beast (the sun and the moon conjoined) between her breasts. With the war now at an end, Crowley and Hirsig, who was already pregnant with their first child, returned to Europe with the intention of refining and forming a new version of the religion of Thelema. Crowley, who had been suffering from recurring bouts of asthma, also had a desire to be closer to his native London and his trusted doctor on Harley Street. More pertinently, however, he needed a place to practise Thelema away from the prying eyes of post-Edwardian England.

In 1920 the Beast and Hirsig travelled to Cefalù in northern Sicily, a town full of fishermen and cobbled streets which retained much of its medieval architecture, and created a temple in an old farmhouse – the Abbey of Thelema – 'officially described as *Collegium ad Spiritum Sanctum*, but in reality was nothing more elaborate than a one-storeyed Sicilian farmhouse, oval in shape, and built in defiance of modern sanitation and comfort'. Hirsig, who had taken the term the 'Ape of Thoth' and the magickal name Alostrael, would indulge in heavy drinking sessions, cocaine and opium addiction, and 'sex-magick' with Crowley; she would also bear him another child, Poupée, who would also die tragically as an adolescent, much to Crowley's despair.

The shocking events that were to unfold at Crowley's 'cesspool of vice' would become the stuff of legend, and even today their legacy lingers to such an extent that the locals believe the now derelict abbey is cursed and advise visitors to stay away from it. Not long after Crowley's arrival, stories of depraved sexual acts at the abbey began to circulate among the locals, and one of the more notorious scandals involved Hirsig sacrificing a goat during copulation. Children allegedly ran around naked with a dog called 'Satan' and witnessed the adults having sex. According to the *John Bull* of 17 March 1923, 'Already five children are in [Crowley's] clutches. Two he claims as his own, but the other three have undoubtedly been kidnapped or lured into his den by his misguided and deluded satellites.' In a later article, the paper claimed that: 'These unhappy children ... are said to be half starved and have already been taught by "The Beast" to indulge in the vilest practises, while they are made to witness sexual debaucheries that are too disgusting to describe.'

In what Crowley called the 'nightmare room', his followers – or the 'Devil's Disciples' – were given drugs and were forced to view his perversely pornographic paintings on the walls (some of which remain today); the idea was that by doing so they would lose their inhibitions and fear.

The main room of the 'Abbey' – which is really a converted farmhouse – is windowless, with a flagged stone floor on which is painted a great orange circle, lined with pale yellow. Inside this 'magical circle' are interlaced black triangles. This room is furnished as a sort of pagan, or Pantheistic, temple, in which are performed not only Cabalistic ceremonies but the most depraved forms of Dionysian rites. (Dionysus was the Greek God of Wine, in whose honour Bacchanalian revels and orgies were given.)

Throughout this period, Crowley and Hirsig continued to travel between Cefalù, Paris and London, lodging, among other places, 'at a horrible hotel in Russell Square thronged with the hustling hooligans of the middle classes', before settling at 31 Wellington Square (31 being his sacred number), Chelsea. It was from here where Crowley would dictate his most successful book, *The Diary of a Drug Fiend*, which he later dedicated to Hirsig.

By 1923, however, the couple had returned to the relative sanctuary of the abbey, where they had made arrangements to receive further guests. A 23-year-old Oxford graduate by the name of Charles Frederick 'Raoul' Loveday arrived at the abbey with his wife Betty May, a denizen of Bohemia and a woman labelled by Crowley as a 'female parasite' and 'an artist's model of the most vicious kind'. 'She was tiny but her angelic appearance belied her violent nature. Those green eyes could blaze with savage ferocity and woe betide the victim of her wrath. She dressed like a gypsy and delighted in shocking people.'

Crowley had previously made Betty May's acquaintance in the Domino Room of Regent Street's Café Royal (where he was well known as the Magus of the Café Royal) in 1914, when she was working as a model and prostitute, and where he was often found dressed in his Highland finery, the 'full panoply of a Scottish chieftain'. 'If he frightened her it was not surprising: about that time he was exhibiting devil-worship in the Fulham Road, mostly to silly old ladies, at exorbitant admission fees.' Throughout the First World War, the Café Royal was 'a fertile territory for lovers' and where 'homosexual women felt accepted among like-minded comrades: modernist poets, exhibitionists, cross-dressers, abstract expressionists, models and nightclub dancers. The Ham and Bone Club and the Cave of Harmony too were full of them. Here they could dance together, unafraid, knowing that the shortage of men had made this a common sight.'

Indeed, the Café Royal has had its fair share of infamous guests throughout its illustrious history, and it is perhaps a point of interest that only twenty years earlier, in December 1894, what the *Daily News* described as a 'Shocking Murder' had taken place at the popular Regent Street eatery. A night porter by the name of Marius Martin, who was known to have clashed with a number of his colleagues during his brief residence at the Café Royal, was found shot dead outside the restaurant's Glasshouse Street entrance. Martin, a burly Frenchman, was also reputed to have been disliked by the restaurant's celebrity clientele, who regarded him as a vindictive gossip. In short, there was an abundance of suspects and the murder remains unsolved today.

Raoul Loveday, whom Crowley had described as 'a brilliant boy, just down from Oxford, where he had distinguished himself by his attainments in history', had a flair for poetry and the occult, and had become obsessed with Crowley's writings and longed to meet the man he so admired. Crowley wrote in his book *The Confessions of Aleister Crowley*: 'for over two years, [Loveday] had studied my magical writings with the utmost enthusiasm and intelligence. His character was extraordinary. He possessed every qualification for becoming a Magician of the first rank. I designed him from the first interview to be my magical heir.'

Loveday, 'a soccer-playing, rag-minded undergraduate of St. John's College', had first met Crowley in London – after the city had 'called for him' – in the late summer of 1922. At this time Loveday and Betty May were living largely on her earnings as a model in the bohemian circles of London's West End. Loveday was already delving into much of Crowley's published writings and was introduced to the Beast by their mutual friend Betty Bickers. According to Betty May, who, in 1929, published her own autobiography entitled *Tiger Woman* after her nickname within the bohemian circles she frequented, Loveday did not return from the meeting with Crowley for two days. When he eventually arrived home, 'his ghostly white face finally appeared at the window: he had climbed up the drain-pipe to the third-floor level of their Beak Street room, and nearly frightened her out of her wits'.

Loveday was 'covered with dust and soot, and his breath reeked of ether. I put him to bed, where he lay in a doped sleep until the middle of the following day. When he awoke I found out that he had spent the whole time he had been away with the great mystic, and that he had taken the drug to excite the mystical activities of his soul.' Interestingly, it was also in *Tiger Woman* where Betty May described how Loveday, her third husband and a keen Egyptologist himself, had taken her to the British Museum to show her the purportedly cursed 'mummy-board' belonging to the priestess of Amen-Ra. Indeed, this scene is re-created in Snoo Wilson's fictional *I, Crowley* where it is portrayed as the pivotal first meeting between Crowley, Loveday and Betty May shortly after the end of the First World War.

Despite their mutual admiration, Crowley could see that Loveday possessed a 'reckless' side that had already left him in hospital fighting for his life after a madcap caper at university went horribly wrong. The Beast believed his relationship with Betty May was another example of Loveday's 'recklessness' – he argued that he 'should not have married her' and that 'it meant the sterilization of the genius of success in life'. Loveday and Betty May lived in a filthy room in Fitzroy Street which Crowley described as a 'foul, frowsty, verminous den, stinking of the miasma of that great class who scrape through the years by dint of furtive cunning in dubious avocations'.

Throughout the previous October, Loveday and Betty May had been ill at frequent intervals, and, during the month, 'the foulness of Fitzroy Street fastened its foetid fangs on [Loveday's] throat. Both he and Betty May had escaped death by a hairbreadth.' (It should be noted that both Crowley and Betty May would later have prominent relationships with the Fitzroy Tavern on nearby Charlotte Street, for whom he would invent the Kubla Khan No 2 cocktail – a drink that consisted of gin, vermouth and laudanum – and where he would scribble mystifying sigils on the walls.)

In October 1922, the Beast returned to Cefalù. En route, he posted a letter to Loveday urging him to join him in Sicily with Betty May in tow:

I hope you will come out p.d.q. and bring Betty. I honestly tell you that the best hope for your married life is to get out of the sordid atmosphere of 'Bohemian' London ...

Does it surprise you that the notoriously wicked A.C. should write thus? If so, you have not understood that he is a man of brutal common sense and a loyal friend. So come and live in the open air amid the beauty of Nature ... Beak Street and Fitzroy Street are horrors unthinkable even in Rome; and Rome is a cesspool compared with Cefalù.

The society of Scholars, of free women and of delightful children will indeed be a great change for Betty; but it is what she needs most. There is in her not only a charming woman, but a good one; and she will develop unsuspected glories, given a proper environment. In London she has not one single decent influence, except your own; and however deeply and truly she may love you, she won't be able to resist 'la nostalgie de la boue' for ever.

Living from hand to mouth in London, Loveday decided to take Crowley up on his offer and travelled to the Abbey of Thelema to join the Beast, Hirsig and the 'Thelemites', a motley band of followers from around the world. They included a Provençal ex-governess called Ninette Shumway, whose less decorative courtesy title was 'Shummy', and the silent film character actress Jane Wolfe. Despite steadfast reluctance from Betty May, the young couple found themselves in Sicily before the end of the year; little did Loveday know at the time that he would never see his beloved London again. 'The responses of husband and wife to Abbey life were fundamentally opposed. For Loveday, it was an opportunity to pursue the path of wisdom under a living master. For Betty May, it was forced confinement in a remote and eccentric household.'

Soon after their arrival at Cefalù, Loveday felt compelled to write a letter to his anxious parents reassuring them that life at the abbey was idyllic, and that the British papers were 'enemies' of the Beast's:

Dear Mum and Dad,
Another line just to let you know how happy and comfortable we both are. Also to let you know that the articles in the *Sunday Express*, about the man in an annexe of whose house we are staying, are absolute lies, and written by an enemy. He was in the Secret Service in America; and had to pretend to be pro-German: hence they have a good opportunity to attack An answer has been sent showing that every word is untrue. He has been as nice to us

as anyone could be; and Robinson Smith is his friend. I thought I'd just send you this so that you could contradict it and needn't worry. Best wishes.

Your loving son, Fred

Indeed, this letter is a good indication as to the extent in which Crowley had brainwashed the gullible young couple. In all, Loveday sent eight naively written letters to his parents, assuring them time and again that the *Sunday Express* had fabricated its stories about the Beast. However, despite Loveday's apparent contentment at the abbey, the growing derision between Crowley and Betty May accelerated as the months went on, and by January 1923 their relationship had sunk to an all-time low. 'Even before the Lovedays arrived at the Abbey, Betty May had made up her mind that she would not comply with the routine of hocus-pocus. Crowley, on the other hand, made up his mind to break her will. He succeeded by threatening to sacrifice her on the "altar" of his temple.' By this time, however, Loveday had fallen drastically ill, and although Betty May initially believed that her husband's condition was brought about by excessive drug use, it later transpired that 'the toxic effect of the consumption of cat's blood as part of a ritual sacrifice in which Loveday presided' was to blame for his sudden sickness and lassitude.

According to Betty May, who had become Crowley's bête noire:

a cat that frequented the Abbey for food scraps was perceived by the Beast to be an evil spirit. Crowley grabbed the cat, which in turn severely scratched his arm. Crowley then resolved that the cat would be sacrificed in three days time by Loveday … Loveday had been supplied by Crowley with a Ghurkha *kukri* – a weapon with a boomerang-shaped blade. Loveday wielded it awkwardly and his first slash at the cat's neck failed to end its life. Despite having been quieted by a dab of ether, the wounded cat now escaped from Loveday's grasp and ran about before being all but decapitated by Loveday's second slash.

Betty May later testified that a bowl captured a large quantity of the cat's blood, which was subsequently consecrated by Crowley. As part of 'The Lesser Banishing Ritual of the Pentagram', Crowley dipped his finger in the blood, traced a pentagram on Loveday's forehead, then scooped the blood into a silver cup and passed it to Loveday, who, Betty May wrote, 'drained it to the dregs'. Soon after, Loveday, who was already 'a frail youth with an unhealthy pallor', contracted a virulent fever and spent many of the ensuing days confined to his bedroom.

By the second week in February, Loveday's illness had become so severe that he had weakened to the point that any physical movement was almost impossible.

He confessed that he had been suffering from fever and diarrhoea for some ten days and that 'it has left me as weak as water'. Loveday also stated his intention to return to England with Betty May as soon as he had recovered sufficiently from his illness. However, unbeknown to her husband, Betty May had written an additional note on the back of a letter that Loveday had written to his parents. It conveyed, for the first time, a warning to his mother of the danger Loveday faced in Sicily under the control and tutelage of Crowley, the manipulative tyrant:

> Dear Mrs. Loveday,
> Raoul doesn't know I am writing and I hope you will not tell him anything I have written on this page to you. I really think Raoul is very very ill and if he doesn't come home soon he will be too weak to be moved.
>   [Crowley] is laying down all sorts of rules, rules that could not possibly be kept. I have never worked so hard in my life as I have here. I am very ill, myself, but I am looking after Raoul as best I can. He wants a good warm bed and nourishment which we cannot get here. If Raoul gets better Crowley thinks of parting us and what can we do? We have got no money and are dependent upon him for our food.

On the same day that Betty May wrote this letter, Crowley had ordered her from the abbey, but she refused to leave, insisting that Loveday remain in her care. On 11 February, following an unsuccessful attempt to lodge an appeal against Crowley with the British consul, Betty May retired to her bedroom to read English newspapers sent on a fortnightly basis by Loveday's mother at his request. As reading was a forbidden luxury – to which both Betty May and Loveday had sworn adherence upon their arrival at the abbey – when Crowley discovered this violation, a fierce and violent argument broke out, as described by Betty May in the following account:

> I had not been reading long when the Mystic strode in, his face twitching with rage. He ordered me to go. There was a terrific scene. I should have said before that there were several loaded revolvers which used to lie about the abbey. They were very necessary, for we never knew whether brigands might not attack it. The Mystic used to shoot any dogs that came anywhere near the abbey with his revolver. He was an extremely good shot. It so happened that I had found one of these revolvers lying about the day before, and it suddenly occurred to me that it would be a wise precaution to hide it under my pillow. I now seized it and fired it wildly at the Mystic. It went wide of the mark. He laughed heartily. Then I rushed at him, but could not get a grip on his shaved

head. He picked me up in his arms and flung me bodily outside, through the front door.

Crowley later acknowledged this argument in his *Confessions*, but described the fight in a less embellished manner. 'I tried to soothe her and abate her violence. Poor Raoul, weak as he was, got up and held her and begged her to be quiet. At last she calmed down, but the room was a wreck.' At this point, Loveday was crucially moved to Crowley's room and Betty May made her departure from the abbey and into Cefalù, where she sought a hotel to spend the night, consoled, as Crowley sneeringly noted, 'by a series of admirers'. The Beast would later write: 'It was imperative to move Raoul to proper surroundings and prevent his being disturbed and neglected by the tantrums of the termagant … For some time he got neither better nor worse, but then, without warning, developed acute infectious enteritis.'

The following day Loveday's condition worsened. On 14 February, a Dr Maggio from the town was summoned to the abbey and made the diagnosis of acute enteritis or, significantly, typhoid fever. Crowley could see 'at a glance that [the doctor] expected a fatal issue. I wrote out a telegram informing [Loveday's] parents so that they might come if they thought fit. Betty offered to take it to the office, but instead of returning, collapsed hysterically in the street before sending it off. It was a common trick of hers to excite sympathy, attract notice or annoy her husband if he happened to say or do anything which she disliked.' The night before this took place, Crowley had recorded in his diary: 'I feel a current of Magical force – heavy, black and silent – threatening the Abbey.' According to Betty May, Crowley had at some point during this tumultuous episode cast the horoscope of Loveday which foretold 'a very gloomy depression. It looks as though you might die on the sixteenth of February at four o'clock.'

According to Crowley's biographer Richard Kaczynski in his book *Perdurabo: The Life of Aleister Crowley*:

Loveday's condition worsened, so on 16 February, the Beast and Betty went into town to fetch Dr Maggio. Returning to the Abbey up the mountain path, Betty fainted from exhaustion. Crowley knelt and gently revived her. When she was able to stand, he helped her to her feet and announced, 'We will make adoration.' She nodded quietly, and Crowley turned to face the sunset … As he spoke the passage from 'Liber Resh,' Betty noticed tears streaming down his cheeks, and she understood the words were also a prayer for Loveday. They marched solemnly back toward the Abbey until [Hirsig] met them on the path, as grim-faced as they. Betty grew concerned. 'Is he worse?' [Hirsig] answered bluntly. 'He's dead.' Betty fainted again.

Raoul Loveday, described by Crowley as the most brilliant disciple to have ever come to Cefalù, died on 16 February at approximately 4 p.m., just as Crowley had predicted.

Betty May found him in bed, laying with his head canted on his arms, just like the deathly apparition in their wedding picture ... Within an hour of death, Loveday's body was placed in a coffin; local law required that the body be disposed of within twenty-four hours. So Crowley spent the night reciting over the clay and rapping with his wand on the side of the box to prepare for his hasty burial ... For Crowley, this was the only funeral over which he had ever presided, and the first funeral he had attended since his father died back in 1887.

In *Confessions*, the Beast described Loveday's final moments: 'Raoul developed paralysis of the heart and died at once without fear or pain. It was as if a man, tired of staying indoors, had gone out for a walk.' This entire episode may well have thrown Crowley, who was already of unsound mind, into a deeper pit of vulnerability. The idea that it didn't is certainly intriguing, and the Beast's bizarre horoscope is all the more peculiar when evoked alongside the other dramatic event that took place on the same day at the very same hour in nearby Egypt. Howard Carter had just broken the threshold of the tomb of Tutankhamun.

8

The Crowley Connection
Part II

The air of London is damp and depressing. It suggests the consciousness of
sin. Whether one has a suite in the Savoy or an attic in Hoxton, the same
spiritual atmosphere weighs upon the soul.

Aleister Crowley, *The Confessions of Aleister Crowley*

Can we really believe that Raoul Loveday, who had just been moved into
Aleister Crowley's care at the Beast's behest, and whose death had been predicted by the Beast to fall on the very hour that Tutankhamun's tomb was
heinously entered, died an innocent death without even the slightest hint
of suspicion? Of course we can't – it is just too much of a coincidence to
think otherwise. Loveday's illness, which developed 'without warning', and
his subsequent death, which was attributed to typhoid, reeks of intrigue and
foul play.

Even though he had enforced a ban on all reading materials in the abbey,
Crowley would no doubt have had access to either Loveday's newspapers or
local gossip and conjecture – making it frankly impossible for him not to have
known of Howard Carter's impending discovery. With Carter's excavation in
Luxor being one of the biggest stories of the age, and with his own morbid
interest in Ancient Egypt piqued, Crowley, spurred on by his conversation with
the mysterious Aiwass in Cairo all those years earlier, would have felt compelled
to act upon Carter's sacrilege by performing a ritual to placate the gods of
Ancient Egypt. It was to be the first in a succession of ritualistic murders carried out by the Beast that were linked to the excavation of King Tut's tomb.

Indeed, Loveday was Crowley's sacrificial lamb, and infecting him with typhoid, or laudanum, as in the case of Bertram Fletcher Robinson, was his modus operandi; in this instance, contaminating the cat's blood and forcing Loveday to drink it would have been straightforward and credulous. Is this why Crowley, when questioned by the authorities, initially denied the sacrifice of the cat had taken place? And why did he insist the sacrifice commence three days after he was attacked by the cat rather than on the spur of the moment? Another puzzling issue is why Crowley murdered Loveday of all people. There was hardly a dearth of potential victims at the abbey for Crowley to choose from who were not as 'brilliant' or as 'intelligent' as Loveday was reputed to have been. The likely answer is that it gave Crowley a chance to spite Betty May, and the outpouring of praise the Beast would later bestow upon Loveday was merely a bluff. This is supported by the fact that there is seldom any mention of Loveday's death in Crowley's Magickal Diaries of 1923, despite its importance in the Beast's subsequent public disgrace, and his grief at losing his 'magickal heir' seems somewhat pithy. It was also well known that Loveday, at Crowley's command, cut himself with a razor every time he used the word 'I'.

Crowley, who would have been greatly assisted by the local law which required Loveday's body to be disposed of within twenty-four hours, had even gone as far as to cover his tracks by insisting that the local water supply was polluted; yet if Loveday's illness was brought about by this so-called contamination, why did none of the other members of the abbey fall sick? The Beast described his own battle with 'Mediterranean fever' during this period, an illness that supposedly infects the liver and spleen, but was this more likely a further effort to mislead his naive 'congregation' into believing that Loveday's death was, quite simply, a tragedy? It is also interesting to note that the last part of Crowley's *Confessions* was written in 1929, although the narrative curiously ends in 1923 (without offering a reason as to why) when it details his forced exile from Cefalù by Benito Mussolini. It also fails to acknowledge the part he played in Loveday's death and the many that were to follow; in hindsight, it was a confession of sorts.

"'I don't charge Crowley with causing Raoul's death," [Betty May] would reflect. "That would be silly." However, by the time she reached London and met reporters at the dock, venom replaced her amity.' It is likely she felt the need to retain a modicum of civility with Crowley to ensure that she could leave Cefalù unscathed. Now that she was safe from the Beast, however, she was free to divulge the truth behind Loveday's death. The newspapers, both in England and Italy, castigated Crowley and his band of 'devil worshippers'. Inevitably, a front-page article ran on Sunday 25 February 1923, with the tiered headline:

NEW SINISTER RELATIONS OF ALEISTER CROWLEY
VARSITY LAD'S DEATH
Enticed to 'Abbey'
Dreadful Ordeal of a Young Wife
Crowley's Plans

The article was a full-blooded assault on Crowley and his practices. 'According to the *Sunday Express*, Betty May had returned to England in a terrible state, "unable to give more than a hint of the horrors from which she had escaped": not only had her husband died under mysterious circumstances, but she had been "left alone to fight the Beast 666" and had witnessed behaviour "too unutterably filthy to be detailed in a newspaper".' While Loveday's death was correctly ascribed to typhoid fever, he was also referred to as one of Crowley's 'latest victims' – along with Betty May herself. The article went on to say: 'Once they were in Sicily, however, they found they had been trapped in an inferno, a maelstrom of filth and obscenity. Crowley's purpose was to corrupt them both to his ends.'

On the very same day in London:

> the Café Royal seemed unusually crowded and excited – and at every table there was at least one copy of that morning's *Sunday Express*. The paper, which had already in the foregoing November printed a somewhat outspoken article about Crowley, now featured an interview with Betty May – the first in a sensational series. Most of the protagonists of her story being well-known to the Café Royalites, the startling disclosures were devoured and debated. Indeed, when Aleister Crowley eventually re-entered the Café Royal [months later] he was greeted with complete silence. All eyes were fixed on him and nobody spoke until the Beast had taken his seat. Only when he called for Brandy, and not freshly killed babies' blood, did the Café resume its normal hubbub.

The *Sunday Express* followed this up by printing an article on 4 March that offered further insight into the lurid deeds taking place within the abbey: 'This man Crowley is one of the most sinister figures of modern times. He is a drug fiend, an author of vile books, the spreader of obscene practices.' Soon after this was printed, the papers dubbed Crowley, among other things, as 'A Wizard of Wickedness', 'The King of Depravity', 'The Wickedest Man in the World', 'a filthy devil in human form' and 'A Cannibal at Large'.

1 The well-known death mask of Tutankhamun (*c.* 1341–23 BC) is made of gold and inlaid with coloured glass and semiprecious stone. *The Art Archive/Egyptian Museum Cairo/Gianni Dagli Orti*

2 Howard Carter: the prominent Egyptologist and archaeologist noted as the primary discoverer of the tomb of Tutankhamun. *The Art Archive/Culver Pictures*

3 Howard Carter and an Egyptian workman examine the recently discovered sarcophagus of Tutankhamun. *Mary Evans Picture Library*

4 A lobby card for *The Mummy*, a 1932 Universal Pictures film starring Boris Karloff. *Universal/The Kobal Collection*

NOUVELLE COLLECTION NATIONALE

CONAN DOYLE

LA MOMIE VIVANTE

Autant de lecture que dans
un volume à 7 francs pour

75 cent.

l'ouvrage complet illustré

5 *La Momie Vivante* (The Living
Mummy); an illustration on the cover
of the French edition of a novel by
Sir Arthur Conan Doyle, published in
Paris 1910–20. *The Art Archive/Private
Collection/Marc Charmet*

6 44 Eaton Terrace,
Belgravia, SW1 (the
middle of the three
properties), the residence
in which Bertram Fletcher
Robinson reputedly died
of typhoid fever. *Author's
collection*

7 Prince Ali Kamel Fahmy Bey, 'the wastrel heir to a great industrialist' and 'a leading society figure in the Egyptian court of King Fuad'. *Getty Images*

8 Marie-Marguerite Fahmy pictured at Prince's Hotel, Jermyn Street, shortly after her acquittal for her husband's murder in September 1923. *Getty Images*

9 The front page of the *Daily Mirror* on 11 September 1923 perfectly exemplifies the feverish interest in the 'Savoy Shooting'. *Author's collection/ Daily Mirror*

10 The entrance to the Savoy Apartments – previously the Savoy Court – where Ali Kamel Fahmy Bey was shot dead by his wife. *Author's collection*

11 Sir Edward Marshall Hall, KC, the famous English barrister and spiritualist who had a formidable reputation as an orator. He became known as 'the Great Defender' on account of his successful defence of those charged with notorious murders. *Getty Images*

12 A recent photograph of Cleopatra's Needle as it undergoes restoration. *Author's collection*

13 The entrance to London's majestic Savoy Hotel pictured here in June 1924, less than a year after the brutal murder of Ali Kamel Fahmy Bey. *Getty Images*

14 A vintage postcard depicting the close proximity between the Savoy Hotel (second building from the left) and Cleopatra's Needle on the Thames Embankment. *Author's collection*

15 Evelyn Waugh, the English novelist, satirist, Bright Young Thing, and Aubrey Herbert's son-in-law, with his wife, Laura Herbert, on their wedding day at the Church of Assumption, London. *Getty Images*

16 A postcard view of the bustling Piccadilly Circus, *c.* 1932, previously home to the Egyptian Hall and where state mummies were once unwrapped. *Author's collection*

17 Members of the excavating team that discovered the tomb of Tutankhamun pose for a photograph at the tomb's entrance. Captain Richard Bethell is second left and Lord Carnarvon is third right. *Getty Images*

18 The former site of the Bath Club on Mayfair's Dover Street before it was destroyed by fire in the Second World War. Now just an office block, it was here where Richard Bethell supposedly succumbed to a 'coronary thrombosis'. *Author's collection*

19 Lord Westbury, 'a well-known racing owner and an excellent game shot', fourth right, at Lord Alington's pheasant shoot in December 1910. *Getty Images*

20 Now part of the Crowne Plaza hotel chain, a recent photograph of St James' Court, Buckingham Gate, SW1E, where Lord Westbury fell to his death from his seventh-floor apartment. *Author's collection*

21 A vintage postcard depicting the British Museum in all its ostentatious glory. *Author's collection*

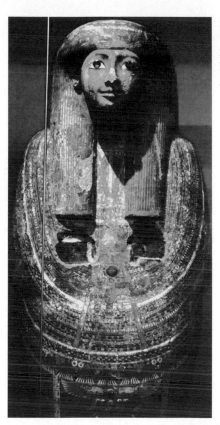

22 The resplendent and allegedly cursed 'mummy-board' belonging to the 'Unlucky Mummy', the priestess of Amen-Ra, can still be found in Room 62 of the British Museum. *Author's collection*

23 A caricature of Sir Ernest Wallis Budge, the former Keeper of the Egyptian and Assyrian Antiquities at the British Museum, complete with an Ancient Egyptian coffin lid, by Powys Evans, 1926. *Mary Evans Picture Library*

24 48 Bloomsbury Street, Bedford Square, WC1B, was once the home of Sir Ernest Wallis Budge and where he died aged 77. *Author's collection*

25 The platform at Holborn underground station where two women mysteriously disappeared on the night of 5 April 1935. The now disused British Museum station, where the screams of an Ancient Egyptian ghost are said to echo, was one stop away on the Central line. *Author's collection*

26 The former site of the British Museum underground station, now the Nationwide Building Society, on High Holborn. It was here where the mysterious sigils appeared on the walls following the disappearance of the two women. *Author's collection*

27 The making of the film *Bulldog Jack* at Shepherd's Bush Studios on 4 January 1935. The fictional Bloomsbury station was based on the British Museum station, and on the night of the film's release the two women disappeared in London. *Getty Images*

28 The 'Great Beast'
Aleister Crowley,
occultist magician,
accomplished chess
player, mountaineer,
author, poet and
murderer, pictured here
on 1 January 1938.
Getty Images

29 The Fitzroy Tavern
on Charlotte Street;
once home to London's
bohemian set and where
Aleister Crowley drew
mysterious sigils on the
walls, created outlandish
cocktails and drank with
Nina Hamnett. *Author's
collection*

30 The Atlantis Bookshop on Museum Street
– London's oldest occult booksellers – was often
frequented by Aleister Crowley when spending time
at the nearby British Museum. *Author's collection*

31 50 rue Vavin, a few doors below the Boulevard
Montparnasse; once the Hotel de Blois, Aleister
Crowley's Parisian base, now Le Parc aux Cerfs
restaurant. *Author's collection*

32 The renowned Parisian music hall Folies Bergère, pictured in July 2010. It was here where Aleister
Crowley made the acquaintance of Marie-Marguerite Fahmy in 1913. *Author's collection*

33 The Café Royal on Regent Street, shortly after its closure in 2008, played host to Aleister Crowley and his eccentric behaviour on numerous occasions throughout his London occupancy. *Author's collection*

34 A rare photograph of Aleister Crowley and his followers performing 'The Lesser Banishing Ritual of the Pentagram' in the 'uncongenial surroundings' of Caxton Hall in 1909. *Mary Evans Picture Library*

35 A poster for the 2008 film *Chemical Wedding*, which starred Simon Callow as a reincarnated Aleister Crowley. *Author's collection*

They even went so far as to suggest that Crowley, during a Himalayan expedition, had killed and eaten two of his native porters and that 'Bestial Orgies' were taking place in Sicily while the protagonists gorged on cakes of goat's blood and honey. Either way, in his *Confessions* Crowley insisted that he was above it all, despite his increasing dependence on heroin, but was unaware that his reputation in his homeland 'had at last been damaged beyond repair'. His most dedicated critic, the *John Bull*, printed an article on 10 March that would prove to be the final nail in the coffin of his quest for public approval:

> Suddenly, [Loveday] became mysteriously ill, leaving the girl-wife alone to fight the Beast. She bravely defied him, and says that Crowley turned her out that night. Within twenty-four hours of his seizure the young husband died. The doctor from Cefalù, who was called, diagnosed the mysterious and fatal malady as acute enteritis, we're told, but 'was puzzled at the case and at certain peculiarities in the nature of the attack' which quickly ended in death.
>
> In the light of the disclosures we have already made, and of those we shall make in subsequent articles based upon authoritative information and documents in our possession, we unhesitatingly demand:
>
> A post-mortem examination by Italian authorities upon this unfortunate young Englishman and a searching inquiry into the activities at the 'Abbey' and of its nefarious Master.
>
> That a close observation be maintained by Scotland Yard of the movements of Crowley's present woman emissary in London and that they see that she leaves the country unaccompanied by anyone.
>
> That the Home Office, which is already in possession of sufficient evidence to justify grave criminal charges being preferred against him, demands the extradition of Crowley.

Although the *John Bull* was notorious for its scandalous spin, the mere fact that the doctor at Cefalù was reported to be 'puzzled' by the 'peculiarities' in Loveday's death is intriguing, as is the fact that they highlighted the need for scrutiny of Crowley's 'present woman emissary in London', a point that would become increasingly significant, and demanded an autopsy on Loveday to determine exactly how he died. A week later, the *John Bull* continued its campaign against Crowley and published the following account from a woman who had partaken in rituals at the Beast's Fulham Road studio in the early 1900s:

> At that time [Crowley] was an attractive and almost handsome man, and his fluent and intensely interesting talk of the strange places he had been to and

the wonderful sights he had seen made a deep impression on the girl (whom we will call Miss. N.). She found herself fascinated by his conversation and became a keenly enthusiastic listener to his dissertations upon the weird and wonderful adventures he had experienced, despite the fact that she was at the time engaged to be married to a young doctor – to whom indeed, she owes the restoration of her reason. Her lover was later killed in the war. With no idea of the true character of the depraved wretch who was cunningly inveigling her into his clutches, as he had inveigled others before, Miss. N. allowed herself to be persuaded to pay a visit to his Fulham Road 'Studio'. When she arrived there she was received by Crowley, who had dressed himself up in a typical magicians robe, and to her amazement, and no little amusement, after showing her around the place, he proceeded to perform a strange sort of religious ceremony, offering up prayers and singing an incantation in a foreign language. Miss N., having come to the conclusion that the man was not entirely in his right senses, started to make a tour of inspection of the weirdly fitted up room. When she opened the cupboard, however, she fell back in horror, for facing her were two grinning skeletons. She swung around to find Crowley gazing down at her with a peculiarly fixed stare. Then in a low vicious voice he said: 'I'll add you to those if you don't do as I tell you.'

The rest of her story detailed the horrifying exploitation she suffered at the hands of Crowley, who repeatedly drugged and abused her. Whether or not 'Miss. N.' was of reliable provenance remains unclear, but there is little doubt that her compelling account of the 'grinning skeletons' gives pause for thought, especially in relation to what would later transpire in London and Cefalù. Arthur Machen, one of Crowley's rivals within the Golden Dawn, added credence to this report when he recalled an anxious meeting with the poet W.B. Yeats in his memoir *Things Near and Far*: 'He described the doings of a fiend in human form, a man who was well known to be an expert in Black Magic, a man who hung up naked women in cupboards by hooks which pierced the flesh of their arms.'

Meanwhile, across the Atlantic, the Beast's supposed friend William Seabrook had written a similar series of damaging articles on Crowley for the *Hearst Sunday* tabloid chain. Featuring headlines such as 'SECRETS BEHIND THE SCENES AMONG THE DEVIL-WORSHIPPERS', Crowley's reputation in America was now similarly in tatters. Worst of all, once the authorities in Sicily learned of Crowley's international infamy, it wasn't long before the abbey was closed to him, and the majority of his followers were deported.

It isn't beyond the realms of possibility that Crowley's congregation were in some way involved in his murderous dalliances, not least because his magickal children did not share his own reluctance to write about the legacy of King Tut. One of his followers, who went by the name of Frater Achad (real name Charles Stansfeld Jones), wrote an abstract book called *The Egyptian Revival* in which he described 'the underlying reason for public interest in the Tomb of Tutankhamun':

> ... in order, if possible, to discover the hidden causes it will be necessary for us to make a brief survey of the Egyptian Current of Thought from the earliest times to the present day. We do not find the public interest centred alone in the treasures found in the tomb of Tutankhamun, but in nearly every instance reference is made to his immediate predecessor King Amenhotep IV, or to use his more familiar title King Khu-en-Aten [actually Akhenaten] ... After his death, Tutankhamun is said to have re-established the old order and the worship of Amen-Ra in place of that of Aten. What was the cause of this controversy, and what is its bearing on the thought of the present day?

Cultural historian Sir Christopher Frayling, in his book *The Face of Tutankhamun*, elaborated on this: 'The answer, for those who had the ears to hear, was that the discovery heralded a major revival of the "influence of the Ever-coming son, the Crowned Child, Lord of the New Aeon", or the cycle of Aquarius, and in addition helped to explicate (always explicate, for some reason, rather than explain) the meaning of the Tarot pack.'

With this in mind, did Crowley see himself as a contemporary King Tut? After all, Tutankhamun was responsible for the restoration of the worship of Amen-Ra and the downfall of the Aten. Did Crowley therefore envisage his bringing down of the old order of Christianity and advancing the worship of Thelema? If so, it is not hard to imagine him forming a rabid connection in his mind to Tutankhamun; a connection strong enough for him to commit murder. The fact that Crowley later expelled Jones from his order indicates that some-where along the way they had a violent disagreement. Was it Jones' writings about both Tutankhamun and Amen-Ra that had so incensed the Beast? It is unlikely we will ever know; although any mention in Crowley's writings of the discovery of the tomb of Tutankhamun, the greatest archaeological discovery of the age, are conspicuous by their absence, and the fact that Crowley, despite his numerous visits to Egypt, never once recorded a visit to Luxor seems most irregular. After all, it was Luxor that was home to the Priest Ankh-af-na-khonsu, who Crowley would later claim to have been a re-embodiment of the magickal current represented by the priesthood to which Ankh-af-na-khonsu belonged.

In fact, the only recorded connections between Crowley and King Tut are an evocative painting that depicted Crowley wearing a *Khepresh* (an Ancient

Egyptian royal headdress) that was modelled on the one Tutankhamun wore; Crowley's belief that he was once the reincarnation of Akhenaten, King Tut's heretical father, and the portrayal of the divine triumvirate of Thelema – Nuit, Hadit and Ra-Hoor-Khuit – in which an enthroned Horus takes the form of Ra-Hoor-Khuit, a hawk-headed king overcome by a cobra headband and a solar disc. It was, of course, the cobra and the hawk that made dramatic appearances on the day the tomb of Tutankhamun was discovered.

Throughout this turbulent time, rumours of ritualistic murder were rife.

Oxford [University] was electrified by Raoul Loveday's death, and Raymond [Greene, the mountaineer and elder brother of the novelist Graham Greene] found himself at the centre of a plan to find out exactly what had happened and, if necessary, exact some kind of revenge on the Beast. He learned that Betty May was holding court at the Golden Cross Hotel, and hurried round to make her acquaintance. She was lying in bed, and he found her 'very attractive in a rare Mongolian way'. She showed no signs of being in a state of shock, but told him how she and Raoul had been taken ill – she thought he might have been persuaded against his will to experiment with drugs, but Crowley claimed that both he and Loveday had been struck down with 'Mediterranean fever' – and after his death she had wandered the bare Sicilian hills all night before making her escape. Betty May's undergraduate admirers were duly outraged, and Peter Rodd – later to become Nancy Mitford's feckless and unsatisfactory husband and the model for Evelyn Waugh's Basil Seal – suggested to Raymond that he should go to Cefalù in the Easter vacation, shoot the atrocious Beast, and make his way to the south coast of Sicily, where Rodd would be waiting with a boat to spirit him away to North Africa. Richard Hughes, later to become a well-known novelist, best remembered for *A High Wind in Jamaica*, heard of Rodd's plan, and wrote to Raymond, urging him to desist. 'Naturally one's first impulse was to assume that Aleister Crowley had murdered [Loveday], and want to retaliate,' Hughes wrote. 'I heard from various sources that you were conspiring. I'm afraid your secret is not particularly well guarded. As for my co-operation, I'm afraid it will be of very little use to you. The only thing of any possible use would be to confront the man and shoot him outright. That I am not prepared to do; and nor are you.' Hughes' cautionary words were uncalled for, since Raymond never had any intention of putting Rodd's half-baked plan into operation.

What really convinced him, however, was a letter he received from Crowley shortly before Easter:

> Dear Sir,
>
>   Do what thou wilt shall be the whole of the law.
> Forgive me if I suggest, from the little experience that I have in such matters, that when one is establishing a spy system it is rather important to prevent one's principal plan coming directly into the hands of the person whom you want watched.
>
>   Love is the law, love under will.
>
>   Yours truly,
>
>   Aleister Crowley
>   Knight Guardian of the Sangraal

In the meantime, Leah Hirsig, convinced that a private detective was following them, stood by the Beast and decided to join him in exile – a journey that would first take them to north Africa. On 1 May, they sailed from Palermo and the following day arrived in Tunis. 'North Africa had served Crowley before as a place in which to test and cleanse his soul. It would do so again.'

By 11 May 1923, Crowley and Hirsig had found inexpensive lodgings in a hotel, Au Souffle du Zephir, in La Marsa Plage, a tourist beach town north-east of Tunis. It was throughout this period that Crowley began to dictate to Hirsig his *Confessions*. With Hirsig often travelling to and from Cefalù to check on the welfare of the remaining members of the Abbey of Thelema, Crowley spent much of his time writing vicious articles and poems about his enemies – Mussolini being the main recipient of his ire and *Schadenfreude*: 'It is the beginning of the end for this upstart renegade with his gang of lawless ruffians, and his crazy attempt to restore the tyranny of the Dark Ages. Only twenty-eight days since he signed the order for my expulsion from Italy, and already he totters.' Several further diary entries confirmed just how deeply affected Crowley had been by his forced exile from a country he adored, and Lawrence Sutin describes how the Beast 'had lost both his Abbey and his reputation, and no longer had a publisher for the massive work on which he laboured'. Instead, his diaries reflect a man on the brink of a mental breakdown and anguished self-analysis. On 19 May, during a session of ethyl oxide, Crowley had sunk to a nadir and contemplated suicide: 'Why drag out a useless life, dishonouring my reputation, discrediting my methods, etc?'

However, with Hirsig frequently away in Cefalù, it would have been around this time that newlyweds Prince Ali Kamel Fahmy Bey and his wife, Marie-

Marguerite, arrived in Tunisia on the next stop of their whirlwind honeymoon, having already taken in the sights of Cairo, Luxor and, in particular, the newly discovered tomb of Tutankhamun. It is not beyond belief to suggest that Crowley and Marie-Marguerite had already crossed paths years earlier in Paris when she was working as a prostitute in the Pigalle district, supplementing her income by singing in the local cafés and bars. By the time she was in her early twenties, Marie-Marguerite was working as an 'ill-mannered' and 'fiery-spirited' hostess at the Folies Bergère – a disreputable cabaret music hall that Crowley was known to frequent.

In 1913, at the same time that Crowley was living in Paris with his lover, Victor Neuburg, Marie-Marguerite began a successful career as a courtesan working for one Madame Denart, who ran a high-class brothel, '*un maison de rendezvous*', at 3 rue Galilée. Denart took great pains to have her protégée groomed, and Marie-Marguerite began to live it up as the paid-for companion and mistress of several wealthy and titled men from Europe and America under the nom de plume Maggie Meller. 'She gave lavish parties, and – usually with a male escort, rarely the same one twice – attended parties given by others of the Smart Set. On most partyless nights, she whiled the time away in exclusive restaurants and expensive nightclubs, often dancing until the small hours at the latter.' The Hermetic Order of the Golden Dawn had also built its Ahathoor Temple in a nearby district.

With Crowley at the height of his practice of Freemasonry, as well as 'sex-magick' with Neuburg (he would later call it his 'Paris Working'), and with Marie-Marguerite working as a 'woman of aristocratic type', the pair would almost certainly have met during this period, quite possibly even forming a friendship or, more likely, a sexual relationship. Indeed, Marie-Marguerite had all the hallmarks and characteristics of a 'Scarlet Woman', as well as a willingness to misplace loyalty.

In his *Confessions*, the Beast recalled that while residing in Paris with Neuburg:

I took Nina and a lady whom I will call Dorothy … Dorothy would have been a *grande passion* had it not been that my instinct warned me that she was incapable of true love. She was incomparably beautiful. Augustus John has painted her again and again, and no more exquisite loveliness has ever adorned any canvas. She was capable of stimulating the greatest extravagances of passion … She was an extremely good friend, though she never allowed her friendship to interfere with her interests. In other words, she was a thoroughly sensible and extremely charming young girl. She was, in addition, one of the best companions that a man can possibly have. Without pretence of being a blue-stocking, she could hold her own in any conversation about art, literature or music. She was the very soul of gaiety, and an incomparable comedienne.

Aside from the fact that Crowley felt the need to protect the mystery woman's identity by referring to her as 'Dorothy', her attributes and personality seem remarkably similar to those that belonged to Marie-Marguerite. Crowley also made reference to 'Dorothy's husband in Montparnasse'; the fact that Marie-Marguerite was also married (to her first husband) at the time corroborates the theory that they were one and the same person, as does the intriguing suggestion that she was painted by Augustus John. There are several sketches by John that depict an anonymous woman who bears an uncanny similarity to Marie-Marguerite, even down to the pronounced mole on her left cheek.

With this in mind, when the Beast and Marie-Marguerite meet ten years later in such strange circumstances at the Tunisia Palace Hotel, and with Crowley having already killed Loveday on the same day and hour that Tutankhamun's tomb was breached, is it not possible that the Beast issued a set of murderous instructions to Marie-Marguerite? Already mentally frail, Crowley would have seen for himself the cruelty that had been inflicted upon her by Fahmy Bey, who had recently insisted they visit the tomb of Tutankhamun twice – a fact that Marie-Marguerite would have been happy to divulge to all and sundry. Fahmy Bey was an ideal target for Crowley: he was rather lacking in diplomacy, was brash and arrogant, had more money than sense, and, most heinously, had brazenly walked into the sacred burial chamber of a dead pharaoh of whom he considered himself to be a descendent.

There is no doubt that Marie-Marguerite fired the fatal shots that killed her husband in the Savoy Hotel, but could there have been an influence or a motive for the murder other than the abuse she suffered at her husband's hands? Indeed, it would have been practically impossible for Crowley to have got close enough to Fahmy Bey to kill him as his retinue followed him everywhere he went. Again, Crowley's presence in this case seems almost too coincidental. It remains highly likely that he would have made Marie-Marguerite's acquaintance in Paris years earlier, and his appetite for murder would have been well and truly whetted by Loveday's death. His latest mission to appease the demands of Aiwass would also have stirred the malaise he suffered since his expulsion from Sicily.

On 11 July, the day of the murder, Crowley revealed in his diary perhaps a telling clue of his involvement in Fahmy Bey's death: 'Half asleep till noon: a wretched state of conflict between "duty" & human weakness. I am far better in health all round, these last 3 weeks, & have done lots of good work.' What 'duty' was he referring to and what was his 'good work'?

On 14 July, Crowley's diaries offer the biggest clue yet as to his complicity. He writes:

10.30 a.m. (Shooting of Ali Fathnay in Savoy Hotel.) Cosmopolitanism evidently involves the conflict of moral codes & the destruction of national & cultural guarantees of good manners & conduct. What is true of Port Said & such Euroclydon centres is now true of the Savoy Hotel. It being possible to revert from Cosmopolitanism, the necessary issue is the establishment of a Cosmopolitan Law. This must be Thelema. This fool was shot for not knowing *CCXX*, I, 41.

Aside from the peculiar spelling of 'Fathnay' and the fact that he refers to him as a 'fool', what this diary entry offers is a genuine link between Crowley and the Fahmy Bey murder. Crowley predominantly used his magical diaries to consolidate the work he initiated in Cefalù and to explore the various techniques of 'sex-magick'. They were therefore short on newsworthy detail at the time, which makes the inclusion of the murder at the Savoy all the more compelling. *CCXX*, I, 41 is a reference to Crowley's *Book of the Law*, the sacred text of Thelema written in Cairo in 1904, which the Beast accredited to Aiwass. *The Book of the Law* I, 41 states: 'The word of Sin is Restriction. O man, refuse not thy wife, if she will! O lover, if thou wilt, depart! There is no bond that can unite the divided but love: all else is a curse.'

So, is Crowley's contempt exacerbated by Fahmy Bey's inability to sexually pleasure his wife? This minutiae would not have been printed in the papers at the time, thus Crowley's knowledge of this facet must have come directly from Marie-Marguerite herself. It is also fascinating to note the use of the word 'curse' in this reference.

On 19 August, Crowley noted in his diary: 'A rather dull day; began poem on Ali Bey & his Wazir.' The mere fact that the Beast continued to make reference to Ali Kamel Fahmy Bey (although no longer referring to him as 'Ali Fathnay') in his diaries over a month after his Savoy Hotel murder is particularly damning. The 'Wazir' he writes about is either Marie-Marguerite or, more likely, Said Enani. Bearing in mind that Crowley had a profound fondness for chess, it could be that the 'Wazir' is a reference to an unorthodox, orthogonal chess piece, or leaper, which is most commonly used in the Muslim variant of the game. Why he would refer to Marie-Marguerite as a 'Wazir' is unknown, but could likening her to an uncommon chess piece allude to a wider implication of her part in his game? This also draws the obvious suggestion that Crowley must have known Marie-Marguerite at a personal level to have made such an obscure reference in the first place. 'Wazir' is also the Arabic word for minister or advisor. Said Enani's relationship to Fahmy Bey would have been akin to that of a wazir to a sheik, so perhaps this is the more probable implication, endorsing the theory that Crowley was *au fait* with the inner workings of Fahmy Bey's attendants.

Consequently, when Marie-Marguerite regaled to Crowley the stories of her two visits to the tomb of Tutankhamun, he would have been inevitably appalled. She would have told him how, in February 1923, she and Fahmy Bey had travelled on a luxury yacht – the *dahabeeyah* – to Luxor and how they had moored outside the opulent Winter Palace Hotel in which a host of impressive guests, including Lord Carnarvon, were staying. 'Lord Carnarvon accepted their invitation to lunch, and the lavish shipboard parties given by the Fahmys during their two visits to Luxor that February were attended by some of the best-known personalities of the "Tutankhamun Season", including Howard Carter, General Sir John Maxwell, the popular and gregarious Maharajah of Kapurthala, a Greek archaeologist, a distinguished Egyptian poet, various financiers and an assortment of local dignitaries.'

It was in between these sumptuous gatherings that the Fahmys, 'gripped by the prevailing Tutankhamun fever', hired a pair of donkeys on which they travelled to Karnak and the Valley of the Kings. On their second visit to the newly opened tomb, Marie-Marguerite marked the occasion by climbing into the nearby open sarcophagus and lay down inside it. 'Clad in a riding habit and with her arms folded in front of her, she became the subject of a zany snapshot.' This blasphemy would have greatly angered Crowley. Demanding retribution, it could have been at this point that he persuaded Marie-Marguerite to murder Fahmy Bey, safe in the knowledge that the stories of the abuse she suffered at his hands would act as a sufficient motive in the eyes of the law and of the public.

As the Beast was himself an 'excellent shot', he would have suggested to Marie-Marguerite that she shoot her husband with her own pistol and then relay to the authorities the details of his cruelty. Although throughout her trial Marie-Marguerite willingly played the part of the downtrodden damsel, acting as if she had never handled a gun before and insisting that she thought it was empty when she aimed it at her husband, a more recent investigation into the Fahmy Bey murder has indicated that she fired a single bullet in the apartment a few moments before killing her husband. Indeed, in Detective Inspector Albert Grosse's statement, he declared that, 'I examined the corridor of the fourth floor. I found a hole in the wall. It was the size of a bullet, and approximately three feet from the door. Some yards farther on I found that the beading of a glass door had apparently been shot away, and I found a hole in the beading through which a bullet had passed.'

Also, why did Marie-Marguerite see fit to shoot at her husband three times? It was undoubtedly excessive and somewhat contradicts her argument that she 'thought the sight of the pistol might frighten him'. Two bullets caused severe damage to Fahmy Bey's brain tissue (from premeditated head shots); the other harmlessly ricocheted into the corridor wall. Marie-Marguerite's lawyer, Sir Edward Marshall Hall:

> suggested that when the pistol was gripped tightly, the slightest pressure on the trigger would fire each shot. But Robert Churchill, Britain's top firearm expert and gunsmith [who coincidentally owned a shop off the Strand and gave evidence at the trial], said, 'The trigger has to be pulled for each shot. It is automatic loading, but not automatic firing.' Marshall Hall also claimed that an ignorant person might not realise that firing a shot, far from emptying the gun, brought the next cartridge case automatically into firing position. Churchill agreed. But as the gunsmith's biographer, MacDonald Hastings, later pointed out, 'it was unlikely … that a woman who thought it necessary to have a pistol for her protection wouldn't have taken the trouble to find out how it worked.'

Percival Clarke, the leading Crown counsel in Marie-Marguerite's trial and son of the famous Victorian advocate Sir Edward Clarke, stated that he believed she 'had fired her pistol out of the hotel window before the shooting … not with the intention of rendering it harmless but to make sure it was in working order'. He also submitted to the judge that he should be allowed, in response to Marshall Hall's passionate decree that Marie-Marguerite was the victim of a deviant sexual predator, 'to dispel the idea that the defendant was a poor child dominated over by this man'. He went on to explain: 'I want to prove that she associated with men from an early age, and that she is a woman of the world in the wildest sense. I submit that I am entitled to ask her how she treated other men. I do not want it to be thought that all the fault was on the husband's side.'

Clarke had earlier asked Marie-Marguerite whether he could correctly describe her as a woman of the world, a woman of experience. 'I have had experience of life,' she sagely replied, a well-placed sob punctuating her every sentence. It later transpired in court that Marie-Marguerite had 'agreed with Marshall Hall that she had been "terrorised" by several of [Fahmy Bey's] employees, including a black valet – but she had to admit to Clarke that the valet was a youth of eighteen who was only five feet tall'.

Indeed, were she cross-examined properly the jury would have discovered that not only had Marie-Marguerite been a teenage prostitute in Bordeaux and Paris, the product of which was an illegitimate daughter when she was just fifteen, but that her husband was not alone in having inclinations towards the same sex. A private detective hired by the prosecution discovered in Paris that Marie-Marguerite 'is addicted, or was addicted, to committing certain offences with other women and it would seem that there is nothing that goes on in such surroundings as she has been moving in Paris that she would not be quite well acquainted with …'

Furthermore, it may also have been Crowley, privy to the Fahmys' London itinerary, who suggested that Marie-Marguerite murder Fahmy Bey in the Savoy Court as the building overlooked Cleopatra's Needle – providing a fitting altar for the impending sacrifice. 'The building, one of the highest in London, was erected by a firm of New York contractors chosen by Rupert D'Oyly Carte and [Sir George] Reeves-Smith. The touch of a bell brought meals from its own kitchens, apart from the services of a chiropodist, hairdresser and manicurist. The heating was thermostat-controlled, then an innovation, and each suite came equipped with telephones and electrical sun beds.'

Moreover, Crowley knew the Savoy and its locale well, having resided there himself over a number of months in between properties and running up a large unpaid bill. In 1911, he attended a 'boisterous' party at the Savoy hosted by the ballerina Isadora Duncan; in his 1917 book *Moonchild*, the dancer Lavinia King stays at the Savoy, and, during Crowley's own residence in the early 1920s shortly before the murder of Ali Kamel Fahmy Bey, he even recorded a list of experiments for his *Amrita* publication – a collection of writings on occult medicine – and wrote a poem on Savoy-headed notepaper called 'Bright's Disease'. It is a point of curiosity that on 22 December 1936, Crowley assembled a group of people by Cleopatra's Needle – 'no doubt chosen for its Egyptian linkage' – to announce the publication of his new book *The Equinox of the Gods*. More of a publicity stunt than anything significant, the Beast:

> paraded a Jew, an Indian, a Negro and a Malayan in a procession to Cleopatra's Needle where, at exactly 6:22am, he proclaimed 'Do what thou wilt shall be the whole of the Law' to all the races of the world. He then gave each individual present a copy of *The Equinox of the Gods*. This stunt would be repeated the following year, almost to the day, again at Cleopatra's Needle.

On this occasion:

> The *Daily Express* of Thursday December 23, 1937 ran an article; '*These Names Make News, Mixed Bag of Early Birds*' by William Hickey, which is

merely an alias used by the noted journalist [Tom] Driberg. The article began: 'An Englishman, a Jew, an Indian, a Negro, a Malayan – no, it's not one of those saloon-bar jokes.' The article is about Crowley assembling a 'mixed bag' of people before Cleopatra's Needle to announce the new release of *The Equinox of the Gods*.

The terrific thunderstorm that broke as Fahmy Bey's murder took place was surely just a coincidental, yet an intriguingly atmospheric, sideshow. Furthermore, it is interesting to note that Crowley was also familiar with the Continental-Savoy Hotel in Cairo, where Lord Carnarvon died, as he resided there himself during his visit with Rose in 1904. On 25 May 1923, Crowley remarked in his diary how he would 'go to sleep with Ethyl, turning my thoughts simply and sacredly towards Aiwass "without lust of result". So long as I make myself one with Him. His thought will infiltrate my consciousness, and determine my Orbit without calculations on my part.' And on 29 June, Crowley wrote, 'I then asked [Aiwass] – as a child might its father – for a good night's rest, & an awakening fit for work, despite all this naughtiness.' On the morning of Tuesday 3 July, a letter postmarked Paris arrived for Marie-Marguerite at the Savoy. It was written in French and unsigned:

> Please permit a friend who has travelled widely among Orientals and who knows the craftiness of their acts to give you some advice. Don't agree to return to Egypt for any object or even Japan. Rather abandon fortune than risk your life. Money can always be recovered by a good lawyer, but think of your life. A journey means a possible accident, a poison in the flower, a subtle weapon that is neither seen nor heard. Remain in Paris with those who love you and will protect you.

It was likely a note from Crowley (the handwriting bore a striking resemblance to his own); a coded message that was designed to give Marie-Marguerite the 'all-clear' to murder her husband; it could also have been perceived as a threat, warning her that if she didn't go through with the murder then she too would feel his wrath. After all, Crowley's treatment of women who rebuffed his demands is perfectly exemplified in *The Book of the Law*, as dictated to him by Aiwass. In chapter three, Crowley writes:

> Let the Scarlet Woman beware! If pity and compassion and tenderness visit her heart; if she leave my work to toy with old sweetnesses; then shall my vengeance be known. I will slay me her child: I will alienate her heart: I will

cast her out from men: as a shrinking and despised harlot shall she crawl through dusk wet streets, and die cold and an-hungered.

This passage may well have been recited to Marie-Marguerite, herself a mother, as a further warning. Either way, Crowley spoke and wrote fluently in French (as indicated by his elaborate French poetry), he was 'widely travelled among Orientals' and 'knew the craftiness of their acts'. Most significantly, he was, by now, spending much of his time in both Tunisia and Paris, where he had written the postcard – or death sentence – sealing the fate of Prince Ali Kamel Fahmy Bey.

On the morning of the 11 July, Crowley would have woken to the newspapers, both in Europe and in England, featuring on their front pages the scandalous story of the murder at the Savoy. The *Daily Mirror's* headline, for example, was simply 'A PRINCE SHOT IN LONDON', and this was typical of its contemporaries. To the *Daily Mirror*, mindful of the year's Tutankhamun discoveries, Fahmy Bey had been a member of 'one of the oldest Egyptian families', a statement which paled in comparison with *The People's* intent on hammering home the link between the curse of King Tut and Fahmy Bey's death. On the first Sunday after the shooting, *The People* declared how Fahmy Bey had been in London some months earlier, helping to revive an Ancient Egyptian dance, a visit at which 'a private, but most allegorical, ceremony was performed to celebrate a festival called Amun Toonh, established ... in 1403 BC ... to celebrate the goddess of the Sun, Ta Aha ... [and] carried on with many mystic movements'.

Articles detailing Fahmy Bey's murder continued to dominate the papers for the following months, right up to the aftermath of Marie-Marguerite's trial, but for Crowley, now back in Tunisia, the article in *The People* newspaper was correct – there was a link between Fahmy Bey's murder and the curse of Tutankhamun, although the link was nothing more than cold-blooded murder, the architect of which was 'reading all about it' safely ensconced hundreds of miles away from London. Indeed, with Crowley avidly scouring the newspapers at the time of Marie-Marguerite's acquittal, in September 1923, merely a week after her exoneration, he would have read about Colonel Aubrey Herbert's complications from an operation in London. As Herbert was Lord Carnarvon's younger half-brother, and with Crowley missing out on delivering vengeance upon the very talisman of the discovery of Tutankhamun's tomb having been waylaid in Cefalù, he would, in his present state of mind, have jumped at the chance to play a part in Herbert's downfall – in a strange way providing him with recompense for having missed the chance of orchestrating the demise of Lord Carnarvon, Crowley's fellow Trinity College alumni.

It would have been simple for him to telegram Marie-Marguerite, his 'present woman emissary in London', instructing her to visit Herbert at the Harold Fink Memorial Hospital, 17 Park Lane, posing as a caring relative, and make certain that he didn't wake from his operation. The newspapers reported that Herbert had succumbed to 'a rare side effect of the operation'. It was blood poisoning, the same method that Crowley had used to dispose of Bertram Fletcher Robinson in London and Raoul Loveday in Cefalù; more pertinently, it not only mimicked the disease that had killed Lord Carnarvon, but it was very rare for someone to die from complications related to a routine dental operation.

On 23 September 1923, on the day of Herbert's death, Crowley, who was often depressed at this time, recorded in his diary: 'My "depression" – as of old! – seems to herald inspiration.' This was followed by the subsequent poem:

The Gods took counsel with the Lords of Fate
'How shall a Master of Mankind dispart
His substance from its shadow, by Our art
Conjoined the grossness of his earth-born state?'
'Let them the little war against the great
That they may purge him of his mortal part
And throne his spirit in the human heart
Above those envies, incommensurate!'
It crossed my mind to draw my dripping scourge
Across a Consul's withers – Demiurge
And donkey – but the Muse cries: 'Nay my Crowley!
The mean malignant baseness of the brute
Serves to remind your honour to dispute
Each inch of ground that gentle blood holds holy!'

Although the nature of the poem is undeniably ambiguous, on the two days that Crowley masterminded Marie-Marguerite to murder in 1923 his mood was markedly upbeat, considering that through much of the year Crowley's depression was at its worst. There are also frequent references to Aiwass in his 1923 diary during the days leading up to and following the murders in question.

By 1924, the Beast was living permanently in France. With his relationship with Hirsig strained by their persistent illnesses, Crowley set sail indefinitely for Paris in December 1923, 'leaving behind an emotionally and financially bereft Hirsig'. Having arrived somewhat inconspicuously in the city, Crowley found lodgings at the Hotel de Blois, 50 rue Vavin, a few doors below the Boulevard Montparnasse and La Rotonde café; it was a hotel run by his old friends, Monsieur and Madame

Bourcier, who allowed Crowley to stay for free. He wrote in his *Confessions*: 'Their hotel had been my headquarters in Paris for over fifteen years and from the very beginning they treated me more like a son than a stranger.'

However, despite living in relative comfort, Crowley's ever-increasing dependence on heroin would spark recurring asthma attacks that damaged his confidence, and when Hirsig decided to visit Crowley in May 1924, the two decided to return to a former haunt, the inn Au Cadrau Bleu at Chelles-sur-Marne, in an effort to cure him. With Crowley suffering greatly from his illness, Hirsig slavishly attempted to maintain herself as the intrepid 'Scarlet Woman': 'In her magical diaries of this period, commenced in autumn 1923 and entitled *Alostrael's Visions*, she vowed to cultivate wisdom worthy of her exalted role. She repeatedly invoked Aiwass and, on 12 December, felt herself "sliding into a vision."'

What Aiwass said to Hirsig is unknown, but she would have undoubtedly relayed his instructions to Crowley. Like Rose Kelly before her, once Hirsig had made contact with Aiwass she was no longer of use to Crowley. It was at this stage, in late August, that Crowley met Dorothy Olsen, 'who would, within weeks, formally supplant Hirsig as the primary "Scarlet Woman".' Abandoned by Crowley, Hirsig sank into a life of prostitution and poverty.

Upon her return to Paris, it is more than likely that Crowley maintained a relationship with Marie-Marguerite Fahmy, too. She slipped back into the social circles with the same zest that was her trademark. However, persistent gossip and rumour-mongering would follow her for the rest of her days and she often found herself at the receiving end of jokes in the French tabloids. In late October 1923, Marie-Marguerite rather surprisingly announced through her lawyer, Maître Assoued, that she was pregnant by her late husband and that she would be returning to Cairo. 'The reason for these bizarre developments is not hard to divine. There had been much gossip in the newspapers about the diminution of Fahmy Bey's fortune by reason of his gross extravagance, but once the dust had settled it had become apparent that he had left an estate valued at some £2.5 million and no will.'

Perhaps it was together with Crowley (who had found himself precariously short of money in Paris) that Marie-Marguerite concocted the elaborate ploy to secure Fahmy Bey's vast fortune? Either way, it was a plan doomed to fail, and an Egyptian court unsurprisingly ruled that his wealth should be shared among his sisters. What this does suggest, however, is that Marie-Marguerite wasn't necessarily the victim she portrayed herself to be, consequently casting her trial in a new light. There was a calculated cunning about her actions, as amply demonstrated by her apparent ability to handle her pistol, despite her claims to the contrary, and her willingness to pretend she bore her dead husband's child in an effort to procure his estate. This made her the perfect foil for Crowley's elaborate machinations.

There was still time for one final drama, however, and in January 1924, the same month in which Crowley had made Paris his permanent home, the body of Said Enani, Fahmy Bey's erstwhile secretary, confidant and lover, was discovered within the city. It was alleged he died of pneumonia, but question marks continue to hang over his death. Indeed, throughout Marie-Marguerite's trial, she made no secret of the hatred she felt towards Said Enani. Could it be that before Crowley settled down with Dorothy Olsen, his new 'Scarlet Woman', he murdered Said Enani as a parting gift for Marie-Marguerite? Or was it because Said Enani had also dared to venture into the sacred tomb of King Tut? Once again, the timelines and locations crucially tally.

Following her unsuccessful bid to purloin her dead husband's fortune, Marie-Marguerite 'lived, prosperously and unspectacularly, latterly in the fashionable Paris suburb of Neilly, which was where she died, aged eighty, in January 1971. The announcement of her death – apparently in only one French newspaper, presumably paid for by her executor – stated only that the burial had taken place, "in the strictest privacy," nearly a fortnight before. Not a word about an incident on the fourth floor back of the Savoy Hotel, London, England, during a thunderstorm.'

By 1926, having already travelled to Germany and Tunisia before returning to Paris, Crowley and Olsen's relationship had, inevitably, come to an abrupt end. Crowley cited both her drunkenness and the jealousy she felt towards his male lovers as the principal reasons behind their split – although it was well documented at the time that Crowley had begun to assault her physically. Taking a host of further lovers and Scarlet Women in Paris, including Kasimira Bass and the 'exotic' voodoo priestess Maria Teresa de Miramar (whom the Beast later married in a ceremony in Leipzig), as well as his own personal secretary, Israel Regardie, it wasn't until 1929 that Crowley finally returned to England after the French authorities declined to renew his identity card.

In February, Crowley travelled to London to assess his legal and publishing options – his arrival was predictably met by a fanfare of profligate tabloid journalism. On 7 February, the *Daily Sketch* reported: 'One of the most interesting and talked of men in Europe is now visiting London after a long absence. He is Aleister Crowley, famed for his knowledge and reputed practice of black magic, who was asked to leave France two months ago. Crowley has an amazing appearance, and eyes which, when you first look into them, are literally terrifying. I hate to imagine what they must be like when he is not in a benevolent mood.'

Unsurprisingly, the *John Bull* of 27 April offered its own unique observation on the Beast's return:

Soon Hell will be the only place which will have you. You were driven out of England, America deported you and so did Sicily. Now France has given you your marching orders. Since I exposed you for the seducer, devil doctor and debauched dope fiend that you are, not a decent country will tolerate you or your sinister satellites.

Hoping to begin work on a new book for Mandrake Press, who had also published the first volumes of his *Confessions* earlier in the year, Crowley – along with de Miramar – moved to Ivy Cottage in Knockholt, Kent, in October, from where they would spend the rest of the winter. With Crowley regularly commuting the 30 miles to London, it was on 15 November that Captain Richard Bethell, the much-publicised personal secretary to Howard Carter in Luxor, travelling companion to Lord Carnarvon and officially one of the first men to enter the tomb of Tutankhamun, mysteriously passed away in his sleep at Mayfair's decadent Bath Club. It is important to remember the circumstances surrounding Bethell's death. Here was a man who was a member of the Scots Guards and who had no previous health complications; it was reported on his death certificate that he had suffered a 'coronary thrombosis', but historian Gerald O'Farrell has since argued that Bethell's death was 'consistent with a pillow being placed over his mouth, smothering him'.

Indeed, now turning his cruel intentions towards the members of the excavating party of Tutankhamun's tomb, Crowley would have had easy access to the Bath Club as he was a regular visitor to many of Dover Street's gentleman's clubs. His close friend, the author W. Somerset Maugham, was a member of the Bath Club and would habitually invite the Beast as his guest when he gave dinner parties there. (Crowley had previously visited the studios at the Bath Club when he posed for a series of photographs with his family.) In order to appease Aiwass, who had since issued a further set of instructions to Leah Hirsig, the Beast had ample motive to murder Bethell, whose position in Luxor under Howard Carter and Lord Carnarvon would have been public knowledge and his responsibility in the desecration of Tutankhamun's tomb untenable. We must also remember that Bethell had covered nearly every wall of his home at Manchester Square (which was in close proximity to the

Fitzroy Tavern, Crowley's regular haunt) with the illegally plundered relics from Tutankhamun's tomb.

The intriguing case of Bethell's servant who was charged with arson at his master's home also throws up an interesting theory. Rather than the servant – whose rather feeble defence that the relics from the tomb had 'got on his nerves' and that he should 'burn down the place so as to get rid of them' does not ring true – could it have been Crowley who was deliberately provoking Bethell by starting conflagrations? The servant in question may well have been one of Crowley's ardent followers who would have done anything he was instructed to do. Indeed, in the Queen of Bohemia, Nina Hamnett's, autobiography, *Laughing Torso*, she described an early meeting with the Beast: 'He asked me to paint four panels with signs representing the elements, earth, air, fire, and water; while I was painting Fire, apparently the Fire Element escaped, and three fires started in mysterious ways in the studio on the same day.' This extract certainly adds credibility to the theory that Crowley had a penchant for starting 'mysterious fires'.

Moreover, it is likely that the Beast had also tormented Bethell's ailing father, Lord Westbury, before killing him, hence Westbury's mention of not being able 'to stand any more horrors' in his suicide note. Were these 'horrors' in actual fact Crowley's cruel and malicious scare tactics? It would have been straightforward for him to send threatening and anonymous telegrams to the bedridden Westbury or to visit him in person. He was, after all, convalescing at his easily accessible home under the watchful gaze of a solitary night nurse. Furthermore, the significance of Lord Westbury's and Richard Bethell's surname would not have been lost on Crowley, the fervent occultist: its biblical connection would have no doubt made their sacrifice that bit sweeter for their assassin. Bethell or Beth-El was a border city described in the Old Testament as being located between Benjamin and Ephraim and is mentioned on numerous occasions in the book of Genesis.

With Crowley's writing career suffering as a result of his murderous machinations, it was becoming increasingly apparent that the publication of his major works were in the balance. Despite these setbacks, Crowley continued to insist on his luxuries, and those who were exasperated by his flamboyance in the face of his hardship 'earned his contempt for lacking the courage to live by a like standard. Dining at the famous Café Royal in Piccadilly [continued to be] one of his favourite extravagances.' And in his *Equinox* publication, the Beast not only showcased his culinary skills, but also highlighted his close association with the restaurant by printing adverts such as:

EPICURES
are invited to taste the Special Dishes invented by
ALEISTER CROWLEY. This can be done at the
CAFÉ ROYAL, REGENT STREET, W.
Pavots d'Amour Cro-Cro
Pilaff de Moules a la Santa Chiara
Crowley Mixed Grill
Soufflé Aleister Crowley.
etc., etc.

'Like another diabolist (albeit of the "Catholic" variety), Enoch Soames, Crowley was irresistibly attracted by the smoke-and-celebrity-laden atmosphere of the Café. Besides, he chased women of any age, race, hue, or even degree of attraction, with unflagging interest. The Café Royal round the turn of the century offered a comfortable, reasonably dignified, and comparatively inexpensive solution to this problem. But he cast envious glances at the coteries straggling round the tables – the painters, the poets, even the pimps and the confidence tricksters. In future years, as it happened, he was to fit in with each category in turn.' Along with his more infamous fellow patrons, the Beast had a personalised chair that he was only too happy to display to his friends, who included the stylist Gwen Otter. Another of his companions at the time, other than the host of nubile women who encircled him, was a jocular, ginger-haired, out-of-work actor by the name of Alec Waters. Waters, much to the Beast's disdain, was known to shout within hearing distance of Crowley: 'If that man was a proper magician, he'd be able to pull a rabbit out of his hat!'

At the Café Royal outlandish tales of the Beast became commonplace, and his eccentric behaviour, which included him tipping a plate of food over his head and striding in wearing full evening dress and a large bronze butterfly plaque that was suspended from his neck on a long cord so it covered his crotch, 'to the delight of the assembled multitude', was periodically reported in the tabloids. It later transpired that the plaque had been stolen from its place censoring a nude statue of Oscar Wilde in Paris. 'There is another strange account – set in this restaurant – which, if true, testifies both to the Beast's outlandish public image and to his own sanguine acceptance of it.' Wearing extravagant yellow robes, mystically inscribed in occult symbols, and a star-spangled conical hat, Crowley anointed his body in scented oil and saffron before marching into the main tea room and performing an adoration to the Egyptian sun god – an 'invisibility rite'. He was working with a sigil from the system presented in a book known as *The Sacred Magic of Abra-Melin the Mage* which purported to bestow invisibility on the operator.

He [Crowley] believed that he possessed a magic cloak which rendered him invisible. One day he appeared in it, a majestic figure in a star-encrusted conical hat and a cloak decorated with the symbols of mysticism, and walked slowly through the Café from Regent Street to Glasshouse Street in an awestruck silence. No one could convince him that the flabbergasted patrons had seen him. 'If they saw me,' he would ask unanswerably, 'why did nobody speak to me?'

Indeed, when asked by two American tourists if he remembered Aleister Crowley, an elderly waiter (having worked at the Café Royal since he was a boy in the early 1930s) recalled another fateful night when the Beast arrived at the famous Regent Street restaurant:

Oh yes! I'd only been working here for a week when this chap came into the Café wearing funny clothes, stood in the middle of the place and started babbling away in some weird language. Nobody paid him any attention, but I asked the Head Waiter if something should be done, but he told me not to worry – it was just Mr Crowley being invisible again.

A further account of this notorious incident described how:

the assembled gentility taking tea in the Café Royal had seen a strangely coloured man in exotic costume walk into the room, make gesticulations and utterance, turn round, and walk out again.

When nobody battered an eyelid, Crowley assumed the ritual had been a success. It had, but this owed everything to upper-crust British disdain and nothing to magic, as the diners munched on, stoically ignoring his existence with typical aplomb.

It was on the evening of 20 February 1930 when this event took place, coincidentally at the same time that Crowley and Mandrake Press had enjoyed a small publishing success with *Moonchild*. It was also on this night that Crowley, having breezed out of the Café Royal believing he was invisible, travelled the short distance to St James' Court where Lord Westbury was under the care of a night nurse. By the morning, Westbury was dead and the manner of his demise shrouded in mystery.

Numerous guests even testified that on the last occasion Crowley dined at the Café Royal – a birthday celebration 'that marked his final exit from that gay haunt of his youth' – he left an unpaid bill of over £100:

Once again a private dining-room had been booked, an even more sumptuous menu bespoken, and the usual sequence of wine and *cognac* preceded by vodka – not out of liquor glasses but *à la Russe* … All his oldest friends were there. Each of them had once been under the spell, if not of his bogus magic, then of his genial personality. Each one had either been stripped of a certain amount of cash or embarrassed in some other way; yet each had somehow forgiven him for it all. The duped, the wronged, and the embarrassed drank his health from the bottom of their hearts. The meal was approaching its end. Soon the sideplates and the crumbs would be whisked away; half-drained champagne glasses would be unobtrusively removed to make way for the demi-tasses and the *ballons*. Solicitous waiters with brandy and cigars would begin their rounds, and a mellow well-being would spread its warm wings over pleasing memories. The host gazed benevolently into his glass, warming it to exact room temperature between his small well-made hands. He looked up and he smiled as he saw his friends about him; his glance wandered from face to face, affectionately. He drained his *ballon*. Then he rose, excused himself, and left the room. He walked down the stairs and up to the cloakroom. He put on his hat and coat, and gave the man half-a-crown. He walked out into Regent Street, hailed a taxi, and drove away. The mellow well-being of his guests received a rude shock when the manager broke the news that their host had left without the formality of paying the bill.

However, his diffident exit on this occasion paled in comparison to the one the Beast made on that bitter, infamous evening in February 1930 when, dressed head to toe in his magical garb, he had murder on his mind.

9

The Crowley Connection
Part III

The city is monstrous and misshapen; its mystery is not a brooding, but a conspiracy. And these truths are evident above all to one who recognises that London's heart is Charing Cross.

Aleister Crowley, *Moonchild*

As was the case with Richard Bethell's death, the newspapers around the world were quick to point out the link between Westbury and Bethell (father and son) and the curse of Tutankhamun. However, historian Gerald O'Farrell remarks in his book *The Tutankhamun Deception* that Westbury, rather than committing suicide, was more likely thrown from his seventh-floor window as it would have been physically impossible for him to jump without assistance – such was the positioning of the window sill and his drugged state. Westbury, who kept a vast collection of Egyptian antiquities within his apartment, including an alabaster vase from the tomb of King Tut given to him by his son, was an obvious target for Crowley.

In what was a premeditated attack, the Beast was able to gain access to Westbury's flat, wait for his night nurse to begin her early morning chores, before entering Westbury's bedroom and throwing the frail old man from the window. Comparable to Bethell's suffocation, Crowley wouldn't have been given the luxury of planning Westbury's murder. His calm approach and modus operandi would have been replaced by an instinctive, opportunistic and more brutal method. It is worth noting that Westbury's residence at St James' Court was in close proximity to Clarence House, a royal residence situated on the

Mall, where mummies were stored by the Prince of Wales, later Edward VII, after he had brought them back from an Egyptian excavation in 1868.

To maintain the illusion of suicide, Crowley then produced two suicide notes, which O'Farrell believes Westbury had no time to write and initially went unnoticed by his night nurse, and swiftly exited before the night nurse reappeared. Witnesses claimed that Westbury performed a somersault motion in the air before plummeting through the glass veranda below, a manoeuvre consistent with being shoved viciously from behind, and that a strange woman was seen lurking by the entrance to Westbury's flat at the time of his death. Who was this woman? The authorities were unable to locate her at the time for questioning so we must draw our own conclusions. Was she an 'emissary' of Crowley's? De Miramar, who was living with Crowley at the time or, possibly, Marie-Marguerite Fahmy are the most obvious candidates for complicity. Let us also not forget how Westbury's night nurse immediately ran downstairs, but, she said, 'They would not let me go further.' No one thought to question her as to who 'they' might be or why they would stop her going to the man she was supposed to be nursing, who was now obviously badly injured. Could 'they' have been Crowley and his accomplice?

Also, the Beast's bizarre display in the Café Royal – which on the face of it was pure theatrical tomfoolery – could well have been an effort to contact Aiwass. This might explain why Crowley, under orders, then marched straight from the restaurant to Westbury's apartment in St James' Court – once again, the timelines tally to such an extent that any suggestion of coincidence is now extraneous. Likewise, the death of Edgar Steele, the British Museum sign-writer, which occurred only four days later and on the same day as Westbury's funeral, could likely be attributed to the hands of Crowley; the Beast had, after all, remained very active within the London social circuit immediately after Westbury's murder. Steele, who was complaining of fever and fatigue, died at St Thomas' Hospital following an unsuccessful stomach operation. He was in charge of handling the relics from the tombs of Luxor – a task that would have greatly provoked Aiwass and Crowley – and his symptoms of blood poisoning were inexplicably similar to those of Bertram Fletcher Robinson, Raoul Loveday and Aubrey Herbert.

The same could be said for Henry (Harry) Reginald Holland Hall, the Keeper of the Egyptian and Assyrian Antiquities at the British Museum, who died at his London residence on 13 October 1930, after catching a common cold that rapidly, yet mysteriously, led to pneumonia. Hall, who was 57 at the time of his death, was not only once the assistant to Sir Ernest Wallis Budge at the British Museum, but had also written extensively about Tutankhamun (once with Budge as his co-author), campaigned to keep Carnarvon's relics in the British Museum and was himself a famed Egyptologist. The boy, Joseph Greer, who was knocked down and killed by Westbury's hearse in Battersea, was surely the unlucky recipient of a chance, although an unquestionably unsettling, accident.

By now, Crowley was beginning to boast to friends that Scotland Yard had built a special room to store his extensive dossier. Only two weeks before Westbury's murder took place, Crowley's planned appearance at the Oxford University Poetry Society was cancelled due to the 'threat of disciplinary action' against its secretary, Hugh Speaight. Speaight wrote a penitent letter to Crowley explaining the decision – the letter was soon reprinted in the newspapers:

> I am writing to tell you that we have unfortunately been forced to cancel next Monday's meeting of the Poetry Society. It has come to our knowledge that if your proposed paper is delivered disciplinary action will be taken involving not only myself but the rest of the Committee of the Society. In these circumstances you will, I trust, understand why we have had to cancel the meeting. I feel I must apologise to you for the trouble I have caused you. I must admit that I had credited the University with more tolerance – or at any rate, with a greater sense of humour. Again many apologies. Perhaps I shall have some later occasion of meeting you. PS – I hope you will understand that no official step has been taken, but it has been made perfectly clear that an official step will be taken if you did come to speak to the Society.

When confronted by a reporter for the *Northern Echo*, Crowley drolly responded by saying:

> I challenge anyone to show why I should not lecture at Oxford today. Full investigations will be made. If there has been a misunderstanding, the lecture will be given later. If the ban is official the lecture will be printed and sold at the street corners of Oxford. There is some underhand business behind this. I had been invited by Mr Speaight to talk to the Society on Gilles de Rais, a medieval magician, who was a contemporary and comrade of Joan of Arc. Perhaps the refusal to let me lecture has come because Gilles de Rais is said to have killed 600 children in ritual murder, and in some way, this was connected with myself, since the accusation that I have not only killed but eaten children is one of the many false statements that have been circulated about me in the past. Probably the authorities are afraid that I may kill and eat 800 Oxford graduates.

The *Northern Echo* article in which this statement appeared also featured this intriguing comment:

[Oxford University] said they thought the whole trouble was the death of Mr Raoul Loveday at Cefalù, in Sicily, while he was Mr Crowley's secretary. Mr Loveday was a young Oxford undergraduate, and in a London newspaper it was alleged that Mr Crowley was responsible, either directly or indirectly, for his death.

Over the next year, while Crowley spent more and more time in London, reports of the curse of Tutankhamun became less frequent and any deaths attributed to it had ceased; this was, in all likelihood, quelled by the British Museum's decision to withdraw several relics from Luxor and the coffin lid belonging to the priestess of Amen Ra from display. In that time, the increasingly eccentric Crowley was often seen out and about in the capital: browsing the esoteric and occult book section in Foyles on the Charing Cross Road (for whom he would later do a talk on 'The Philosophy of Magick' at the Foyles Literary Luncheon), in the Atlantis Bookshop on Museum Street, Watkins Books in Cecil Court (where the proprietor, Michael Houghton, challenged him to demonstrate his magick powers) and the British Museum's Reading Room; partaking in heavy drinking sessions in numerous London hostelries, most notably in the Fitzroy Tavern where he would drink alongside the likes of the bohemians Nina Hamnett and Dylan Thomas; and taking lodgings at 89 Park Mansions, Knightsbridge, and 20 Leicester Square.

Indeed, it was in the French House pub on Soho's Dean Street where it is said that Crowley first encountered the Welsh poet Dylan Thomas, scribbling frantically in a notebook. (It was also in the French House where Thomas would later leave the manuscript of his radio play *Under Milk Wood* beneath his chair.)

One day [Thomas] and Theodora Fitzgibbon sat at the bar drawing doodles; then they turned each other's doodles into a cartoon. They were interrupted when the barman brought them a sheet of paper, sent by a mysterious figure sitting across the room. It was an identical drawing. [Thomas] immediately grabbed Theodora and rushed out into Dean Street, where he explained that the man was the Great Beast himself, Aleister Crowley, up to his tricks. He had no wish to get involved in Crowley's magical workings.

Indeed, it is widely believed that Thomas refused to go anywhere near the Beast after this incident.

It was during his tenure in Knightsbridge that Crowley found himself short of both money and inspiration. He was also concerned that Raoul Loveday's widow, Betty May, had published her autobiography – *Tiger Woman* – in which the notorious deeds at the Abbey of Thelema in Cefalù came under particular scrutiny, once again attracting the attentions of the rabid British tabloid press who were keen to exploit her notoriety. Crowley put his concerns to Anthony Powell (a former associate of the Bright Young Things), the editor of the book for Duckworth Press, at a luncheon meeting at none other than Simpsons-in-the-Strand, next to the Savoy Hotel and behind which Cleopatra's Needle still stands.

Powell was uncertain about the meeting, wondering: 'whether I should be met in the lobby by a thaumaturge in priestly robes, received with the ritual salutation: "Do what thou wilt shall be the whole of the Law"; if so, whether politeness required the correct response: "Love is the Law, Love under Will."' In fact the 'big weary-looking man' who 'rose from one of the seats and held out his hand' was 'quietly, almost shabbily, dressed in a dark brown suit and a grey Homburg hat'. His figure seemed 'intensely sinister' due to the 'unusual forma-tion of his bald and shaven skull'. They dined on mutton, and Crowley had a glass of milk. After fully stating his case against the 'inaccuracies and vulgari-ties of phrase' marring *Tiger Woman*, Crowley expounded in general upon 'the hard life of a mage, its difficulties and disappointments, especially in relation to the unkindness and backbiting of fellow magicians'. They parted amicably, and Crowley took no further action against the Betty May book.

Worsening Crowley's general melancholy throughout this period, de Miramar was often drunk, had made little effort to learn English and would flirt lasciviously with male visitors. Crowley was in desperate need of a calling, having made no reference to any communication with Aiwass since that fateful night in February 1930. On 1 June of that year, he penned a 'sharply satiric self-portrait in verse':

> Bury me in a quicklime grave!
> Three parts a fool, & one part a knave.
> A Superman – bar two wee 'buts'
> I had no brains, & I had no guts.
> My soul is a lump of stinking shit,
> And I don't like it a little bit!

With his relationship with de Miramar breaking down, Crowley moved back to Germany alone and left instructions with his London solicitors to begin divorce proceedings. Immediately he felt at home in Berlin and again took numerous lovers, both male and female. 'Some of their names survive whole – Hanni Jaeger [with whom Crowley later went missing at Boca de Inferno, Portugal, supposedly committing suicide much to the delight of the British press], Louise Aschaetzsch, Renate Gottsched and, most prominently, Hanni Richter.' As he wrote to his friend, Gerald Yorke, in June 1931: 'The idea of my coming to England unless someone will give me £1,000,000 per day to do it – in which case I will come for 10 days with a flock of Eagles – is the idea of someone who has never been in Berlin.'

The previous month, on 3 May, the *Berliner Tageblatt*, much like its American, French and English counterparts had previously done, deemed it prudent to herald Crowley's arrival in their paper:

This fifty-five year old personality is at present staying amongst us, in order to prepare for the exhibition of his paintings which is to take place in Berlin this Fall. Aleister Crowley is a painter by passion. He became one because as an Alpine Climber he has seen air and light effects, which previously were hardly accessible to human eyes … In England Crowley, the gentleman bohemian, is a much contested personality. One group consider him as a revolutionary philosopher, another as a foolish artist; that this mountaineer, chess player, poet-philosopher and painter is one of the most peculiar person-alities is denied by nobody.

It was during his stay in Berlin that Crowley, according to his friend, the novel-ist Christopher Isherwood, 'walked up to a very tough-looking youth in an open shirt, standing by the bar, and scratched the boy's chest deeply with his nails. Only a sizable gift of money succeeded in restraining the boy from beat-ing him up on the spot.'

Having squandered his funds, Crowley was ejected from the latest in a series of Berlin flats for non-payment of rent, forcing him to return to London on 22 June 1932. The Beast gathered together enough money to rent a new flat at 27 Albemarle Street, off Piccadilly and adjacent to Dover Street (and the now infamous Bath Club), from where he would attempt to drum up interest from British publishers for his new books. It was also during this period that Crowley split from his secretary, Israel Regardie (who would himself become a successful writer on the occult), but became acquainted with the young black magician Rollo Ahmed, a West Indian of Egyptian descent, who fired his fading love for the occult. Ahmed, who was a member of the Golden Dawn in Bristol, could conceivably have been responsible for stirring Crowley from his melan-choly and into committing his subsequent macabre endeavours.

Yet it would be another factor that would this time precipitate Crowley's stay in London: desperate for money, he developed a litigious nature that had already seen him sue a bookshop on Praed Street for displaying a misleading card in their shop window concerning his book *Moonchild*. However, the following year Crowley would begin legal proceedings against his former friend and drinking partner Nina Hamnett. It would prove to be a trial that would keep the Beast in England for the rest of his life.

In 1932, Hamnett, the self-proclaimed Queen of the Fitzroy and Bohemia, wrote *Laughing Torso*, a book that would go on to become a best-seller in both Britain and the United States. In the book, Hamnett made numerous remarks about Crowley and his practising of black magic in Cefalù, allegations that Crowley strenuously denied. The libellous passage stated:

Crowley had a temple in Cefalù in Sicily. He was supposed to practice Black Magic there, and one day a baby was said to have disappeared mysteriously. There was also a goat there. This all pointed to Black Magic, so people said, and the inhabitants of the village were frightened of him.

In another passage, Hamnett described her initial meeting with the Beast:

He was supposed to be very clever and very wicked. I was taken to his studio and introduced to him. I found him extremely intelligent and he did not strike me as being very bad … It was said that Crowley was so wicked that no young thing could remain alone in the same room with him in safety.

Perhaps the most intriguing extract from *Laughing Torso* regards Hamnett's views on Raoul Loveday's and Betty May's occupancy at the Abbey of Thelema:

They were on their way to Cefalù as Crowley had offered him a job as his secretary. He was very much intrigued with Crowley's views on magic. He had been very ill the year before and had had a serious operation. I had heard that the climate at Cefalù was terrible; heat, mosquitoes, and very bad food. The magical training I already knew was very arduous. I urged them not to go. I succeeded in keeping them in Paris two days longer than they intended, but they were determined to go and I was powerless to prevent them. I told Raoul that if he went he would die, and really felt a horrible feeling of gloom when I said 'Good bye' to them. After five months I had a postcard from Betty on which was written, 'My husband died last Friday; meet me at the Gare de Lyon.'

In the ensuing 'Black Magic Libel Case', Crowley *v.* Constable & Co., Limited and Others, which began in April 1934 (coincidentally presided over by Mr Justice Rigby Swift, who famously took the chair for the trial of Marie-Marguerite Fahmy), Hamnett and her publishers defeated Crowley, who, as a result, was left bankrupt, vilified and reprimanded. On the first day of the trial, the Beast took to the stand and was asked to swear on the Bible. It was a hollow and futile vow on a book that he didn't recognise, yet he gladly obliged:

'Are you familiar with the words "Do what thou wilt shall be the whole of the Law"?' John Eddy [Crowley's counsel] asked at one point.

A smile crossed Crowley's face in spite of himself. 'I am.'

'Did they have any reference to [the Abbey of Thelema]?'

'They are the general principles on which I maintain all mankind should base its conduct.'

'What do they mean?'

'The study of those words has occupied the last thirty years of my life,' Crowley explained proudly. 'There is no end to what they mean, but the simplest application to practical conduct is this: that no man has a right to waste his time on doing things which are mere wishes or desires, but that he should devote himself wholly to his true work in this world.'

'Have those words anything to do with black magic?'

'Only indirectly. They would forbid it, because black magic is suicidal.'

Asked about the difference between black and white magic, Crowley continued, 'In boxing you can fight according to the Queensberry rules or you can do the other thing.'

Malcolm Hilbery, for the defence, interjected, 'Does this mean that his definition of black magic is the same as all-in wrestling?' Laughter filled the courtroom.

'I approve of some forms of magic and disapprove of others,' Crowley elaborated.

Eddy continued with his questions. 'What is the form you disbelieve?'

'That which is commonly known as black magic, which is not only foul and abominable, but, for the most part, criminal. To begin with, the basis of all black magic is that utter stupidity of selfishness which cares nothing for the rights of others. People so constituted are naturally quite unscrupulous. In many cases, black magic is an attempt to commit crime without incurring the penalties of the law. The almost main instrument of black magic is murder, either for inheritance or for some other purpose, or in some way to gain personally out of it.'

'On the third day [of the trial], one of the counsel [an incredulous Irishman named Martin O'Connor] blandly invited [Crowley] to make himself invisible and prove that he was not an imposter. Crowley declined with dignity.' Mr Justice Swift's blunt summation left no doubt as to his feelings towards the Beast and his practices, and he vehemently declared:

> I thought that I knew of every conceivable form of wickedness. I thought that everything which was vicious and bad had been produced at one time or another before me. I have learnt in this case that we can always learn something more if we live long enough. I have never heard such dreadful, horrible, blasphemous and abominable stuff as that which has been produced by the man [Crowley] who describes himself to you as the greatest living poet.

'Still, there was a bright spot, as he left the London courtroom, a nineteen-year-old girl named Deidre MacAlpine ran up to [Crowley] and asked, "Couldn't I be the mother of your child?"' The Beast benevolently granted MacAlpine her wish, and young Aleister Ataturk MacAlpine, Crowley's magical heir, was born three years later. Indeed, Swift's pitiful opinion of Crowley was reciprocated, and:

> a diary entry over three years later – on October 19, 1937, the day Crowley learned of the death of Mr. Justice Swift – makes clear that anger had lingered, and also provides a clue as to what had buoyed him on that day of defeat. 'The drunken blackguard Swift is dead. N.B. the sot's swinish injustice gave me the best thing that ever happened: Deidre and Ataturk!'

As for the fate of Nina Hamnett; when, on 16 December 1956, she tragically fell from her apartment window and was impaled on a wrought-iron fence 40ft below, many questioned the gruesome manner of her death: was it suicide or was she pushed? Her last words were believed to have been, 'Why don't they let me die?' Although Hamnett won the case against Crowley, the repercussions of the trial profoundly affected her for the rest of her life and she became a rampant alcoholic, spending many of her last years at the bar (usually that of the Fitzroy Tavern) trading anecdotes for drinks. It was even whispered among bohemian circles that Crowley, himself now nine years dead, had placed a magick curse upon her; either way Crowley indubitably enjoyed the last laugh.

Throughout the year of the trial, and the two years preceding it, Crowley had been spending much of his time at Museum Street, opposite the British Museum, which played host to his publisher, Mandrake Press, and two of his favoured London haunts – the Plough public house and the Atlantis Bookshop. 'When the Black Magic case came before the King's Bench, Crowley was 59-years-old. The constant intake of drugs had left its mark on his constitution; it is said that his daily dose of heroin eventually rose to eleven grains – an enormous quantity. The public ostracism which he had invited by his constant boasting of wickedness had become an obsession. It was a paranoiac fighting back who brought this case. He foresaw utter humiliation and destruction for his "enemies"; nor was he entirely unmindful of the financial possibilities.'

It was perhaps unsurprising then that during this period Arthur Weigall, the respected Egyptologist and journalist, and Sir Ernest Wallis Budge, a former Keeper of the Egyptian and Assyrian Antiquities at the British Museum, both succumbed to 'illnesses'. With both men having extensive links to the British Museum (as well as being at loggerheads with one another), and with Budge living a mere stone's throw away from it at Bloomsbury Street, Bedford Square, Crowley had easy access to the frail old man he once admired.

Only months before Budge's death, in the autumn of 1933, Arthur Weigall was diagnosed with terminal cancer and was moved to a room within the London Hospital. Crucially, it would have been common knowledge that Weigall, scathingly described by fellow curse victim Mervyn Herbert as 'a filthy little fellow of German name', was present at the opening of the tomb of King Tut in 1923 as he was reporting on the events for the *Daily Mail*, and this detail wouldn't have been overlooked by Crowley. In the autumn of that year, Weigall went on a tour of Britain and America, 'Lecturing on the romance of finding the tomb of King Tut'. The following year, on 23 April – St George's Day – Weigall supervised the construction of a complete replica of the tomb of Tutankhamun for the British Empire Exhibition at Wembley Stadium – an exhibition that was opened by King George and Queen Mary. Howard Carter, who was already feuding with Weigall following the discovery of the tomb in Luxor, was strongly opposed to the exhibition and made several moves to have it closed down:

> When he got to hear about it, Carter was absolutely furious. The day before the Exhibition opened, when Carter had just arrived in New York for his lecture tour, the *Daily Express* ran the headline 'Carter's Wembley Bombshell – Attempt to Close the Pharaoh's Tomb'. What had happened was that Wembley Amusements Ltd had received a writ from Carter's solicitors, stating that the archaeologist 'objects to the wood and plaster replica of the tomb in the Amusements Park ... on the grounds that it violates certain copyrights held by him'.

However, his desperate pleas fell on deaf ears, and the contents of the tomb, which were arranged in the exact same position in which they were found at Luxor, were available for the public to view. The exhibition itself was covered extensively by *The Times*:

Having bought their tickets, visitors entered a long, low and white construction, got up to resemble the rock cliffs of Thebes, and were shown, by a gentleman in a red tarboosh, full-colour and full-sized facsimiles of the contents of the antechamber. Then, having turned left and seen the antechamber from another perspective, they walked down the corridor and were shown the golden shrine and stone sarcophagus (unopened, of course). Then, along another corridor to the exit and the Flying Machine ... The replicas in the tomb had, apparently, been made by William Aumonier with the help of twelve skilled craftsmen, and had taken six months to produce in a studio off the Tottenham Court Road, 'from photographs and sketches Mr. Arthur Weigall took at Luxor'. The smallest hieroglyphics were reproduced so faithfully that they could be read by Egyptologists. And it was estimated, said the publicity, that gold and gold-leaf worth nearly £1,000 had been used to colour the shrine and couches.

In his 1924 diaries, Evelyn Waugh described the exhibition thus:

We lunched at Previtali, borrowed £1 from Chapman & Hall, and found ourselves at about tea-time at the Empire Exhibition at Wembley. We went to the Palace of Arts and walked through a blazing nightmare of colonial paintings to some peculiarly charming period rooms ... I saw a sculpture and desired with all my heart to become a sculptor and then I saw jewels and wanted to be a jeweller and then I saw all manner of preposterous things being made in the Palace of Industry and wanted to devote my life to that too.

Quite possibly in Crowley's eyes a heinous and gaudy replica such as this would have been construed as the ultimate sacrilege and Weigall the main instigator. It is also important to remember that Weigall had masterminded a play that was intended to portray the reincarnation of the heretical pharaoh Akhenaten, Tutankhamun's father, by appeasing the ancient god of Amen-Ra and lifting the curse that had condemned Akhenaten to a ceaseless wandering after death. Could Weigall's depiction of Akhenaten in his subsequent book about the heretic pharaoh, in which he not only compared him to Moses but also cast him as a visionary who had dared to challenge the ancient priesthood, have provoked Crowley's indignation, too? As the Beast once considered himself to be the reincarnation of Akhenaten, there is every chance that this was indeed the case.

With Weigall's illness and his location frequently mentioned in the newspapers, Crowley would have found it uncomplicated and logical to murder him at this particular time, not only because the hospital was renowned for its sheer frequency of patients and visitors, but also because Weigall was in a vulnerable condition. Indeed, it was noted that his death, in January 1934, was 'extraordinarily intense, and his end rapid' – a report that gives credence to the notion that foul play was involved. But, as ever, any suspicion of murder was suppressed by the mitigating circumstances surrounding the case, in this instance Arthur Weigall's terminal illness. Crowley was either very shrewd or very lucky (or perhaps a combination of the two) as he, and the charge of murder, could always evade suspicion. Given Weigall's connection to the tomb of Tutankhamun, it was predestined that his death would make the headlines in the newspapers, and the curse of Tutankhamun was once again at the forefront of the public's collective anxiety. This would have pleased Crowley greatly as his 'work' was contributing to espousing the myth of the age. And when we consider that Weigall's cancer was exacerbated by his renowned drug habit, we must not ignore the possibility that he already knew Crowley and mingled in similar bohemian circles.

There is one final postscript concerning the suspicious death of Arthur Weigall. On 20 March 1923, shortly before Carnarvon's death, the journalist H.V. Morton wrote in the *Daily Express* (under the double headline 'Lord Carnarvon Poisoned – Is Pharaoh at Work?'):

> More than one authority believes that if we could go back a few thousand years and consult an Ancient Egyptian magician we would find him a very disappointing person, whose stock-in-trade was an unconvincing mass of Mumbo Jumbo designed to impress the ignorant. Still, the fact remains that there's a strange atmosphere ... I was riding back from the tomb of Tutankhamun with a friend the day after it had been opened. Inside the dark chamber, faced by the blue and gilt foot of the gigantic coffin, we had apparently both experienced the same eerie feeling. 'Something will happen, you mark my words,' he said. 'Tutankhamun will get even with us for disturbing him!' 'Do you honestly believe that?' I asked him. 'Well, only half and half!' he replied.

The friend in question was none other than Arthur Weigall. Perhaps he knew at the time what peculiar and grim fate would befall him? So when, in September 1934, Crowley read in *The Times* of Sir Ernest Wallis Budge's investigation into

'Mummy Wheat', Budge, whose translation of the Egyptian *Book of the Dead* was so revered by the Beast, was now a prime target of his. Indeed, it was Budge's *The Nile: Notes for Travellers in Egypt*, written for Thomas Cook in 1890, that had a significant impact on Crowley's concept of the gods – the spellings of which Crowley would later replicate in *The Book of the Law*. Nonetheless, there is little doubt that the Beast would have deemed Budge's experiment sacrilegious; an experiment that took the sanctified wheat from inside an Ancient Egyptian tomb to see if it could germinate. Furthermore, in Budge's autobiography, *By Nile and Tigris*, he boasted of his 'adventures in smuggling huge quantities of antiquities out of Egypt'. Crowley would also have been privy to Budge's participation in the promotion of the Tutankhamun excavation. Having been encouraged by Lord Carnarvon, it was Budge who, in 1923, wrote *Tutankhamun: Amenism, Atenism and Egyptian Monotheism*, a book that detailed the possible relationship between the Amarna period, the story of Moses and the Exodus from Egypt, and who, after Carnarvon's death, labelled the curse of Tutankhamun as 'bunkum'.

Moreover, in *Sword of Wisdom*, a biography of Samuel Liddell McGregor Mathers, author Ithell Colquhon suggests that Budge was a member of the Hermetic Order of the Golden Dawn in London, and it was in Budge's 1930 book *Amulets and Superstitions* where he would make frequent references to the occult and Ancient Egypt. So, aside from the fact that Crowley dutifully studied Budge's numerous works on Ancient Egypt, it is likely that he was also an acquaintance of his. This would have made access to his Bloomsbury Street home, where the ailing Budge lay waiting, uncomplicated and credulous. Not long before his death, Budge laconically declared: 'I have dug up mummies in many lands and yet no curse has descended on me.' It would appear he spoke too soon. Budge subsequently left his vast estate to both Oxford and Cambridge Universities to provide bursaries for burgeoning Egyptologists.

As previously stated, initial newspaper reports at the time suggested that throughout the course of 1934, Egyptology recorded a heavier loss of life among its leaders than had occurred in any other single year of the century, and five of the seven who died were Englishmen. What role Crowley played in these deaths is unclear, although Budge reportedly died at home on 23 November 1934, the month in which Crowley was in court in London yet again, this time appealing the verdict and judgement of Mr Justice Swift in favour of Nina Hamnett and her publishers. His appeal was later dismissed. It should be noted that Crowley, who was residing in the heart of London's West End at Carlos Place, Grosvenor Square, and Upper Montagu Street, Marylebone, throughout this period, was also in court during July 1934 when he represented himself in a trial accusing him of receiving stolen letters belonging to Raoul Loveday's widow, Betty May (now Sedgewick) – the woman who had accused the Beast of complicity in her husband's death. He was found guilty and was ordered to pay a sum not exceeding 50 guineas towards the cost of the prosecution and was warned of future imprisonment.

It is probable that these incriminating letters, addressed to 'Bumble Toff', one of Betty May's nicknames, in some way implicated Crowley in Raoul Loveday's murder and he understandably wanted them destroyed – at any cost. Newspapers reported that Crowley 'received the letters between June 21, 1933, and April 10, 1934'.

> In June, 1933, Mrs Sedgewick was living in Seymore [sic] Street. There was also living there a man named [Eddie] Cruze, and you will hear that in her possession at Seymore [sic] Street were four letters which had passed between her and the solicitors who were arranging for her to be called as a witness [in the trial between Crowley *v.* Nina Hamnett]. They disclosed that she had been receiving money in respect of expenses. These letters, together with other personal documents, were put by her in an attaché case. Towards the end of June she went to a cottage in the country and had occasion to open the attaché case. She found the documents which it formally contained had disappeared. Those letters were never seen by her from the end of June 1933, until April 1934, when they were produced in court by the council for Crowley. Mr Stevenson said it was not known who stole the letters. The only person who was likely to have any interest in their possession was Aleister Crowley, and it was for him to give an explanation of his possession of them … Mrs. Sedgewick said the last time she was with Cruze was in a public house off Tottenham Court Road [the Duke of York] in March. She then accused him of stealing the letters, as she had heard he was showing them around saying he could get £100 for them … Detective-sergeant Davidson said that there was a summons against Cruze charging the alleged larceny of two envelopes, one addressed to Betty May and the other to Mrs Ricksworth, but it had not yet been served. The first witness for the defence, George Mather, a merchant, of Cambridge-terrace, W., said he told Crowley that Capt Cruze told him he (Cruze) had quarrelled with Miss May and was anxious for Crowley to have the use of the letters. Cruze told him (witness) that he was advancing money to Miss May, and the letters were part of the security.

Who was this Captain Eddie Cruze and why was he colluding with Crowley? Was there more to these letters than just financial gain? Shortly after this article was printed, an unknown newspaper ran the eye-catching headline 'BLACK MASS CULT IN LONDON' and included the following in its article:

> In no other civilised country in the world are weird and unseemly practices more freely indulged in than in Great Britain ... Secret orders, with one of which, having world-wide connections, Aleister Crowley has admitted association, perform all manner of queer rites, most of which are at least inimical to the Church and State. These rites, carried on in great secrecy, have been known to be the cause of insanity and in some cases suicide of the 'disciples.' Devotees of these underground creeds prey upon society for their own gain ... Young men and women, often touching the fringe of under-society for the first time by way of a 'rag' or jaunt, have been led to drink, drugs, and perverted practices until they reach the uttermost depths. Only recently it was revealed that young and impressionable visitors to one of these so-called temples had been led into profound studies with an apparent honest endeavour to read the hidden mysteries of the Universe. These soon degenerated into erotic orgies. This happened in the Earl's Court district. Certain London cults practice the Black Mass, where black bread, black wine, and black candles are used, worshippers confess every good deed as a sin, and do penance ... Today, just as fervently as it was in the Dark Ages, alchemy is practised in London.

On 5 April 1935, just as *Bulldog Jack* (the film that 'spoofed 1933 press reports that the British Museum station was haunted by an Egyptian ghost') opened in the UK cinemas, two 'young and impressionable' women of the 'under-society' allegedly disappeared from a platform at Holborn – the same platform along which the screams of the Ancient Egyptian ghost were said to echo. The women were never to be seen again, and strange, indecipherable marks were later found on the tiled walls belonging to the disused British Museum station a mere stop away. It bore all the hallmarks of the Beast, who was known to have scribbled similar mysterious sigils on the walls of the nearby Fitzroy Tavern, and who would have crucially been aware of the station's nefarious reputation and its bond with Ancient Egyptian mythology. It was also, incredibly, twelve years to the day since Lord Carnarvon succumbed to blood poisoning in Cairo.

It seems almost too unbelievable to consider these disappearances a coincidence; instead, it is rather more likely that they were planned by Crowley to coincide with the anniversary of Carnarvon's death. Moreover, Holborn underground station is situated just yards from Lincoln's Inn Fields, the largest public space in London, which is believed to have been laid out by Inigo Jones based on the exact dimensions of the Great Pyramid of Giza. It was, of course, in the Great Pyramid where Crowley spent a night meditating on his honeymoon with Rose, later claiming that the walls began to glow a shade of blue. Lincoln's Inn Fields also plays host to Sir John Sloane's Museum, a museum of architecture that was formerly the home of the neo-classical architect of the same name. Not only exhibiting drawings, models, paintings and antiques, the museum also houses a collection of rare Ancient Egyptian antiquities, including the sarcophagus of Seti I, two Egyptian stelae and a wooden mummy case.

In February, Crowley had entered into involuntary bankruptcy proceedings, his total debts amounting to £4,695, and his assets – aside from the ill-foundered claim against his former friends – were nil. His only income now would come in the form of 'small trust payments, donations from disciples, sporadic gifts from friends, rare sums from the few souls who came to him seeking magical healing and the Elixir of Life – these were the tenuous means of maintaining a frayed gentility that befitted a Prophet awaiting his Aeon'. In other words, Crowley had enjoyed plenty of time to engage in his morbid pursuits for Aiwass.

However, by the mid-1930s, Crowley firmly believed that he had been abandoned by his Holy Guardian Angel, as reported by Shri Gurudev Mahendranath in *The Londinium Temple Strain*, where he recalls the following conversation he had with Crowley:

> The Magus often visited me in a little flatlet I had on the King's Road front at Brighton. He frequently came down from London and stayed at the Ship Hotel. One afternoon I put to him the question, 'Where is Aiwass now?' Crowley looked at me and gave his head a minute shake and then spread his arms with upturned palms as if to say, 'Where?' or even 'God knows!' Then he spoke, 'I think the fault is mine.'

This makes perfect sense. By the second half of 1935 any deaths attributed to the curse of King Tut had ceased, crucially coinciding with the Beast no longer communicating with Aiwass. Aiwass, who was often referred to by Crowley as his deity, was no longer issuing instructions to his chosen minion, 'the prince-priest the Beast'.

With his communication with Aiwass now at an end and reports of the curse of Tutankhamun in the newspapers ceasing, Aleister Crowley lived the last decade of his life as a bastion of British eccentricity, barely resembling the menacing character that had graced the 1920s and early 1930s club scene. He still found time to frequent his favourite London haunts, including the Café Royal on Regent Street, and 'the last phase of the Beast's story was enacted partly in London, and partly in the highly respectable environment of seaside resorts'.

'By that time Crowley had realised that "Crowleyanity" was not, after all, to supplant Christianity in the foreseeable future, and that the Cult of the Will was definitely not gaining the expected public support.'

His friend, the American occultist Grady Louis McMurty, confirmed this thus:

> it is a habit in England for school-boys to go around in small groups at Xmas time and sing carols at your front door, and, as has been said, 'they will not go away until they are paid!' Well, they did that time. Go away, that is, without being paid. We were sitting there at 93 Jermyn Street playing chess and rapping one wintry afternoon just before Xmas of '43 e.v. when we heard this raucous noise at the door. Crowley said, 'I wonder what that is,' in some annoyance, and went and opened the door. Here were four English school-boys bawling away. Crowley flew into a temper, slammed the door, and came storming back into the room raging, 'TO THE LIONS WITH THEM! TO THE LIONS WITH THEM!' Of course if they had been singing 'Oh little house of Boleskine', as someone was at a recent Crowleymas party, he might have felt differently.

Madeline Montalban, a journalist working for the *Daily Express*, remembered an interview that took place with the Beast in the late 1930s on esoterica and Thelema. 'He was living at Half Moon Street at the time, and invited [me to] lunch at the Café Royal restaurant in Regent Street. At the end of the meal, Crowley suddenly discovered he had no money to pay for it and [I] had to foot the bill.' Indeed, this habitual nuance would become something of a familiar character trait of his.

There is another incident which took place in the Café Royal shortly after the Montalban interview that perfectly exemplified the Beast's ambivalent attitude and conduct in later life.

> In 1937, when Crowley had decided that it was time for him to celebrate his sixtieth birthday (in which he was unquestionably right, considering that he was already sixty-two), he was anticipating a happy combination of pleasure with business. A foreign lady of uncertain but obviously advanced years had shown an interest in purchasing from Crowley a small pot of his Celebrated Magical Sex-Appeal Ointment for the (as he said) ridiculously small sum of £2,000. She was to be the guest of honour at his birthday party. A large private dining room was booked; printed invitations were issued, commanding each man to bring a lady friend; the succession of courses was debated with the banqueting manager and chef; and instructions were given for the

progress of drinks: Montrachet – Richebourg – Veuve Clicquot – Napoleon Brandy. On the night of the party, about two dozen guests assembled at a neighbouring tavern for a preliminary drink, after which Crowley and his First Concubine of the moment shepherded them over to the Café Royal. The meal, ordered with all the mastery of an accomplished connoisseur and prepared and served with equal skill, was hugely enjoyed. But the party, on the whole, was a disappointment to the host. Crowley was just not making any headway with the foreign lady. From time to time, as he sat beside her, it seemed to him that the pot of Celebrated Magical Sex-Appeal Ointment was as good as sold. But every time the lady changed the subject. Had he lost his magic touch? Deftly he would steer the conversation back to the restorative of fading charms. The lady listened – then shied off again. Crowley was defeated. The dinner was over. The bill was asked for, and as arranged, put down before the Whore of the Stars who of course was to foot it.

It was later to the Beast's chagrin that he was unable to sell the ointment to the lady and, feeling as though he had finally lost his appeal to members of either sex and writing of his 'weakening erections', he resigned himself to a life that would soon be full of frailty, illness, destitution and war. Some might say an unfitting end to such a colourful, eventful and depraved life. And yet, with the build-up to the Second World War imminent, Crowley continued to spend much of his time frequenting his favourite of places – London's West End – unperturbed by the looming threat of the Luftwaffe's bombing campaign. Taking several flats in London and one in Richmond, including premises at Welbeck Street, where he was later ejected for antisocial behaviour, and Hamilton House in Piccadilly, before settling into 93 Jermyn Street (the third time the street would play host to the Beast), Crowley was, by now, an old man plagued by recurring illnesses. In the summer of the previous year, from another of his London apartments at the time:

Crowley launched his own brief public practice as a health provider. His home office at 6 Hasker Street offered not only Elixir of Life pills but also osteopathic treatment, body vibrators, infrared rights and 'Zotofoam' equipment. At least one defaulted creditor of his short-lived enterprise claimed that Crowley had represented himself as a doctor. The Beast resided at his Hasker Street address for eight months. His young landlord, just turned twenty, had dropped his studies at Cambridge to pursue an acting career. Crowley persuaded him to provide free lodgings and office space and agree to a shared expenses arrangement (the young man bearing the brunt of it) in exchange for a proposed year of magical training. But by February 1939, arguments over money and the young man's growing mistrust of the Beast led to an end of this arrangement.

By the summer of 1939, Crowley was happy to be seen as a jingoistic figure in the public eye, and even agreed to pose as Winston Churchill in a collection of photographs (it was for Churchill who the Beast later claimed to have created the 'V for Victory' hand sign). This was a far cry from the defector with German sympathies who had fled his native Britain to travel to New York at the outbreak of the First World War. He was keen to lend his support to the British cause, and even composed a poem, *England, Stand Fast!*, which was issued as a pamphlet on 23 September 1939:

England, stand fast! Stand fast against the foe!
They struck the first blow: we shall strike the last.
Peace at the price of Freedom? We say No.
England, stand fast!

Despite being rebuked again by the British Secret Service after appealing to interrogate their prisoner Rudolph Hess, whose ramblings at the time were said to be riddled with occult references, Crowley's patriotism didn't diminish, and during one German bombing raid in the winter of 1943, Crowley's then landlady, a Miss Manning, reported that while her tenants were huddled in the kitchen, 'the Beast proceeded – at his own suggestion – to read in devout manner the Twenty-third Psalm of the Bible to the group. This was, according to Miss Manning, an evident reversion to the Christian faith of Crowley's childhood.' Taking into account his mental illness, perhaps this was an attempt by Crowley to make amends for the crimes he had committed. 'It was also here at 93 Jermyn Street that a German bomb landed in his back yard, blowing glass from the window all over his bed, and as he said to me at the time, "If I had been home, I would have been killed." This shook his nerve a bit.'

His close friend John Symonds visited him these final couple of years and noted that he looked fatigued. Still greeting him with the Thelemic salutation, 'Do what thou wilt shall be the whole of the law', Symonds remarked that the Beast 'was not much more than medium height, slightly bent, and clad in an old-style plus-4 suit with silver buckles below the knee … he had a thin goatee beard and a moustache … a brooch with the image of Thoth was on his silk tie. He wore a large ring with Egyptian hieroglyphics. He had a sweet smell from Abramelin oil … he talked of the end of the world, the prophecies of Nostradamus. His daily intake of heroin was likely enough to have killed a roomful of run-of-the-mill addicts.' Indeed, aside from his drug addiction, it would appear that his sinister attraction to Ancient Egypt continued into old age. His sense of humour, too, had not deserted him, and, on 20 February 1943, Crowley made a brief note in his private diary that simply read: '… shaved head: barber terrified as usual.'

While his friend, the British spy Maxwell Knight, compassionately described the Beast during this period as 'a well-dressed middle-aged eccentric with the manner of an Oxford don', by 1946, however, when interviewed by the author E.M. Butler for her new book, *The Myth of the Magus*, Crowley was depicted as being 'more repulsive than I had expected, and his voice was the ugliest thing about him: thin, fretful, scratchy – a pedantic voice and a pretentious manner … I could not take him seriously'. 'When her book was finally published, the year after Crowley's death, we find that the Beast is only briefly mentioned as being the "amanuensis of Aiwass," nothing more.'

By the time he died on 1 December 1947, at Netherwood, a boarding house in Hastings, the Beast was 72 years old. His description of his fellow residents as 'the most appalling crowd of alleged human beings that have ever been got together in one place' indicates that his cantankerous nature and scathing wit lasted to the bitter end. According to one source, as he succumbed to a respiratory infection, his last words were reputed to be: 'I am perplexed.' However, as legend has it, when he died on a still day, the curtains allegedly blew out across the room and a great peel of thunder rumbled in the sky – much in the same way as it did when Ali Kamel Fahmy Bey was murdered at the Savoy Hotel. Also, Crowley's physician, a Dr William Brown Thompson, who had refused to continue his patient's robust opiate prescription, died within twenty-four hours of the Beast at his Mayfair apartment – Crowley having supposedly placed a curse on him three months earlier. 'The supreme satisfaction is to be able to despise one's neighbour and this fact goes far to account for religious intolerance. It is evidently consoling to reflect that the people next door are headed for hell,' Crowley wrote shortly before his death.

Indeed, tales of the 'Curse of the Beast' still circulate today, and when a television production company filmed a documentary on Crowley called *Beast of Boleskine*, the art director pulled out at the eleventh-hour following a warning from a white witch. Perhaps more urban myth than anything tangible, the Loch Ness locals still advised the film crew to avoid passing Boleskine after dark as various strange happenings occurred to those connected with it. Allegedly a coachman became an alcoholic, Crowley's housekeeper vanished and a workman went mad and tried to kill the Beast. There is also a tale of a butcher accidentally killing himself when he cut off his own hand with a cleaver after reading a note from Crowley.

On 10 April 2005, *The Observer* published an article entitled 'THE DARK HISTORY OF A SEASIDE TOWN IS BROUGHT TO LIGHT'. In the article, the journalist William Shaw examines the posthumous impact the Beast had upon Hastings, the town in which he died:

Reu Hickman still feels nauseous whenever he returns to Hastings. He had a miserable time. Growing up there, he believed Hastings had been cursed by the occultist Aleister Crowley. He was in his teens when he first heard the story. At the time, Reu (pronounced 'Roo') found that easy to believe.

It turned out Crowley, the famous dabbler in 'sex magick', had ended his days in a boarding house there in 1947. Reu's friends pointed to a spooky house built against the cliff where he'd supposedly lived. Actually, the Victorian house known as Netherwood had been demolished decades earlier. Facts and rumours mix easily at that age. A heroin addict, the self-dubbed 'Great Beast' had run out of friends and money; he ended his days in Room 13 – appropriately.

There was a big goth scene in Hastings when Reu lived there; they all used to go to the club the Crypt, looking for the dark heart of Hastings, swapping stories about Crowley. There were rumours of animal sacrifices. He'd made furniture out of human skin, they said. And he'd cursed the town. It seemed likely. To Reu, Hastings was the town in the Morrissey song: the seaside town they forgot to close down.

Crowley wasn't the only heroin addict to wind up there. To this day, Reu believes the place has a higher than average murder rate. Remember Billie-Jo Jenkins, murdered in Lower Park Road in 1997? Or the teenager who killed a retired vicar in 2001 and left his dismembered body behind the Summerfield Leisure Centre? In the Eighties, when the British stopped taking their holidays at home, the guesthouses filled with the unemployed and the mentally ill. As far as he was concerned it was a stinkhole for people whose lives weren't going very well. Like him. There was nothing for teenagers to do there; especially in the winter. He left home at 16 – he and his mum were always at each other's throats – and started dossing at friends' houses.

It wasn't nice. At first, all he had was a carpet to sleep under. He wasn't a nice person, then, either. On the dole, drinking, taking speed, ecstasy and magic mushrooms. Going out on a Saturday night. Getting into fights. Going home. Drinking some more. You can get caught up in a dead-end town. Reu dreamed of getting away.

They said that the Crowley curse was that if you lived in Hastings you could never leave; if you tried you'd always come back. Reu found it a terrifying thought.

It would seem that even in death the Beast's peculiar legend was, and perhaps still is, something to be feared by all who crossed him. His upbringing, too, is worthy of further examination: his parents were members of the Plymouth Brethren fundamentalist Christian sect, an austere and devout Protestant fellowship, and their overbearing and domineering influence upon his childhood may have provided the catalyst for the bizarre adolescent behaviour that would shape the rest of his adult life. Let us not forget that John George Haigh, who earned the sobriquets the 'Acid Bath Murderer' and the 'Kensington Vampire' for murdering nine people throughout the course of the 1940s before disposing of their bodies in drums of acid, was brought up by parents who were also dedicated members of the Plymouth Brethren. Incredibly, John Bodkin Adams, the doctor and suspected serial killer who reputedly murdered up to 160 of his patients, was also a member of the Plymouth Brethren Christian sect, and, much like Crowley, his father was a preacher within a local congregation. Was there something in the manner of their authoritarian and dogmatic upbringings that triggered an impulse for murder?

So why had the Beast chosen London's West End as his hunting ground? Unable to gain access to the many others who had so scandalously desecrated the ancient tomb of Tutankhamun, London's West End, apart from seemingly attracting many of the wealthy dilettante Egyptologists, was the site where the tale of the mummy's curse reputedly originated during the 1820s with an English author and a bizarre theatrical striptease act during which mummies were unwrapped. The show took place in the very heart of the West End near Piccadilly Circus in 1821, the same district in which Crowley not only stalked his prey, but also made his domicile. Indeed, the Beast was later quoted as saying that he 'loved Piccadilly because the prostitutes were so plentiful and available at any time of the day'.

Furthermore, Piccadilly was also once home to the Egyptian Hall ('a museum of spectacular and magical and curious objects') – before its demolition in 1905 – a museum that housed a collection of magical curiosities brought back from South Seas by Captain Cook and later by the famed archaeologist Giovanni Belzoni. It was the first building in England to be influenced by the Egyptian style, partly inspired by the success of the Egyptian Room in Thomas Hopes' house in Duchess Street. With this in mind, there is no denying that Piccadilly and the West End provided Crowley with the most perfect and apposite of settings for him to indulge in such wickedness, much in the same way Whitechapel and the East End was the ideal stage for Jack the Ripper's bloodbath in 1888. And with the Beast having moved to London in 1887, could the 'Autumn of Terror' have contributed to the young Crowley's murderous machinations?

10

Aleister Crowley and Jack the Ripper

Five white dress ties soaked in blood.

Aleister Crowley, *Jack the Ripper*

When writing the graphic novel *From Hell*, Alan Moore, the celebrated comic book writer and occultist, used historian Stephen Knight's theory that the Whitechapel murders were part of a conspiracy between the Freemasons and the Royal Family as the basis for his story. He also decided to give Aleister Crowley a cameo as the teenaged Beast who bumps into Detective Inspector Abberline outside the mortuary where the autopsy is being carried out on a Ripper victim. Wearing short trousers and sucking on a candy cane, Crowley lectures the police about magic and tells Abberline that he's read that a man is killing ladies to make himself 'magic and invisible'. When Abberline vehemently dismisses young Crowley's claims, the Beast simply replies: 'You're wrong. Goodbye.' In the graphic novel's extensive notes, Moore remarks: 'Crowley moved with his mother to London in 1887 when he was thirteen. Given that in later life he showed more than a passing interest in the Whitechapel murders, it seemed possible that he may have been drawn to them as a spectator during his childhood.'

Could it be that Crowley's murderous instinct was born and nurtured in the late summer and autumn of 1888 when he was a mere 'spectator' of the Whitechapel murders, travelling regularly from his home in Streatham to East London? In *Confessions*, Crowley casts his mind back to the time when 'London was agog with the exploits of Jack the Ripper. One theory of the motive of the murderer was that he was performing an Operation to obtain the Supreme Black Magical Power. The seven [actually five] women had to be killed so that their seven bodies formed a "Calvary Cross of seven points" with its head to the west. The theory was that the killing of the third or fourth, I forget which, the murderer acquired the power of invisibility, and this was confirmed by the fact that in one case a policeman heard the shrieks of the dying woman and reached her before life was extinct, yet she lay in a *cul-de-sac*, with no possible exit save the street; and the policeman saw no sign of the assassin, though he was patrolling outside, expressly on the look-out.'

Indeed, the links between Jack the Ripper and occultism are extensive. While Crowley, who was only the tender age of 13 at the time of the murders, was never a likely suspect, authors Paul Woods and Gavin Baddeley, in their book *Saucy Jack*, believe that 'Crowley is the joker in the ripperology pack – a wild card who many feel inherently damages the credentials of any theory he's associated with. Yet the elements he brings to the mix – of forbidden blood rites and strange sex ceremonies – has proven too heady a witch's brew for some to resist, though it inevitably makes for a very murky concoction.'

In his *Confessions*, Crowley makes a brief reference to the Ripper when discussing his own growing media notoriety, stating: 'I enjoy the joke thoroughly. I can't believe that anything can hurt me. It would hurt my pride to admit it, I suppose. When a newspaper prints three columns, identifying me with Jack the Ripper, it never occurs to me that anyone in his senses would believe such rubbish.' Although the Beast attempts to rebut the suspicion of him as a murderer in this reference, there is plenty of evidence to suggest that he may have at least known the identity of Jack, owing in no small part to his own significant ties with the occultist underworld in London. Shortly before his death in 1947, the Beast wrote an essay simply titled 'Jack the Ripper'; in it he reinforced his strong belief that a notable part of Jack's modus operandi was influenced by the occult and black magic – a 'second-hand' opinion he no doubt 'repeated from cronies and rivals within the gossipy occult community'. It was enough to inspire Frater Achad Osher subsequently to write and publish an obscure pamphlet entitled 'Did Aleister Crowley Know the Identity of Jack the Ripper?'

There are also curious parallels between Jack and the Beast that are worthy of further examination. For example, they were both tabloid sensations of their respective eras, and Woods and Baddeley discuss this in *Saucy Jack*:

Whilst the Ripper suckled the infant tabloid press in the 1880s, in the 1920s Crowley presided over British yellow journalism's coming of age. The Beast was arguably the first consummate tabloid villain, 'a man we'd like to hang', 'king of depravity', and, most famously, 'the wickedest man in the world', according to *John Bull* magazine, among his most determined detractors.

And it was the *Sunday Express*, who, in 1922, labelled his practices as being 'the lowest depths that human depravity can reach'. However, it was in another vicarious newspaper, the *Pall Mall Gazette*, where an unnamed journalist wrote a front page story entitled 'The Whitechapel Demon's Nationality: and Why He Committed the Murders'. On 1 December 1888, and identifying himself inexplicably as 'One Who Thinks He Knows', the author (who Crowley later suspected was Jack the Ripper himself) based his supposition on the mysterious, allegedly anti-Semitic graffiti that was discovered chalked on a wall in Goulston Street shortly after the murder of Catherine Eddowes. He argues that the unusual spelling of 'Juwes' points to a French culprit, following a tenuous line of reasoning:

Frenchmen are 'notoriously the worst linguists in the world', allowing for a grammatical problem with his theory, while he eliminates a French-speaking Swiss or Belgian Ripper on the basis that 'the idiosyncrasy of both those nationalities is adverse to this class of crime.'

Furthermore, 'in France, the murdering of prostitutes has long been practised, and has been considered to be almost peculiarly a French crime.' Unsurprisingly, few subsequent ripperologists have paid much attention to this 'Jacques le Ripper' theory as to the killer's identity. The writer's speculations on the motive, however, have aroused substantial subsequent interest.'

'Now, in one of the books by the great modern occultist who wrote under the *nom de plume* of [Eliphas Levi], *Le Dogme et Rituel de la Haute Magie*, we find the most elaborate directions for working magical spells of all kinds,' notes the *Pall Mall*'s correspondent. 'The second volume has a chapter on Necromancy, or black magic, which the author justly denounces as a profanation. Black magic employs the agencies of evil spirits and demons, instead of the beneficent spirits directed by the adepts of *la haute magie*. At the same time he gives the clearest and fullest details of the necessary steps for evocation by this means, and it is in the list of substances prescribed as absolutely necessary to success that we find the link which joins modern French necromancy with the quest of the East-end murderer. These substances are in themselves horrible, and difficult to procure. They can only be obtained by means of the most appalling crimes, of which murder and mutilation of the dead are the least heinous. Among them are strips of the skin of a suicide, nails from a murderer's gallows, candles made from human fat, the head of a black cat which has been fed forty days on human flesh, the horns of a goat which has been made the instrument of an infamous capital crime, and a preparation made from a certain portion of the body of a *harlot*. This last point is insisted upon as essential and it was this extra-ordinary fact that first drew my attention to the possible connection of the murderer with the black art.'

The author of the article, later revealed as one Dr Robert (Roslyn) D'Onston Stephenson, proceeds to explain the Ripper's true motive:

Here we find perhaps the first instance of the idea of the murders being committed in specific locations, determined by the desire to plot a mystical symbol across the map of London using the bodies of his victims. Did the murderer, then, designing to offer the mystic number of seven [sic] human sacrifices in the form of a cross – a form which he intended to profane – deliberately pick out beforehand on a map the places in which he would offer them to his infernal deity of murder? If not, surely these six *coincidences* are the most marvellous event of our time.

Indeed, some ripperologists have gone further and, much like Crowley, have named D'Onston Stephenson as a likely suspect due to his far-fetched theories, his practising of the 'black arts', and his article in the *Pall Mall Gazette* that was written to gloat over his crimes whilst throwing the police off the scent.

His most dogged accuser is the ripperologist Melvin Harris. D'Onston Stephenson had a colourful past before he became a freelance journalist, according to Harris, 'he had panned for gold in the United States, witnessed devil worship in the Cameroon and hunted for the authentic rope trick in India. For a while he even courted danger as a surgeon-major with Garibaldi's army.' Having said that, Harris admits, '[D'Onston Stephenson's] newspaper writings are packed with deception; biographically, they are of limited use and his tales of magic in Europe, Asia and Africa are just too exaggerated to be true.'

It is almost certainly D'Onston Stephenson whom Ivor Edwards identifies as the man behind *Jack the Ripper's Black Magic Rituals*, and, more pertinently, who Crowley is referring to in his revelatory Ripper essay. So why was it that Crowley believed D'Onston Stephenson to be Jack the Ripper? 'Harris establishes that his suspect [D'Onston Stephenson] was in the vicinity at the time, though convalescing at The London Hospital on Whitechapel Road' – where Crowley would later murder Arthur Weigall.

He was suffering from neurasthenia, a very nineteenth-century complaint whereby the sufferer's nerves come under such pressure as to render them a physical invalid. It was a popular diagnosis among Bohemian artists, as it implied an excess of sensitivity, and some saw it as illustrating the thin line between genius and madness. In [D'Onston Stephenson's] case it seems likely that his chronic alcoholism was exacerbated by the toxic preparations he took in order to try and control the side effects of his heavy drinking.

It is likely that Crowley shared Harris' theory. Along with a confession the Beast procured from Vitorria Cremers (a colourful Italian occultist who claimed D'Onston Stephenson confided in her the part he played in the Ripper murders), this formed the basis of the most popular theory of Jack the Ripper as a black magician. Moreover, Cremers declared that she had discovered five blood-stained neckties among D'Onston Stephenson's possessions. This was the 'story later repeated by Crowley – who claimed to have had possession of the incriminating neckties – and the story reported periodically in the press in various forms'. Furthermore, Woods and Baddeley write that:

> Melvin Harris is adamant that [D'Onston Stephenson] was only ever playing the fool in order to throw people off the scent, presenting the journalist W.T. Stead as a character witness who believed that [D'Onston Stephenson] was more just a plausible fantasist. It was Stead who commissioned his infamous Ripper article for the *Pall Mall Gazette*, and according to D'Onston Stephenson it was Stead who furnished him with the dubious insider information about the sodomy of Jack's final victim.

'He has been known to me for many years,' wrote Stead, introducing some of D'Onston Stephenson's journalism in an 1896 edition of the *Borderland* quarterly:

> He is one of the most remarkable men I ever met. For more than a year I was under the impression that he was the veritable Jack the Ripper; an impression which I believed was shared by the police, who at least once had him under arrest; although, as he completely satisfied them, they liberated him without bringing him to court.

Coincidentally, it was Stead, another famed sensationalist, who concocted the story of the cursed 'mummy-board' belonging to the priestess of Amen-Ra at the British Museum, and who died onboard the *Titanic* after regaling the tale of its infamous legend.

Furthermore, in *From Hell's* notes, Alan Moore goes on to state that: 'Elsewhere, [Crowley] ascribes the murders to the founder of theosophy [and his great predecessor], Madame Blavatsky.' Like Stead, Blavatsky was also previously mentioned in relation to the cursed 'mummy-board' at the British Museum when she was summoned to perform an exorcism at the home belonging to the owner of the artefact. 'Can you exorcise this evil spirit?' asked the owner. Blavatsky replied, 'There is no such thing as exorcism. Evil remains evil forever. Nothing can be done about it. I implore you to get rid of this evil as soon as possible.'

It is perhaps no coincidence then that the 'mummy-board' itself makes an appearance in *From Hell* when the murderer, Sir William Gull, pays a visit to the British Museum. Addressing the portly curator (possibly Sir Ernest Wallis Budge), Gull argues against the removal of the 'mummy-board' from the museum, stating that, 'What better place for the artefact than here in this Museum, next to [Nicholas] Hawksmoor's Bloomsbury Church?' He then continues his tour before crossing paths with W.B. Yeats and deriding Dr William Wynn Westcott's 'little group', the Hermetic Order of the Golden Dawn. The importance of the 'mummy-board' and its frequent re-emergence in this book is perhaps unsurprising when we consider the role it played in Crowley's first murder, that of Bertram Fletcher Robinson in 1907.

However, there are further links between Aleister Crowley and the Whitechapel murders (other than his suspicions as to the identity of Jack) that are important to consider. The Beast himself confessed to bedding his family's chambermaid in his mother's bed when he was in his early teens, and the said chambermaid was subsequently dismissed by the doctrinaire Crowley family before becoming a prostitute. She allegedly went on to become one of Jack the Ripper's victims. Intriguingly, Lord Carnarvon suffered similar scandalous gossip when he was rumoured, as a young man, to have been involved in a sexual tryst with Mary Jane Kelly, the Ripper's final and most notorious victim.

Also, in 1888, the year of the Ripper murders, the Hermetic Order of the Golden Dawn was founded in London by Samuel Liddell McGregor Mathers and Dr William Wynn Westcott. It was, of course, within the Golden Dawn where Crowley would serve his 'occult apprenticeship'. Drawing heavily from Eliphas Levi's scholarship, whose work was also referred to by D'Onston Stephenson in his infamous Ripper article, the Golden Dawn flourished and had attracted thirty-two members by the end of 1888.

Levi was certainly a highly influential occult authority, whose reputation had grown since he died in poverty in 1875. The Theosophical Society, founded that same year, incorporated many of his doctrines into their sprawling cosmology, whilst the Great Beast Crowley claimed to have been his reincarnation (sharing a date of birth with the French occultist's date of death).

As one of the Golden Dawn's founders, Westcott, a London coroner himself, was a man with vast medical knowledge who just so happened to form his occult order in the year of the Ripper crimes – but was it mere coincidence? One reporter argues that it wasn't:

> Journalist Christopher Smith has concocted a theory he calls 'Jack the Ripper: The Alembic Connection', which has Westcott presiding over the churchyard sacrifice of the Ripper victims before his hooded Golden Dawn minions dump their bodies in the backstreets of the East End. It's an implausible theory for numerous reasons – more a gothic flight of fancy than informed criminological speculation – but even though the Golden Dawn may be wholly blameless, might not another organisation or individual have committed the Ripper crimes with satanic intent?
>
> Nigel Cawthorne's overheated true-crime paperback, *Satanic Murders*, deals with pre-twentieth-century 'murder, madness and mayhem' in a chapter entitled 'From Early Satanism to Jack the Ripper'. With circumspection not always evident in his study, Cawthorne describes Jack as 'a killer who performed ritual murders which seem to have had some occult overtones … Interestingly, if you plot the five murders on a map, they mark out the points of a pentagram, the five-pointed star.'

Indeed, in Alan Moore's *From Hell*, Sir William Gull takes the reader on a tour of London's landmarks, describing their hidden symbolism, and finally reveals that they are laid out across the city in the form of a giant pentagram. One of these landmarks is Cleopatra's Needle, behind which the Savoy Hotel ominously overlooks the Thames, and this fact would have been of significant interest to Crowley. It was, of course, the Savoy Hotel that played host to the murder of Prince Ali Kamel Fahmy Bey. Another of these landmarks is none other than Nicholas Hawksmoor's St George's church, Bloomsbury, which is but a stone's throw from the British Museum and Bloomsbury Street, where Sir Ernest Wallis Budge met his grisly end at the hands of Crowley. The church, built in the style of Egyptian and Greek architecture, even houses a copy of the original pyramid from the sarcophagus at Halicarnassus.

Hawksmoor, a revered British architect who worked under the tutelage of Sir Christopher Wren, is the subject of a poem – 'Nicholas Hawksmoor: His

Churches' – by Iain Sinclair, which appeared in Sinclair's collection of poems *Lud Heat* (1975). Sinclair argues that Hawksmoor's churches formed a pattern consistent with the forms of Theistic Satanism. Historian Peter Ackroyd in his book *Hawksmoor*, and Alan Moore and Eddie Campbell in *From Hell*, developed this idea further, with the latter speculating that Jack the Ripper used Hawskmoor's buildings as part of ritual magic, with his victims as human sacrifice. The authors also brought notoriety to Hawksmoor's famous London churches. The argument includes the idea that, when dotted up on a map, the churches produce an Eye of Horus, and that this has some ritual significance.

With broad ties to Westcott, D'Onston Stephenson, W.T. Stead and the Golden Dawn, and having spent time as a scholar of the murders, there is little doubt that Crowley would have drawn inspiration from Jack the Ripper's rampage – as well as his mystical and occult leanings – without resorting to copycat killings. When the Whitechapel murders are evoked alongside Crowley's own killing spree in London's West End all those years later, we can begin to discern incredible parallels. For example, when five of the locations of Crowley's West End murders are drawn upon a map of London, a five-pointed star, an almost perfect pentagram, is astonishingly revealed.

These are, in chronological order, the murder of Ali Kamel Fahmy Bey at the Savoy Hotel; the murder of Richard Bethell at the Bath Club; the murder of Lord Westbury at St James' Court; the murder of Edgar Steele at St Thomas' Hospital and the murder of Sir Ernest Wallis Budge at 48 Bloomsbury Street, Bedford Square. What provoked Crowley to initiate the pentagram at this stage is unclear, bearing in mind he had already committed at least two other murders, but whatever the cause it is patent that we are well beyond the realms of coincidence now, especially when we consider the fact that the streets off Piccadilly, the district around which Crowley had chosen as his hunting ground due to its extensive ties with Ancient Egypt, are in the heart of the pentagram. Also in its centre is the Admiralty, with whom the Beast had either worked for or was hounded by – depending on which report you believe – throughout the First World War, and Nelson's Column and Charing Cross station, two landmarks that were of esoteric importance to Crowley. In his novel *Moonchild*, Crowley described the station thus:

> The city is monstrous and misshapen; its mystery is not a brooding, but a conspiracy. And these truths are evident above all to one who recognizes that London's heart is Charing Cross ... but it is to be observed that Nelson, on his monument, is careful to turn his gaze upon the Thames. For here is the true life of the city, the aorta of that great heart of which London and

Westminster are the ventricles. Charing Cross Station, moreover, is the only true Metropolitan terminus … Honestly, Charing Cross is the true link with Europe, and therefore with history … This terminus is swathed in immemorial gloom; it was in one of the waiting-rooms that James Thomson conceived the idea for his *City of Dreadful Night*; but it is still the heart of London, throbbing with a clear longing towards Paris.

As for the Beast's victims, it could be argued that he had been directly responsible for the deaths – or disappearances – of eleven individuals in London. Was

1. Savoy Hotel

2. Bath Club, Dover Street

3. St James' Court

4. St Thomas' Hospital

5. Bloomsbury Street

this number significant to him in any way? In *The Book of the Law*, Crowley wrote: 'my number is 11, as all their numbers who are of us. The Five Pointed Star, with a Circle in the Middle, & the circle is Red. My colour is black to the blind, but the blue & gold are seen of the seeing. Also I have a secret glory for them that love me.'

In another essay about Jack the Ripper, Crowley writes how:

the number of murders involved in the ceremonies was five, whereas the Whitechapel murders so-called, were seven in number; but two of these were spurious ... These murders are completely to be distinguished from five genuine ones, by obvious divergence on technical points. The place of each murder is important, for it is essential to describe what is called the averse pentagram, that is to say, a star of five points with a single point in the direction of the South Pole. 'From this point Crowley refers to himself in the third person, presumably in an effort to give this theory an air of scientific respectability.'

The investigation has been taken up by Bernard O'Donnell, the crime expert of the Empire News; and he has discovered many interesting details. In the course of conversation with Aleister Crowley this matter came up, and the magician was very impressed with O'Donnell's argument. He suggested an astrological investigation. Was there anything significant about the times of the [Ripper] murders? O'Donnell's investigation had led him to the conclusion that the murderer had attached the greatest importance to accuracy in the time. O'Donnell, accordingly, furnished Crowley with the necessary data, and figures of the heavens were set up ...

Crowley thought this an excellent opportunity to trace the evil influence of the planets, looking naturally first of all to Saturn, the great misfortune, then to Mars, the lesser misfortune; but also to Uranus, a planet not known to the ancients, but generally considered of a highly explosive tendency. The result of Crowley's investigations was staggering; there was one constant element in all cases of murder, both of the assassin and the murdered. Saturn, Mars, and Herschel were indeed rightly suspected of doing dirty work at the crossroads, but the constant factor was a planet which had until that moment been considered, if not actively beneficent, at least perfectly indifferent and harmless – the planet Mercury.

Crowley went into this matter very thoroughly and presently it dawned on his rather slow intelligence that after all this was only to be expected; the quality of murder is not primarily malice, greed, or wrath; the one essential condition without which deliberate murder can hardly ever take place, is just this cold bloodedness, this failure to attribute the supreme value of human life. Armed with these discoveries the horoscopes of the Whitechapel murders shone crystal clear to him. In every case, either Saturn or Mercury were precisely on the Eastern horizon at the moment of the murder (by precisely, one means within a matter of minutes). Mercury is, of course, the God of Magic, and his adverse distorted image the Ape of Thoth, responsible for such evil trickery as is the heart of black magic, while Saturn is not only the cold heartlessness of age, but the magical equivalent of Saturn. He is the old god who was worshipped in the 'Witches' Sabbath.'

With Crowley's theory in mind, one wonders how the planets aligned on the nights of his West End murders. Unquestionably, these planetary alignments bear as much significance to him as the locations of the murders, and Crowley's essay lays bare the extent in which his meticulous research into the Whitechapel murders directly inspired his own efforts as a serial killer.

In Patricia Cornwell's 2002 book *Portrait of a Killer: Jack the Ripper – Case Closed*, she argues that the acclaimed artist Walter Sickert was the man responsible for the Whitechapel murders, citing an alleged defect in his penis as one of the motivating factors. During her research, Cornwell famously went so far as to purchase thirty-one of his paintings to test for DNA to corroborate her theory. Sickert, much like Crowley, had taken a keen interest in the nefarious activities of Jack the Ripper, and even believed that at one time he had lodged in a room used by Jack. He subsequently painted the room, entitling it 'Jack the Ripper's Bedroom', and portrayed it as a dark, brooding and almost unintelligible space.

Prior to Cornwell's controversial disclosures, author Jean Overton Fuller, in her 1990 book *Sickert and the Ripper Crimes*, had identified Sickert as Jack, and ripperologist Stephen Knight, in his revelatory 1976 title *Jack the Ripper: The Final Solution*, had argued that Sickert was forced to become an accomplice in the Ripper murders. Whether or not Sickert had any part to play in Jack's chilling rampage remains unclear, but it is certainly significant that both Sickert – a viable Ripper suspect – and Crowley drank together at the Fitzroy Tavern during the period in which the Beast was at the height of his own murderous endeavours. So, with this in mind, were Crowley's very public and overt suspicions of Robert D'Onston Stephenson as the Ripper merely a bluff in order to protect the inspirational Sickert?

Though [Crowley] was a customer at the Fitzroy, his presence was not encouraged by Annie [the landlady], as he was a dangerous man. He did contribute to Annie's autograph book, and in September 1941 he was to give to her a signed copy, No 89 out of the 100 copies that were printed of his book *Thumbs Up*, a pentagram and a pentacle to win the war.

Indeed, although Crowley mentions the Ripper depicted an 'averse pentagram' comprising the locations of his killing spree, this was not actually the case, and the pentagram of sorts that overlaid Whitechapel in 1888 and London's West End years later represented the microcosm – the Kingdom of Malkuth (the 'Tree of Life').

As well as being used symbolically in many other religions, Crowley continued to make regular use of both forms of the pentagram in his Thelemic system of magick; for example, an adverse or inverted pentagram represents the descent of spirit into matter, whereas the regular pentagram represents the opposite. In his *Confessions*, Crowley, recalling his 'Magical Workings' and, crucially, referring to Aiwass, writes:

> Asked for a messenger, Aiwass appears. F., suspecting him, puts a pentagram on him; he blurs and becomes dirty and discrowned ... F. uses pentagram and shrivels him up to a black charred mass ... 'I am the God of Vengeance. I am thy Guardian Angel. I would have thee seek thine own soul in silence and alone. Take no aid with thee; take no mortal soul but retire and depart from mankind.' Pentagram makes him brighter: he grows firmer.

It is fascinating to note the connection between Aiwass, Crowley's 'Guardian Angel', and the pentagram, as well as the Beast's belief that Aiwass was 'the God of Vengeance', considering his murderous mission was one born of retribution.

Crowley contradicted his old comrades in the Hermetic Order of the Golden Dawn, who, following Levi, considered the adverse orientation of the symbol evil and associated it with the triumph of matter over spirit. Either way, it is evident that the Beast had an association with the mystical properties of the pentagram that began long before he committed his West End murders. Indeed, such was his obsession with the pentagram star and its religious significance that Crowley not only wrote instructions for 'The Greater Ritual of the Pentagram' on a train destined for India in 1906 (the year before Bertram Fletcher Robinson's murder), but he also recorded a piece of oratory dedicated to it in 1910. He later composed a poem, 'The Pentagram', which was written to commemorate the first European flight of a 1km circuit by Henri Farman in January 1908, and was dedicated to his friend, the writer George Raffalovich:

In the Years of the Primal Course, in the dawn of terrestrial birth,
Man mastered the mammoth and horse, and Man was the Lord of the Earth.
He made him an hollow skin from the heart of an holy tree,
He compassed the earth therein, and Man was the Lord of the Sea.
He controlled the vigour of steam, he harnessed the lightning for hire;
He drove the celestial team, and man was the Lord of the Fire.
Deep-mouthed from their thrones deep-seated, the choirs of the æons declare
The last of the demons defeated, for Man is the Lord of the Air.
Arise, O Man, in thy strength! the kingdom is thine to inherit,
Till the high gods witness at length that Man is the Lord of his spirit.

Also, let us not forget that Crowley, shortly before King Tut's tomb was discovered in 1923 and as part of 'The Lesser Banishing Ritual of the Pentagram', dipped his finger in cat's blood and traced a pentagram on Raoul Loveday's forehead, before scooping the blood into a silver cup and passing it to Loveday, who 'drained the contents to the dregs'. Furthermore, Crowley's flat in Chancery Lane, which was under constant police surveillance at the time, was reputed to have two temples within it, one dedicated to the practice of white magic and the other to the practice of black magic. Both were covered with pentagrams, and the black magic temple even contained a skull that Crowley fed with scraps of food, small birds and blood. From his flat at 124 Victoria Street, as well as at the nearby Caxton Hall (these buildings being a stone's throw from St James' Court where Lord Westbury was pushed to his death), Crowley would again perform 'The Rites of Eleusis' as well as 'The Lesser Banishing Ritual of the Pentagram' – the single most important ritual in the Beast's system – as was eloquently described by *The Looking Glass* publication who had gained covert admittance to Caxton Hall. Moreover, 'the evening service [at the Abbey of Thelema] – the Pentagram – [has since been described as] an elaborate affair, during which Crowley lashed himself into a frenzy with his chanting, and broke into an *enchaînment* of ecstatic dances'.

These are important pieces of evidence, and the first even links the pentagram and Loveday's murder in Cefalù to those that took place within London's West End soon after. Indeed, Crowley's reference to the Ripper murders in his *Confessions*, 'that the killing of the third or fourth, I forget which, the murderer acquired the power of invisibility', leaves a chilling reminder of his performance in the Café Royal restaurant on the night of Lord Westbury's murder. 'Walking slowly in through the swing doors, Crowley marched solemnly through the rows of tables to the exit, and out into the Nirvana of Glasshouse Street', before heading south to St James' Court where Westbury lay waiting.

Crowley demonstrably believed that he had garnered 'the power of invisibility' from his third murder, that of Richard Bethell at Mayfair's Bath Club, and that his magic cloak would now protect him as he went about his further macabre pursuits. He could have killed Bethell on numerous occasions in any of his London residences or clubs (including his home at Manchester Square), but to maintain the rigidity of the pentagram and for geographical purposes the Bath Club on Dover Street was chosen. To obtain the 'Supreme Black Magical Power', much like Jack the Ripper did in 1888, Crowley would have to murder a further two people, starting with his fourth victim, Bethell's father, Lord Westbury, and finishing with his fifth victim, Sir Ernest Wallis Budge, whose death at his home on Bloomsbury Street completed the pentagram.

Crowley's murder sites were chosen, fortuitously in some cases, to form the spiritual connection to the pentagram, and, despite two of Jack the Ripper's murders being described as 'spurious' by Crowley, the murders that didn't comprise the star, such as Aubrey Herbert's at the Harold Fink Memorial Hospital on Park Lane and Arthur Weigall's at the London Hospital, Whitechapel, would have nevertheless been deemed justifiable due to the victim's connivance with the violation of King Tut's tomb. However, unlike Jack the Ripper's bloodbaths, the Beast cunningly ensured that the deaths of the majority of his victims bore the hallmarks of natural causes consistent with those who had reputedly fallen victim to the curse of Tutankhamun.

It would certainly seem as if Crowley was obsessed with making himself invisible and would go to great lengths to satisfy this rampant curiosity of his. With this in mind, it is important to recall his previous attempt to acquire the power of invisibility when he was in Mexico in 1900. He experimented with Freemasonry and various rituals before he became satisfied that his reflection in the mirror was growing weaker. Finally, he truly believed that he was invisible to everyone. Moreover, when cross-examined during the Nina Hamnett trial, Crowley revealed that he had rendered himself invisible to 'evade detection after shooting an assailant in India'. However, in hindsight, Crowley was clearly dissatisfied with these experiments, hence his further trials and use of ritualistic murder in subsequent 'experiments'.

Before his ashes were sent to his disciples in America, perhaps the words from Crowley's infamous poem 'Hymn to Pan', which were read out during his funeral service in 1947, acted as some sort of posthumous confession for these barbaric acts? The words included: 'I rave; and I rape and I rip and I rend, Everlasting, world without end!' It was Crowley who also wrote, 'I want none of your faint approval or faint dispraise. I want blasphemy, murder, rape, revolution, anything, bad or good, but strong.'

Depicting the peculiar ceremony that took place in a Brighton crematorium, authors Paul Woods and Gavin Baddeley offer a suitably morose description of the final moments of the Beast's interment:

> The unorthodox congregation file out, witnessed by a small press contingent already trying to wring one last line of sinister scandal. Finally, as if on cue, the heavens open with shards of lightning and hammering rain as the smoke rises from the chimney of the Brighton crematorium. Is this the thunderous applause of forsaken deities or a final rumble of divine disapproval?

11

The Aftermath: Howard Carter, Allies and the Ones Who Got Away

He had ordered the canary brought to the site, to encourage the workmen as they cleared away the rubble. It was also – Carter would not deny this to himself – a feeble attempt to calm his own raging nerves, for since his boyhood he had always been a lover of birds, and found in their singing a source of great comfort. But although his expression, that first long day and the next, appeared perfectly composed, his thoughts remained a tumult of terrors and wild hopes, and he barely heard the canary's song. Nothing filled his ears but the chink of spade upon rock, as slowly, step by step, a stairway was revealed.

Tom Holland, *The Sleeper in the Sands*

So why was it that 64-year-old Howard Carter, the man responsible for discovering the tomb of Tutankhamun and the very first person to enter his sacred chamber, defied the curse – or Crowley's wrath – when he died in 1939 of lymphoma at his home at 19 Collingham Gardens, Kensington? The archaeologist's death, so long after the opening of the tomb, despite being the leader of the expedition, is the most common piece of evidence put forward by sceptics to refute the idea of a curse plaguing the party that violated King Tut's burial chamber.

Also, why was it that Crowley saw fit to spare Carter, a man who was surely the most deserving of the charge of sacrilege and the most likely to incite the indignation of Aiwass? Perhaps the fact that Carter spent much of 1924 on a tour of America, far away from Crowley, or the respect he had shown to both the tomb and to King Tut's legacy, both in his writings and later in his opposition to Arthur Weigall's garish Wembley replica, had persuaded the Beast to let him live? After all, Crowley had previously spared the life of Marie-Marguerite Fahmy, who had not only heinously entered the sacrosanct burial chamber with her husband, but who had also posed for a 'zany snapshot' within the open sarcophagus. Marie-Marguerite later proved to be a valuable 'emissary' for Crowley when she was in London, so did Carter also provide Crowley with a service that was worth sparing his life for? We must remember that although Carter was terminally ill, Crowley showed Weigall no mercy despite him having a similar prognosis. Indeed, is there a connection between Carter and Weigall's long-standing and bitter rivalry and Weigall's murder?

What is certain, however, is that by the time Howard Carter passed away in 1939, Crowley had lost all contact with his Holy Guardian Angel – Aiwass – who had been issuing him with murderous commands since they first made contact in Egypt in 1904. Crowley had seemingly been cured of his mental illness, and by 1935 any deaths attributed to the curse of King Tut had ceased, crucially coinciding with the Beast no longer communicating with Aiwass. However, it is certainly more intriguing if we consider the theory that Howard Carter was in some way linked to Crowley's macabre undertakings.

In his book *The Tutankhamun Deception*, historian Gerald O'Farrell believes that Carter was a very murky figure, who, along with his patron, Lord Carnarvon, plundered King Tut's tomb of four-fifths of its treasures before making the discovery official. They then went on to commit a 'string of necessary murders', disguised as the 'Curse of the Pharaohs', in which those who had knowledge of the precious papyrus documents found in the tomb were disposed of. In their book *Tutankhamun: The Exodus Conspiracy*, authors Andrew Collins and Chris Ogilvie-Herald draw a similar conclusion in which Howard Carter threatened to reveal the truth behind this secret papyri that held the 'true account' of the biblical exodus from Egypt. They argue that at a time when Arab hostility towards Britain's support for the establishment of a Jewish homeland in Palestine was spilling on to the streets of Jerusalem and Jaffa, such actions on the part of Carter would have caused untold chaos across the Middle East.

Moreover, both books not only paint Carter as an illicit figure who had retained bounty from Tutankhamun's tomb for himself, but also raise the theory that the curse was nothing more than cold-blooded murder. Collins and Ogilvie-Herald even go as far as to suggest that Carnarvon himself exhibited distinct signs of toxic poisoning in his final days, which included

his teeth falling out, and the fact that he knew full well of the discovery of
the papyri advances the notion of the involvement of foul play. They also
highlight Carnarvon's fascination with the occult, and how this interest 'was
not unique for his era':

> Many wealthy, well-to-do people in British society shared a belief in the
> omnipotent powers of Ancient Egypt. To them this distant land, beneath the
> hot desert sun, was an exotic paradise, where the ancient gods still lived on in
> the invisible world. These very humanlike deities were seen not simply as the
> product of the superstitious fears of a bygone race, but as the power and moti-
> vation behind the great civilisation that built the Great Pyramid and flourished
> for nearly 3,000 years before its decline at the time of the Roman Empire.
>
> It is certain that, had he lived, the fifth Earl of Carnarvon would have
> believed in the curse of Tutankhamun, for it seems that the British aristo-
> crat was deeply influenced by spiritualism and the occult. He was also an
> active member of the London Spiritual Alliance. On numerous occasions
> Carnarvon organised séances in the East Anglia Room at Highclere Castle.
> Present would be his daughter, Lady Evelyn Herbert, the politician and lawyer
> Sir Edward Marshall Hall KC; Lady Cunliffe-Owen and, when in the coun-
> try, Howard Carter. In his published memoirs the sixth Earl of Carnarvon
> says that his father became 'keenly interested in the occult' as he and Howard
> Carter waited restlessly for hostilities to cease during World War One.

Incredibly, it was Sir Edward Marshall Hall who not only represented Marie-
Marguerite Fahmy in her questionable trial for the murder of her husband,
Ali Kamel Fahmy Bey, but also the clairvoyant and occultist Cheiro (whom he
would have met at Carnarvon's séances), who had pleaded for his help 'after he
was named as a co-respondent in a case brought against him by the husband of
a woman client who had become infatuated by the celebrated palmist. In the
end the petitioner withdrew his claim, and paid the damages and costs, but only
after [Cheiro] was able to prove his innocence. At the time, the fortuneteller
revealed to Marshall Hall psychic imagery that would foreshadow, and even
predict, his election win at Southport some sixteen months later in October
1901.' It was, of course, Cheiro who had predicted Lord Carnarvon's death and
who was also well acquainted with Richard Bethell and Lord Westbury. And
with Crowley occasionally crossing paths with the London Spiritual Alliance,
was there a connection between Marshall Hall, Cheiro and the Beast, too? It
was common knowledge that both Crowley and Cheiro believed they could
invoke Tutankhamun's father, Akhenaten, the heretic pharaoh.

Could Crowley have procured Marshall Hall's redoubtable services to ensure that Marie-Marguerite, another of his allies, was exonerated? Marshall Hall was not only one of the finest legal minds of his generation, but he was also at ease socialising with and even representing well-known occultists. His 'bigoted portrayal of Fahmy Bey as a monster of amoral Eastern bisexual depravity' seems, in retrospect, rather premeditated, especially when we consider the fact that Marie-Marguerite was also known to have had bisexual relationships. It is also very peculiar that upon helping clear Marie-Marguerite of the charge of murder, Marshall Hall insisted upon celebrating their victory at the Savoy Hotel – the very scene of the crime. If the conspirators were indeed that saddened by what had transpired, for the sake of appropriateness it is rather more likely they would have decided to celebrate elsewhere, or perhaps not celebrate at all. But Marie-Marguerite, 'for a few days following her trial, was busy in the West End of London: partygoing and interview-giving'.

Furthermore, it seems a little too coincidental that Cheiro, himself a renowned occultist, should have known so many of Crowley's victims and allies. It is a point of interest that Marshall Hall had previously defended and had acquitted the likes of Robert Wood in the trial of the Camden Town Murder, Ronald Light in the case of the Green Bicycle Murder, and the English solicitor Harold Greenwood, who had been charged with murdering his wife by arsenic poisoning. Indeed, he would later become known as 'the Great Defender' on account of his successful defence of those charged with notorious murders. However, even Marshall Hall's formidable powers couldn't save the likes of Dr Crippen, Frederick Seddon or George Joseph Smith, the 'Brides in the Bath' murderer, from the gallows. Four years after representing Marie-Marguerite Fahmy in her trial, Marshall Hall died at the age of 68, from complications related to pneumonia and heart disease. It would seem as if pneumonia continued to make its mark on those directly connected to the curse of Tutankhamun years after the discovery of his tomb.

Aside from crossing paths at the London Spiritual Alliance, Crowley and Howard Carter would have also met regularly when they were both members of the South London Association of Gentlemen. This would have given Carter ample time to forge a relationship with the Beast, endorsing the hypothesis that Carter was somehow tangled up in his devilish undertakings. It is quite remarkable how the lives of such a small cast of characters are so frequently intertwined. For example, W.T. Stead, another habitually reappearing player in this melodrama (in particular in the case of the 'mummy-board' at the British Museum), was a regular lecturer who addressed the eccentric collective of London spiritualists. Crowley was also acquainted with the impious Stead, and he mentions in his *Confessions* that during one particular meeting 'Stead broke off every minute or two to indulge in a lustful description of some passing flapper and slobber and how he would like to flagellate her'. In addition, is there any link between Crowley and these so-called mysterious missing papyri?

Also, what of Lady Evelyn Herbert, Lord Carnarvon's daughter, who, along with Carter, his assistant, Arthur 'Pecky' Callender, and her father, was in the initial group of people to enter King Tut's tomb? Lady Evelyn lived until 1980 when she passed away at the ripe old age of 79. Although it is perhaps no coincidence that the majority of Crowley's victims were male, Lady Evelyn's presence at the illegal opening of the tomb wasn't public knowledge until years later, thus making it highly unlikely that Crowley ever knew of her illicit association.

In 1987, seven years after Lady Evelyn's death, an extraordinary discovery was made at Highclere Castle – the country seat of the Herbert family, the earls of Carnarvon. Behind oaken wall panelling, the present Earl of Carnarvon discovered a cubbyhole which contained a hidden cache of Ancient Egyptian artefacts – pre-dating the discovery of Tutankhamun's tomb – which came from the fifth earl's early excavations with Howard Carter. They were missed when the fifth earl's widow, Lady Almina, sold the bulk of his Egyptian plunder to the New York Metropolitan Museum. When interviewed at the time, the present earl, George Herbert, said: 'My grandfather was superstitious and did not want to talk about Egypt, so he took the Egyptian collection out of sight. It remained hidden away in a cupboard between two rooms down below the cellars for some 65 years.'

So why did the sixth Earl of Carnarvon (the fifth earl's son, the former Lord Porchester) see fit to conceal these Egyptian treasures in particular? Perhaps the fact that he had been at his father's deathbed in Cairo, seeing firsthand the hospital lights go out the moment Lord Carnarvon passed away, had precipitated his desire to conceal all of his Egyptian antiquities? Among the artefacts currently on display at Highclere Castle is a splendid 3,500-year-old painted coffin of a woman named Irtyru, from Deir el-Bahri, a calcite shabti showing the head of Amenhotep III, silver bracelets from the Delta, faience bowls, a 5,000-year-old calcite dish used in priestly offerings, coffin faces carved in wood, alabaster vessels found at the entrance to the tomb of King Merneptah, the son of Ramesses II, and even the razor that caused the blood poisoning that led to the death of Lord Carnarvon.

Sir Flinders Petrie, the 'Father of Egyptology', who was a guest of Howard Carter's at the opening of King Tut's tomb, died in 1942 at the age of 89, 'and

Professor Percy Edward Newberry, who had also entered the tomb, lived until 1949, when he died at the age of 80'. Arthur Callender was another of the original excavators who evaded Crowley's retribution. A former official of the Egyptian railway lines, Callender, an American, retired from his post in 1920 when he was invited by Howard Carter to join his expedition in the Valley of the Kings. As a trained architect and engineer, his experience was invaluable during the disassembly of the wooden chest containing the gold anthropoid sarcophagus, which, in turn, contained the mummy of Tutankhamun. There are well-documented photographs that appeared in *The Times* showing Callender at work alongside Carter within Tutankhamun's tomb. These would have been easily accessible for Crowley to view. Although Callender (who interestingly discovered the canary being eaten by the cobra at Howard Carter's Egyptian home) died in 1936, there is little coverage of the details of his death. It is therefore likely that he returned to his native America once the excavation had come to an end, making it frankly impossible for the Beast to enact his revenge. By the 1930s Crowley was living in relative penury, so a trip to America would have been out of the question.

Yet, despite him spending more and more time in London, Crowley still maintained his fearsome reputation both overseas and at home – and this remains the case today. Indeed, as the author Jake Arnott remarked in an article written for the *Daily Telegraph*:

> It was now open season on Crowley, as his legend became the stuff of gaudy thrillers. The best of these is Dennis Wheatley's *The Devil Rides Out* (1934), where he is clearly the Satanist Morcata. He also appears in Warwick Deeping's *Exiles* (1930), H.R. Wakefield's *He Cometh and He Passeth By* (1930), and Dion Fortune's *The Winged Bull* (1935), which contains the marvellously melodramatic announcement: 'London, Paris, New York, Berlin are full of all sorts and conditions of organisations experimenting and researching and playing about generally with the Unseen.'

Indeed, 'among the book-reading public of the day, and of many days to come, the occult was very popular: Dennis Wheatley enjoyed enormous success with *The Devil Rides Out*, in which a black mass is celebrated near Stonehenge and there is a euphemistic but unambiguous description of black magicians pissing into a chalice containing pieces of holy wafer'.

Evelyn Waugh, the erstwhile novelist, Bright Young Thing and flamboyant raconteur, was another author to embrace the occult and draw inspiration from the Beast when he wrote *Brideshead Revisited* in 1945, a book that depicts the unique friendship between two Oxford University undergraduates of vastly differing social backgrounds. In the book, the character of Anthony Blanche, a stuttering, homosexual aesthete, is referred to as 'having practiced black art in Cefalù'. Cefalù was, of course, the home to Crowley's Abbey of Thelema where Raoul Loveday had died. In Waugh's autobiography, *A Little Learning*, published in 1964, he writes of his election as secretary to Oxford University's Hypocrites Club: 'My predecessor in the office, Loveday, had left the university suddenly to study black magic. He died in mysterious circumstances in Alistair [sic] Crowley's community and his widow, naming herself "Tiger Woman", figured for some time in the popular press, where she made "disclosures" of the goings-on at Cefalù.' Fascinatingly, the Bright Young Things' Hypocrites Club has since been described as being 'reminiscent of ... Sir Francis Dashwood's Hellfire Club, another group of hedonistic, dissolute, and aristocratic young men.

In his autobiography, Waugh describes a larger-than-life hostess of many of the parties he attended in London shortly after leaving Oxford University: 'There was Mary Butts, a genial, voluptuous lady of the avant-garde who wrote short stories and at the time consorted with a man who had been in Alistair [sic] Crowley's black-magical circle at Cefalù.' And historian D.J. Taylor, in his biography of the Bright Young Things, *Bright Young People*, writes: 'Among home-grown figures who operated on the Bright Young People's fringe, Mary Butts was an opium addict and the author of "Fumier", a semi-fictional account of the mechanics of opium use.' In his 1925 diaries, Waugh depicts one of these outlandish parties at Butts' home in Belsize Park:

> The party at Mary's was quite fun ... At last he arrived and after we had drunk some beer in a slum bar we went on to Mary's where we found some very odd painters quite drunk and rather naked. They were for the most part what Mary called 'Paris Queers'.

In fact, Butts had spent twelve weeks in the middle of 1921 at the Abbey of Thelema herself, but found the practices there so shocking that she subsequently fled and came away with little more than rampant drug addiction and bad memories. 'The climate and food nearly killed Mary, and when [she] came back to Paris [she] looked like a ghost and [was] hardly recognisable.' Crowley would later refer to Butts in his *Confessions* as 'a large, white, red-haired maggot'.

> A great deal has been written, by Waugh himself, by his contemporaries, by his later commentators, about those [Oxford University] days, but some

important evidence is lacking. Waugh kept a diary for part of his time at Oxford, but it is no longer available to us:

'I have been living very intensely the last three weeks. For the past fortnight I have been nearly insane ... My diary for the period is destroyed ... I may perhaps one day tell you of some of the things that have happened. It will make strange reading in the biography.' Christopher Sykes' biography of Waugh describes his going through an 'extreme homosexual phase [at Oxford] ... unrestrained, emotionally and physically'. Were entries pertaining to this period what prompted Waugh to destroy the diary? Quite probably yes – in part. But there may have been something more, something that would later provide material for his first novel: some kind of involvement in the occult.

When we consider that these diaries were written in 1923, not only the year in which Tutankhamun's tomb was opened but when Waugh's future father-in-law, Aubrey Herbert, was murdered on the orders of Crowley, the contents of the missing diary become increasingly tantalising.

Evelyn Waugh may have participated in satanic ritual at Oxford and been possessed by a 'demon' in one or another sense for the rest of his life. The supernaturalism he espoused as a Roman Catholic may have pre-dated his conversion and been based on a terrifyingly personal experience. He described possession once in his novels, in *Helena* (1950), a literary treatment of the story of St Helena, the discoverer of the true cross. The novel is set between the third and fourth centuries AD and makes use of 'certain wilful, obvious anachronisms which are introduced as a literary device.' Indeed, in Humphrey Carpenter's biography of the Bright Young Things, *The Brideshead Generation*, he writes how: 'Waugh's Catholicism was a force that saved him from ... this "demon of destructiveness" ... which might otherwise have destroyed him.'

With this in mind, it is possible that [Waugh's] acquaintance with Crowley was not entirely third-hand, as we can see from examination of a short story called *A Step Off The Map* that he wrote in 1933. Waugh's short stories are not particularly good, for the most part, and *Out of Depth*, as *A Step Off The Map* was later renamed, does not stand out even amongst them for its literary merit. It is however of extraordinary interest from the point of view of this article, for it describes a dinner party encounter had by a lapsed American Catholic with a man called Jagger [later renamed Kakophilos] who is unmistakably based on Crowley: 'an elderly, large man, quite bald, with a vast white face that spread down and out far beyond the normal limits ... a little crimson smirking mouth'. The American, Rip, is introduced to the bald man. 'Do what thou wilt shall be the whole of the law,' said Dr Kakophilos, in a thin Cockney voice.

'Eh?'

'There is no need to reply. If you wish to, it is correct to say, Love is the Law, Love under will.'

Rip does not take Kakophilos seriously, but finds himself unable to resist the force of his personality and becomes involved in an occult experiment that projects him 500 years into the future, to a London in which 'great flats of mud, submerged at high water, stretched to his feet over the Strand'. Europe has reverted to barbarism; Rip is treated almost as a pet by the savages inhabiting the ruins of London, and is eventually presented to a party of black African anthropologists for study at a coastal military base. He finds only one sane and familiar thing in this new world: a Roman Catholic mass conducted in Latin by a black priest at the base. Somehow he returns to the twentieth century. The story ends with him speaking with another Roman Catholic priest in a most curious fashion, considering that his involvement in the time-hop had been quite involuntary: 'Father,' said Rip. 'I want to make a confession … I have experimented in black art …'

In another of Waugh's short stories, *Mr. Loveday's Little Outing*, published in 1936, the protagonist, Angela Moping, visits her mentally ill father in a psychiatric hospital and becomes charmed by his loyal (and 'kindly lunatic') secretary, Mr Loveday, who, despite killing a woman on a bicycle years earlier, appears perfectly sane and rehabilitated. When Angela successfully campaigns for his release, Mr Loveday is free to commit the same crime all over again. More comparisons can be drawn here: Lord Moping, who is dressed in a black frock and often writing beleaguered letters to the Pope, and who had 'habitually threatened suicide', is no doubt based on Crowley; while his secretary, Mr Loveday, is an obvious nod to Raoul Loveday. In 1925, Waugh described his novel *The Temple at Thatch* as being 'a book about madness and magic'. Later, he writes: 'I also wrote some pages of a novel I had begun … it was named *The Temple at Thatch* and concerned an undergraduate who inherited a property of which nothing was left except an eighteenth-century classical folly where he set up house and, I think, practised black magic.' The undergraduate in question was based on his own experiences at Oxford.

So why had Waugh drawn so much inspiration from Crowley and his followers, and why were his novels and short stories riddled with clues alluding to his relationship with the Beast? When we remember that he was Aubrey Herbert's son in law, this extensive link to Crowley, Herbert's murderer, becomes even more beguiling. Indeed, was Waugh somehow in collusion with Crowley against his future father-in-law? It would certainly seem as if their association was more than 'third-hand', given their numerous mutual acquaintances and Waugh's propensity for writing in detail about the Beast, the occult and later dismissively about 'Tutmania'. In 1929, Waugh remarked that the re-creation of Tutankhamun's tomb at the British Empire Exhibition at Wembley 'had been a particularly retrograde step: In the mind of the public, the tomb became a second Queen's Doll's House full of "quaint" and "amusing" toys.' And when we bear in mind that Waugh was at first unwelcome in the Herbert family due to his failed marriage to Evelyn Gardner, Aubrey Herbert's niece, we cannot ignore the distinct possibility that the two men were somehow bound by their experiences with the occult.

In 1954, in a letter to the novelist Nancy Mitford (whose husband, Peter Rodd, had plotted with Raymond Greene to have the Beast assassinated following Raoul Loveday's death), Waugh wrote that a 'frog' newspaper had announced, at the time of Aubrey Herbert's death, that his father-in-law had committed suicide. However, there is no evidence of this article having ever been written, nor any further reference to Herbert's 'suicide'. So why did Waugh feel compelled to draw Mitford's attention to it? Indeed, much like Crowley, Waugh was 'a bully and a snob', and, according to his brother-in-law, Auberon Herbert, he could be 'an awful shit'. The similarities don't end there: in 1966, when Waugh suffered a fatal heart attack at the age of 62, he was an alcoholic drug addict, a lifetime's exuberance having taken its toll on a weakened constitution. Moreover, we must keep in mind that Anthony Powell, Waugh's close friend and fellow Bright Young Thing and Oxford alumni, had arranged a 'clear-the-air' meeting with the Beast at Simpsons-in-the-Strand when he was an editor for Duckworth Press (who had recently published Betty May Loveday's 'slanderous' autobiography, *Tiger Woman*).

> After fully stating his case against the 'inaccuracies and vulgarities of phrase' marring *Tiger Woman*, Crowley expounded in general upon 'the hard life of a mage, its difficulties and disappointments, especially in relation to the unkindness and backbiting of fellow magicians.' They parted amicably, and Crowley took no further action against the Betty May book.

Had Waugh's influence played a part in Crowley's eventual affability?

Furthermore, in 1935, when Waugh was working as a correspondent covering the second Italian war in Abyssinia (his experiences later providing him with the inspiration for his 1938 novel *Scoop*), he just so happened to employ a local man by the name of Wazir Ali Bey who acted as his interpreter and informant. Although it later transpired that Wazir Ali Bey was, in fact, in the pay of the many other foreign journalists sent by their editors to cover the war in Abyssinia, it remains likely that this is the name Waugh bestowed upon the local man in an effort to provide him with anonymity. Why had he chosen this particular alias? When we recall that Crowley had written a poem in 1923, shortly after Prince Ali Kamel Fahmy Bey's murder at the Savoy Hotel, 'on Ali Bey & his Wazir', perhaps it is no coincidence. This would suggest that Waugh, Raoul Loveday's successor as secretary to Oxford University's Hypocrites Club, had access to Crowley's magical diaries of the period in question – a period in which Waugh claimed to have been 'living very intensely' and going 'nearly insane' – and took a scrupulous interest in the passages concerning Fahmy Bey's death. Yet there is little doubt that in spite of his numerous allusions to Crowley in his literary work, Evelyn Waugh was meticulously vigilant not to refer to the Beast in his personal diaries and correspondence.

Crowley and Waugh may well have been introduced by one of their mutual acquaintances, most likely the flamboyant journalist and MP Tom Driberg or the stylist Gwen Otter, who would have been quick to point out the intriguing Oxford University connection between Waugh and Loveday. Waugh himself would later write how he 'began to frequent the Café Royal in the evenings. My brother Alec introduced me to a bohemian world among whom I found cronies. My name was not on the lists of any conventional hostesses. No engraved cards summoned me to the thriving world of Pont Street. Most of the parties I attended were impromptu or assembled at very short notice by word of mouth.' It is likely that Waugh made Crowley's acquaintance at one such 'party'.

Also, with the Beast regularly taking common or garden flats on Jermyn Street, and with the Cavendish Hotel – central to the Bright Young Thing mythology – on the same thoroughfare, Crowley and Waugh would have had ample chance to meet and plot their devices. The two men were clearly well known for their reciprocal affection for Regent Street's Café Royal and La Rotonde café in Paris, where they dined frequently throughout the same period, the obscure country pub the Bell Inn in Aston Clinton, where they habitually visited, and Port Said in Egypt, where they travelled extensively.

Even James Bond creator Ian Fleming, after spending time with Crowley when he worked for the naval intelligence at MI5, used the Beast as a:

template for Le Chiffre, the first Bond villain in *Casino Royale* (1953). This was to be the final study in his lifetime and a fitting climax to the absurd double narrative of his existence ... After the Second World War, Crowley's status as the wickedest man in the world seemed faintly ludicrous, and his eligibility as a literary villain began to wane. Indeed, by the Sixties he had been reinvented as a hero to the counter-culture movement, which questioned traditional morality just as he had done.

Sidney Blackmer, who played the charming Satanist Adrian Marcato in Roman Polanski's *Rosemary's Baby*, reportedly based his performance on tales of the Beast and the Chicago-born Satanist Anton La Vey. Crowley would, of course, go on to feature on the cover of The Beatles' *Sergeant Pepper* album and in the lyrics of David Bowie, The Doors, Ozzy Osbourne, Black Sabbath and Led Zeppelin (guitarist Jimmy Page, an ardent follower, even bought Crowley's Boleskine House on the shore of Loch Ness). His work was introduced to the Rolling Stones by underground filmmaker Kenneth Anger; more recently, he appeared in Alan Moore's graphic novel *From Hell* and the popular comic *2000AD*; he was reincarnated as Simon Callow in Bruce Dickinson's and Julian Doyle's film *Chemical Wedding*; and served as inspiration for the macabre characters of Reverend Henry Kane (also known as the Beast) in the *Poltergeist* films, Mal'akh in Dan Brown's novel *The Lost Symbol* and Lord Blackwood in Guy Ritchie's unique reimagining of *Sherlock Holmes*. In Ritchie's film, Lord Blackwood carries out a series of ritualistic murders and ceremonies – the sites of which encompass the pentagram – with each murder supposedly granting Blackwood special powers. Perhaps the writers of the film had drawn similar conclusions about Crowley?

Continuing the Sherlock Holmes theme, the Beast makes further appearances in no less than five of Moonstone Books' *Sherlock Holmes Mysteries*; titles include *The Loch Ness Horror, The Case of the Philosopher's Ring, Return of the Devil* and, most intriguingly, *Doctor Watson and the Invisible Man*, in which Crowley aides Watson, Mycroft Holmes and the police hunt for a killer. Indeed, the legacy of Crowley as a fictional character stems from the early 1900s when writers were drawn to the Beast when he was in the infancy of his hedonistic career.

W. Somerset Maugham's *The Magician* (1908) featured the sinister Oliver Haddo, whom Maugham admitted was based on Crowley. They had both frequented the same dining club in Montparnasse. 'I made my character more sinister and ruthless than Crowley ever was,' Maugham insisted … There is some debate as to whether Crowley is the basis for the evil alchemist Karswell in M.R. James' ghost story *Casting the Runes* (1911). This tale came at a moment when Crowley was still forming his alter-ego and there are prophetic lines in James' yarn. Karswell is said to have 'invented a new religion for himself', which is precisely what the Beast went on to do.

Indeed, in *Casting the Runes*, the character of Karswell even makes an appearance in the Select Manuscript Room of the British Museum, having performed research into the great authorities on alchemy. Another of James' infamous characters, Mr Abney, who appears in his chilling story *Lost Hearts* (1895), also bears some familiar Crowley characteristics. In the story, Mr Abney is obsessed with the occult and sacrifices two children in an attempt to gain immortality – his plans to sacrifice a third child, his young cousin, are only scuppered when the ghosts from his previous victims enact their terrible revenge.

> He lives retired from society, 'a man wrapped up in his books', with a library full of works on the mysticism of the Late Classical period. He is a writer of articles, recognised by academics for his learning And within him the pursuit of knowledge has warped into something terrible. Immersed in the world of the mystics, he has lost his moral sense – or at least put it aside. What is this thing he plans to do? He writes of 'enacting certain processes', 'absorbing the personalities', and 'removal'. It may seem barbaric to the modern mind, but he, a man of philosophic temperament, is merely engaging in experiment, testing the truth of an old receipt of Hermes Trismegistus': that one may attain the powers known to Simon Magus by a simple method, 'by the absorption of the hearts of not less than three human beings below the age of twenty-one years.' The best method is to cut out the living heart, reduce it to ashes, and drink it down in some port; the psychic portion of the souls thus absorbed may be an annoyance for a while, but can be disregarded.

Perhaps, in developing the characters of Karswell and Mr Abney, James knew something about Crowley that everyone else had failed to notice?

It is this author's conclusion that there was never a 'curse' wreaking havoc in London, neither any spectral pharaoh's retribution nor King Tut's vengeance. Aside from the astonishing occurrences in Egypt and the rest of the world, which this author is certain will never be truly explained, what took place within London's West End throughout the 1920s and '30s were, quite simply, the morbid deeds of a madman – and his allies – believing he would acquire powers beyond his mortal being, and who manipulated the legacy of the 'Curse of Tutankhamun' and its hold over the fragile British public for his own corrupt ends.

Moreover, aside from his victims, it is uncanny that so many people who came into direct contact with the Beast should die in such tragic circumstances. Ever since the climbing accident in the Himalayas in 1905, in which four of Crowley's party died, 'it is not difficult to feel that Crowley went through life trailing some cloak of death and insanity behind him'. In the accident, he reputedly heard a commotion, but did not investigate or help, claiming his companions had been making a noise all day and that he did not realise anything was wrong. Crowley just calmly left the scene and drank tea. Later in Calcutta, the Beast shot dead two of a group of robbers who had attempted to mug him. Furthermore, many of Crowley's mistresses and followers ended up in a sorry state: either in asylums, as alcoholics, working as prostitutes or even dead.

Soon after leaving him in 1912, Hanni Jaeger committed suicide. Joan Hayes, the mistress of Crowley's erstwhile lover, Victor Neuburg, who went by the professional name of Ione de Forest, shot herself at her home in Chelsea following the performance of the Rites of Eleusis at Caxton Hall; and let us not forget that the Beast had threatened to hire a bunch of thugs to kill W.B. Yeats, his rival within the Golden Dawn, and sacrifice Betty May Loveday on the 'altar' of his temple at the Abbey of Thelema in Cefalù. Crowley would later claim that he placed a curse on Joan Hayes two days prior to her death, much in the same way he threatened his physician, Dr William Brown Thompson, his former drinking partner, Nina Hamnett, and his former mentor, Samuel McGregor Mathers. Indeed, aside from having the disposition of a murderer, it would seem as if casting 'curses' occupied a significant part of Crowley's adult life. His friend and fellow occultist Evan Morgan, the second Viscount Tredegar, summoned the Beast to his home, Tredegar House in Monmouthshire, to take part in a ritual that was designed to curse the commanding officer who court-martialled him following a security breach in the Second World War. 'And, amazingly, the commanding officer soon contracted some mysterious illness and nearly died.' Also, Norman Mudd, a devotee of the Beast's, who had left his well-paid job to study with Crowley at the Abbey of Thelema, and who spent time promoting Crowley's interests, committed suicide in Guernsey in 1934 after being abandoned by his master and left penniless.

Indeed, for a man who had a predilection for travelling the globe on a regular basis, it is, quite frankly, a remarkable set of coincidences that either he, or one of his 'emissaries', should always be in the very same place at the very same time when a death ascribed to the curse of King Tut occurred in either London or Paris. Yet the name Aleister Crowley would continue to dominate the pages of the tabloids well after his death.

12

A Curse Returns

It is definitely possible that the Ancient Egyptians used atomic radiation to protect their holy places. The floors of the tombs could have been covered with uranium. Or the graves could have been finished with radioactive rock. Rock containing both gold and uranium was mined in Egypt. Such radiation could kill a man today.

Louis Bulgarini

In 1966, just as plans were being finalised to transport the relics from the tomb of Tutankhamun to Paris, Mohammed Ibrahim, the Egyptian Director of Antiquities, began a frantic campaign to keep the treasures in Cairo. Allegedly suffering from recurring nightmares of a grim fate befalling him if the relics left the country, Ibrahim pleaded with his government to take immediate action. Following a tempestuous meeting with government officials, Ibrahim reportedly stepped out on to what looked like a clear road on a bright sunny day and was hit by a car, killing him instantly.

Only four years later, Richard Adamson, the sole surviving member of Howard Carter's 1923 expedition, who had previously lost his wife within twenty-four hours of publically speaking out against the curse and whose son had later broken his back in an aircraft crash, gave an interview on British television for an Anglia programme. As a security guard at the excavation site, Adamson, in the interview, repeated his view that despite what had happened to him he still did not believe in the curse. Later that evening, as he left the television studios, he was involved in a near-fatal accident when his taxi crashed just outside Norwich, leaving him in hospital with fractures and bruises. Adamson, who was thrown from the taxi and narrowly avoided being run over by a lorry, was later quoted as saying, 'In the past, when I have disclaimed the curse, disastrous things have happened in my family. You can say that this has given me food for thought.'

In 1972, the curse of Tutankhamun made a dramatic reappearance just as the treasures from King Tut's tomb were being transported from their home in Cairo to a prestigious exhibition at none other than the British Museum in London. Dr Gamal Mehrez, Mohammed Ibrahim's successor as the Egyptian Director of Antiquities, scoffed at the idea of the curse, saying that his whole life had been spent in Egyptology and that all the deaths and misfortune through the decades associated with the curse of King Tut had been the result of 'pure coincidence'. Incredibly, Mehrez died the night after supervising the packaging of the relics for transport to England by a Royal Air Force plane, and numerous members of the crew, who had previously been in perfect health, suffered death, injury, misfortune and disaster in the years that followed their cursed flight. Flight Lieutenant Rick Laurie died in 1976 from a heart attack. His wife declared: 'It's the curse of Tutankhamun – the curse has killed him.'

Perhaps most extraordinarily, Ken Parkinson, a flight engineer, suffered a heart attack at the same time each year as his Britannia aircraft flight that brought the treasures to England commenced. Tragically, he had a final fatal one in 1978. Before their mission to Egypt, neither of the servicemen had suffered any heart trouble and had been pronounced fit by military doctors. During the flight, the chief technical officer, Ian Lansdowne, accidentally kicked the crate that contained the death mask of King Tut. 'I've just kicked the most expensive thing in the world,' he quipped. Later on, as he disembarked from the aircraft on another mission, a ladder mysteriously broke beneath him and the leg he had kicked the crate with was badly broken. It was in plaster for nearly six months.

Flight Lieutenant Jim Webb, who was also aboard the aircraft, lost everything he owned after a fire devastated his home. A steward, Brian Rounsfall, confessed to playing cards on the sarcophagus of Tutankhamun on the flight home and suffered two heart attacks. And a woman officer onboard the plane was forced to leave the RAF after having a life-saving operation.

Eventually, on 30 March 1972, the exhibition was opened by Queen Elizabeth II, and, perhaps aided by the somewhat infamous press it had harvested (which included a front page spread in the *News of the World*), saw over 1.5 million visitors pass through the doors of the British Museum. 'As if the world of the pharaohs wasn't already exciting enough with its scarabs and cobras, its falcons and sphinxes, its bandaged corpses and its brain-extracting hooks, here was the mystery of a handsome boy-king and his tomb full of treasures. Here were rumours of murder and a real-life mummy's curse. The modern-day blockbuster exhibition was born.'

In 2007, as part of its worldwide tour, plans were unveiled to open the *Tutankhamun and the Golden Age of the Pharaohs* exhibition at London's O2 Arena. On 15 November, and for the following nine months, the treasures from King Tut's tomb (apart from the famous gold death mask that was deemed too valuable to travel) were on display for an enthralled new generation of Londoners, and the O2 Arena itself was lit with a golden hue, the main entrance flanked by two colossal figures of Anubis. Despite having its own unique version of Monopoly created for the event, this time, however, there were no tales of death curses that followed in the exhibition's wake. (At least none as this book went to press ...)

The experimental years of the 1960s and '70s unsurprisingly saw a vast number of writers and musicians soaking up Aleister Crowley's work for stimulation. One such musician was the pioneering record producer and songwriter Joe Meek (he of *Telstar* fame), who was heavily influenced by the occult and the idea of 'the other side'. Fearing he was to be evicted from his Holloway Road home and studio, Meek shot dead his landlady, Violet Shenton, on 3 February 1967, before turning the gun on himself. Coincidentally, it was eight years to the day since Buddy Holly, Meek's hero, died in the infamous plane crash at Mason City Airport. Aged just 37, Meek was heavily in debt and suffering from manic depression; he was 'a gay, speed-addicted, devil-worshipping, tone-deaf Gloucester farmhand who built a little recording studio over a shop, and made one of the biggest-selling records of all time'. His homosexuality, which was illegal in Britain at the time, put him under additional pressure, and four years earlier he had been charged with 'importuning for immoral purposes' after an incident in a public toilet at Madras Place, London, which subsequently led to a blackmail scandal.

Meek, who has since been described as being 'psychologically unstable; delightful company one minute, uncontrollably furious the next', was known to regularly solicit rent boys, and many believe that his irrepressible behaviour culminated in the tragic events that were to take place at 304 Holloway Road, North London. In January 1967, police in Tattingstone, Suffolk, discovered two suitcases in a field containing the mutilated body of 17-year-old Bernard

Oliver, a local rent boy, who was an associate of Meek's. Fearing implication in Oliver's murder after the Metropolitan Police issued a statement in which they declared their intention to interview all known homosexuals in the city, Meek spiralled into despair and helplessness, somewhat aggravated by his unbridled drug addiction. Still agreeing to a recording session the following week, his friends and colleagues noted his increasing 'paranoia', and by the beginning of February Meek was an emotional wreck. On the 2nd:

> [he] had another visitor ... Ritchie Blackmore, who went on to fame and success with Deep Purple and Rainbow, was a member of The Outlaws, and rented a flat from [Meek]. He was on tour, but [Meek] was friends with his German wife, Margaret. She came round later that night, and is convinced [Meek] had been indulging in the black arts. She tells how [Meek] said: 'There's somebody around me – I can feel it. There's somebody in the air.' She believes that Aleister Crowley's spirit was lurking in the flat that night. Margaret also describes how a picture [Meek] had painted, of a woman crying, was 'full of blood ... like someone tried to get some blood in it. It was like someone said goodbye to something.'

Aside from having a rabid fascination with the occult, Meek also believed he was, at one time, possessed by the Beast.

The following day, the gunshot-riddled bodies of Joe Meek and Violet Shenton, the landlady who ran the leather goods store below, were found at the Holloway Road flat (which Meek believed was haunted), and despite interviewing over 100,000 people, the Metropolitan Police never caught Bernard Oliver's murderer. Could it be that he died that day in North London in February 1967? Furthermore, another case that attracted the attention of the British tabloids was that of Graham Bond, the musician widely regarded as being the founding father of the English rhythm and blues boom of the 1960s, who, believing he was Aleister Crowley's son, became increasingly involved in the occult due in no small part to the Beast's writings. Already suffering from depression and drug addiction, Bond threw himself underneath an underground train at Finsbury Park station on 8 May 1974.

Just over twenty years later, on 28 November 1994, the naked body of Rikki Neave, a 6-year-old boy from Peterborough, was found in local woods – he was spread-eagled in a posture identical to Leonardo da Vinci's drawing of the Vitruvian Man. Upon being charged with Rikki's murder, the court heard how his mother, Ruth Neave, a drug addict, owned a book entitled *Magic* by Aleister Crowley, which gave details of human sacrifice. Although she was subsequently found not guilty of her son's murder, Ruth Neave was jailed for seven years having been deemed culpable of child cruelty and neglect. Barely two years later, a self-confessed German disciple of the Beast, who was not only charged with spreading Crowley's message, was found guilty of rape and jailed for six years. However, four years after that took place, a more lurid and shocking crime would occur, this time in London's West End.

On 7 May 2000, seven years before the *Tutankhamun and the Golden Age of the Pharaohs* exhibition opened at the O2 Arena, an appalling murder took place in the heart of the West End at Covent Garden. The victim was Diego Piniera-Villar, a 12-year-old boy from London's Spanish community, who was stabbed repeatedly in broad daylight in front of hundreds of horrified shoppers by Edward Crowley. 'Local restaurant worker Anwar Khan witnessed the attack. "There was no mercy," he said. "It was very cold. Just jab, jab, jab."' At the subsequent trial, the court heard how Crowley, a 52-year-old man who had a long history of mental illness, had not only struck up a friendship with Piniera-Villar, but had also claimed to be a disciple of his namesake, Aleister Crowley. He had reputedly become obsessed with Piniera-Villar and could not accept the boy's desire to end their platonic friendship.

Although the British tabloids insisted that Piniera-Villar's murder was an 'occult sacrifice', it is important to consider the facts that Crowley was an indigent and a homeless drifter and had been reliant upon the British mental health system for twenty-eight years. During his time in London leading up to the murder, Crowley began to descend the slippery slope of destitution. He lost his home and had become dependent upon church communities in central London for food, water and shelter. Earlier he had fallen into the hands of priests in Westminster Abbey who, he declared, exorcised him. How this experience impacted upon Crowley's already delicate state of mind is unknown, but it is worth recalling that in previous instances of impromptu exorcism, murders have followed. In one infamous case in Barnsley in the early 1970s, a man was exorcised by church ministers and promptly strangled his wife to death.

At his trial the prosecution insisted that Edward Crowley was carrying an inscription in Latin which read 'Diego must die' and diagrams relating to sacrifices. They also claimed that he emulated the infamous occultist Aleister Crowley and murdered Piniera-Villar because he was influenced by the instructions on ritual sacrifice in the magical workbook titled *Magick in Theory and Practice*, originally published by the Beast in 1929. In the book, Aleister Crowley, referring to himself as Frater Perdurabo (I shall endure), describes how: 'for the highest spiritual working one must accordingly choose that victim which contains the greatest and purest force. A male child of perfect innocence and high intelligence is the most satisfactory and suitable victim.' Crowley continues: 'the bloody sacrifice, though more dangerous, is more efficacious; and for nearly all purposes human sacrifice is the best.' Although many Thelemites believe the 'sacrifice' in question is a euphemism for masturbation, if Piniera-Villar's murder was indeed an 'occult sacrifice', it is more than likely that this is the passage Edward Crowley drew his inspiration from.

Moreover, the jury rejected Edward Crowley's plea of insanity – despite hearing how he had attempted suicide on no less than eight separate occasions and that he had often sought help from occult healers – and found him guilty of Piniera-Villar's murder. Although he had a personality disorder, he was not psychotic, and so could not be held in custody under the Mental Health Act; he was subsequently jailed for life. One wonders whether Aleister Crowley, having had to face the same prosecution and culpability for his murders, would have been incarcerated for life or handed a reprieve due to his own mental health issues.

The Piniera-Villar case intriguingly takes us full circle, back to the Beast's own West End murders, how they were consistent with what he had written in *Magick in Theory and Practice* and how his coded words displayed his personal apathy towards murder. Remembering that Aleister Crowley's victims were, for the most part, male and that he believed 'a male child of perfect innocence and high intelligence is the most satisfactory and suitable victim', the Beast writes how:

> there is another sacrifice with regard to which the Adepts have always maintained the most profound secrecy. It is the supreme mystery of practical Magick. Its name is the Formula of the Rosy Cross. In this case the victim is always – in a certain sense – the Magician himself, and the sacrifice must coincide with the utterance of the most sublime and secret name of the God whom he wishes to invoke … For this reason FRATER PERDURABO [Crowley] has never dared to use this formula in a fully ceremonial manner, save once only, on an occasion of tremendous import, when, indeed, it was not He that made the offering, but ONE in Him. For he perceived a grave defect in his moral character which he has been able to overcome on the intellectual plane, but not hitherto upon higher planes. Before the conclusion of writing this book he will have done so … One word of warning is perhaps necessary for the beginner. The victim must be in perfect health – or its energy may be as it were poisoned. It must also not be too large: the amount of energy disengaged is almost unimaginably great, and out of all anticipated proportion to the strength of the animal.

It was this passage that was greatly scrutinised during, and possibly cost Crowley, the 'Black Magic Libel Case' in which he attempted to sue Nina Hamnett. Shortly before *Magick in Theory and Practice* was published in 1929, the Beast murdered Richard Bethell at Mayfair's Bath Club, prophesising his own oblique words: 'before the conclusion of writing this book he will have done so.' Bethell, a member of the Scots Guards, was a man in perfect health, of high intelligence and who was not particularly tall or thickset. Raoul Loveday also fit the same criteria. Could Loveday's murder have been the one sacrifice that Crowley was referring to? Recalling Loveday's illness in Cefalù, it was Crowley who took it upon himself to care for his ailing disciple, giving him ample time to perform his sacrificial ritual without being disturbed or suspected by the other members of the abbey.

However, it was his murders in London that shaped the pentagram that were truly the actions of a deeply troubled, sometimes brilliant, yet malevolent mind. Ultimately, it was Crowley, again in the significant year of 1929, who wrote in his *Confessions*, 'To know, to do, and to keep silent'. Silent, until now.

In 1946 [the year before Crowley's death], George Orwell sat down and penned an essay lamenting 'The Decline of the English Murder.' The country's so-called 'golden years' for killing had long since passed, he wrote, arguing the years spanning 1850 to 1925 represented a high watermark for the ultimate in crime. Jack the Ripper, Dr Crippen, and other notorious fiends, had set, in Orwell's estimation, the standard by which all other murderous acts should be judged.

He might well have added the macabre genius of Aleister Crowley to that list, propelling the 'Great Beast' into the dark pantheon of Britain's most enigmatic killers.

Select Bibliography

Listed below is a selection of the more useful books that formed a part of the research for this book.

Ackroyd, P., *Hawksmoor* (Penguin, 2002)

———, *London: The Biography* (Chatto & Windus, 2000)

Arnold, C., *Necropolis: London and its Dead* (Pocket Books, 2007)

Arnott, J., *The Devil's Paintbrush* (Sceptre, 2009)

Booth, C., *The Curse of the Mummy: And Other Mysteries of Ancient Egypt* (Oneworld, 2009)

Brandon, D. & Brooke, A., *Haunted London Underground* (The History Press, 2008)

Carter, H., *The Tomb of Tutankhamun* (National Geographic, 2003)

Clark, J. & Ross, C., *London: The Illustrated History* (Allen Lane, 2008)

Coates, G., *Discovering Gin* (NewLifeStyle, 1996)

Collins, A. & Ogilvie-Herald, C., *Tutankhamun: The Exodus Conspiracy* (Virgin, 2003)

Conan Doyle, A., *Tales of Unease: Tales of Mystery & the Supernatural* (Wordsworth, 2008)

———, *The Hound of the Baskervilles* (Penguin, 2004)

Connor, J.E., *London's Disused Underground* (Capital Transport, 2001)

Crowley, A., *Magick in Theory and Practice* (Dover, 1986)

———, *Moonchild* (Samuel Weiser, 1988)

———, *The Confessions of Aleister Crowley* (Arkana, 1989)

———, *The Book of the Law* (Red Wheel, 2004)

———, *The Magical Diaries of Aleister Crowley 1923* (Samuel Weiser, 1981)

Deghy, G. & Waterhouse, K., *Café Royal: Ninety Years of Bohemia* (Hutchinson, 1956)

Fiber, S., *The Fitzroy: An Autobiography of a London Tavern* (Temple House Books, 1995)

FitzHerbert, M., *The Man who was Greenmantle: A Biography of Aubrey Herbert* (John Murray, 1983)

Frayling, C., *The Face of Tutankhamun* (Faber & Faber, 1992)

Furneaux, R., *The World's Strangest Mysteries: Happenings that have Intrigued and Baffled Millions* (Odhams, 1961)

Glinert, E., *London's Dead* (Collins, 2008)

——, *West End Chronicles: 300 Years of Glamour and Excess in the Heart of London* (Penguin, 2008)

Goodman, J., *Murder on Several Occasions* (The Kent State University Press, 2007)

Haag, M., *The Rough Guide to Tutankhamun: The King, The Treasure, The Dynasty* (Rough Guide, 2007)

Hamnett, N., *Laughing Torso: Reminiscences of Nina Hamnett* (Kessinger, 2004)

Hankey, J., *A Passion for Egypt: Arthur Weigall, Tutankhamun and the 'Curse of the Pharaohs'* (I.B. Tauris, 2002)

Hattersley, R., *The Edwardians: Biography of the Edwardian Age* (Abacus, 2006)

Herbert, A , *Mons, Anzac and Kut* (Pen & Sword, 2009)

Hobhouse, H., *Regent Street: A Mile of Style* (Phillimore & Co., 2008)

Holland, T., *The Sleeper in the Sands* (Little, Brown, 1998)

Howse, G., *Foul Deeds & Suspicious Deaths in London's West End* (Wharncliffe, 2006)

Jackson, S., *The Savoy: A Century of Taste* (Muller, 1990)

James, T.G.H., *Howard Carter: The Path to Tutankhamun* (I.B. Tauris, 2001)

Jenkins, A., *The Twenties* (Book Club Associates, 1974)

Kaczynski, R., *Perdurabo: The Life of Aleister Crowley* (North Atlantic Books, 2010)

Kohn, M., *Dope Girls: The Birth of the British Drug Underground* (Granta, 2003)

Lewis, J., *Shades of Greene: One Generation of an English Family* (Jonathan Cape, 2010)

Macintyre, B., *Operation Mincemeat* (Bloomsbury, 2010)

Meyrick, K., *Secrets of the 43 Club* (Parkgate, 1994)

Miles, B., *London Calling: A Countercultural History of London Since 1945* (Atlantic, 2010)

Moore, A. & Campbell, E., *From Hell* (Knockabout, 2008)

Morton, J., *Gangland Soho* (Piatkus, 2008)

Murphy, R., *Smash and Grab: Gangsters in the English Underworld* (Faber & Faber, 1993)

Nicholson, V., *Singled Out: How Two Million Women Survived Without Men after the First World War* (Penguin, 2008)

Oates, J., *Unsolved London Murders: The 1920s and '30s* (Wharncliffe, 2009)

O'Farrell, G., *The Tutankhamun Deception* (Pan, 2002)

Pugh, M., *We Danced All Night: A Social History of Britain Between the Wars* (Vintage, 2009)

Read. S., *Dark City: Crime in Wartime London* (Ian Allan, 2010)

Reeves, N., *The Complete Tutankhamun: The King, The Tomb, The Royal Treasure* (Thames & Hudson, 2007)

Robins, J., *The Magnificent Spilsbury and the Case of the Brides in the Bath* (John Murray, 2010)

Roland, P., *The Crimes of Jack the Ripper: An Investigation into the World's Most Intriguing Unsolved Case* (Arcturus foulsham, 2006)

Rose, A., *Scandal at the Savoy: The Infamous 1920s Murder Case* (Bloomsbury, 1991)

Seabrook, W., *Witchcraft: Its Power in the World Today* (Harcourt Brace, 1940)

Smith, S., *Underground London: Travels Beneath the City Streets* (Abacus, 2005)

Spence, R., *Secret Agent 666: Aleister Crowley, British Intelligence and the Occult* (Feral House, 2008)

Sugden, P., *The Complete History of Jack the Ripper* (Robinson, 2002)

Sutin, L., *Do What Thou Wilt: A Life of Aleister Crowley* (Griffin, 2002)

Taylor, D.J., *Bright Young People: The Rise and Fall of a Generation: 1918–1940* (Chatto & Windus, 2007)

Wallis Budge, E.A., *The Egyptian Book of the Dead* (Penguin, 2008)

Waugh, E., *A Little Learning: The First Volume of an Autobiography* (Chapman & Hall, 1964)

——, *The Diaries of Evelyn Waugh* (Weidenfeld & Nicolson, 1976)

——, *Vile Bodies* (Penguin, 2000)

White, J., *London in the Twentieth Century: A City and its People* (Vintage, 2008)

Woods, P. & Baddeley, G., *Saucy Jack* (Ian Allan, 2009)

Newspaper and Periodical Sources

Berkeley Daily Gazette
Berliner Tageblatt
Bizarre
Daily Express
Daily Mail
Daily News
Daily Record
Daily Sketch
Daily Telegraph
Hearst Sunday
John Bull
Murder Casebook: Shots in the Dark Marguerite Fahmy and Lock Ah Tam
New York Times
New York World
Northern Echo
Pall Mall Gazette
Sunday Express
Tatler
The Equinox
The Looking Glass
The Mirror
The Observer
The People
The Referee
The Sunday Morning Star
The Times
The Washington Post
The World's Most Notorious Women
Time Out

Notes

1 Of Curses Newspapers, Writers and Books

'in an attempt to persuade him …' Andrew Collins & Chris Ogilvie-Herald,
    Tutankhamun: The Exodus Conspiracy (Virgin, 2003), p. 151.
'Much to his own chagrin …' Christopher Fraying, *The Face of Tutankhamun*
    (Faber & Faber, 1992), p. 53.
'The four pages of excellently worded information …' Ibid.
'The story quickly became legend …' Julie Hankey, *A Passion for Egypt*
    (I.B. Tauris, 2002), p. 137.
'This was carried to the dig-house …' Charlotte Booth, *The Curse of the Mummy:
    And Other Mysteries of Ancient Egypt* (Oneworld, 2009), p. 199.
'from the 1890s onwards …' Collins & Ogilvie-Herald, *Tutankhamun: The Exodus
    Conspiracy*, p. 93.
'The society palmist and "seer" Velma …' Frayling, *The Face of Tutankhamun*, p. 43.
'The public in the 1920s …' *The World's Most Notorious Women* (Chancellor Press,
    2001), p. 378.
'Mass produced accessories …' Frayling, *The Face of Tutankhamun*, p. 19.
'there was a story …' Ibid., p. 12.
'the black-bearded …' Alan Jenkins, *The Twenties* (Book Club Associates, 1974), p. 220.

2 Golden Twenties and Bright Young Things

'were grand affairs …' Alexander Scrimgeour, *Scrimgeour's Small Scribbling Diary*
    (Conway, 2008), p. 12.
'BLACK DEVILS AND WHITE GIRLS …' Andrew Rose, *Scandal at the Savoy*
    (Bloomsbury, 1991), p. 11.

'Waugh's novels evoked the zeitgeist ...' Geraldine Coates, *Discovering Gin* (NewLifeStyle 1996), p. 75.

'Interwar cinemas were typically called ...' Frayling, *The Face of Tutankhamun*, p. 20.

'Cinemas, such as, in the London area alone ...' Ibid.

'fairyland interiors with glades of autumnal trees ...' Cathy Ross & John Clark, *London: The Illustrated History* (Allen Lane, 2008), p. 257.

'mahogany-coloured horseshoe or lemon-shaped bar' Jerry White, *London in the Twentieth Century: A City and its People* (Vintage, 2008), p. 335.

'the underworld and the aristocracy ...' Robert Murphy, *Smash and Grab: Gangsters in the English Underworld 1920–1960* (Faber & Faber, 1993), p. 8.

'This may have saved ...' James Morton, *Gangland Soho* (Piatkus, 2008), p. 50.

'[Meyrick] was by no means ...' Ibid., p. 48.

'used to chew gum ...' Marek Kohn, *Dope Girls: The Birth of the British Drug Underground* (Granta, 2003), p. 124.

3 Prince of Darkness

'So it was with a mixture ...' *Murder Casebook: Shots in the Dark* (Marshall Cavendish, 1991), p. 3071.

'However, the wedding wrought a transformation ...' Ibid., p. 3066.

'"Madame Meyrick, Madame Meyrick," she burst out ...' Kate Meyrick, *Secrets of the 43 Club* (Parkgate, 1994), p. 61.

'the very crack of doom' Ibid.

'On an oddly still, humid evening ...' Rose, *Scandal at the Savoy*, p. 65.

'No doubt to the relief ...' Ibid., p. 66.

'The two men then went back ...' Ibid., p. 67.

'The tidiness of the woman ...' Jonathan Goodman, *Murder on Several Occasions* (Kent State University Press, 2007), p. 27.

'very bad state of nerves' Ibid., p. 29.

'Grosse was just the sort ...' Ibid., p. 30.

'unnatural sexual acts ...' Geoffrey Howse, *Foul Deeds & Suspicious Deaths in London's West End* (Wharncliffe, 2006), p. 173.

'Marshall Hall was the most sought-after ...' Jane Robins, *The Magnificent Spilsbury and the Case of the Brides in the Bath* (John Murray, 2010), p. 82.

'His silver hair curled at the temples ...' *Murder Casebook: Shots in the Dark*, p. 3077.

'One needs to remember ...' Goodman, *Murder on Several Occasions*, p. 35.

'After an hour's ride ...' Rose, *Scandal at the Savoy*, p. 49.

'I have had a somewhat unpleasant time ...' Margaret FitzHerbert, *The Man who was Greenmantle: A Biography of Aubrey Herbert* (John Murray, 1983), p. 242.

'... the club committee ...' D.J. Taylor, *Bright Young People: The Rise and Fall of a Generation: 1918–1940* (Chatto & Windus, 2007), p. 64.

'was the haunt of artists ...' Ben Macintyre, *Operation Mincemeat* (Bloomsbury, 2009), p. 189.

'wrote so dismissively of the whole phenomenon ...' Frayling, *The Face of Tutankhamun*, p. 23.

4 1929–30: The Second Coming

'an astute, intelligent and extremely charismatic man ...' Collins & Ogilvie-Herald, *Tutankhamun: The Exodus Conspiracy*, p. 148.
'on nearly every wall ...' Ibid., p. 149.
'Apparently, a close friend ...' Ibid.
'consistent with a pillow ...' Gerald O'Farrell, *The Tutankhamun Deception* (Pan, 2002), p. 175.

5 Museum Macabre and the 'Unlucky Mummy'

'The return to the previous capital ...' Hankey, *A Passion for Egypt*, p. 152.
'... a Mrs. Gordon ...' Ibid.
'Apparently, a small avalanche of parcels ...' Frayling, *The Face of Tutankhamun*, p. 59.
'The British Museum ...' Ibid.
'This legend is echoed ...' Stephen Smith, *Underground London: Travels Beneath the City Streets* (Abacus, 2005), p. 282.
'three or four articles for them ...' Hankey, *A Passion for Egypt*, p. 150.
'Weigall is an oddity ...' Ibid.
'extraordinarily intense ...' Ibid., p. 339.
'encouraged by Lord Carnarvon ...' Collins & Ogilvie-Herald, *Tutankhamun: The Exodus Conspiracy*, p. 189.

6 The Golden Dawn and the 'Wickedest Man in the World'

'In 1900, Mathers was exposed as a fraud ...' Ed Glinert, *West End Chronicles: 300 Years of Glamour and Excess in the Heart of London* (Penguin, 2008), p. 95.
'Crowley's initiation into the grade ...' freemasonry.bcy.ca/aqc/crowley.html
'Crowley's behaviour ...' www.robotwisdom.com/jaj/irishlit.html
'The prolix, labyrinthine machinations ...' Glinert, *West End Chronicles: 300 Years of Glamour and Excess in the Heart of London*, p. 96.
'a hotchpotch of all the established ...' Guy Deghy & Keith Waterhouse, *Café Royal: Ninety Years of Bohemia* (Hutchinson, 1956), p. 179.
'Crowley described the unearthly voice ...' Lawrence Sutin, *Do What Thou Wilt: A Life of Aleister Crowley* (Griffin, 2002), p. 123.
'body of fine matter, or astral matter ...' Ibid.
'one of the most remarkable ...' Aleister Crowley, *The Confessions of Aleister Crowley* (Arkana, 1989), p. 546.

7 The Crowley Connection Part I

'these magicians and magi ...' Frayling, *The Face of Tutankhamun*, p. 42.

'While his spiritual life soared ...' Richard Kaczynski, *Perdurabo: The Life of Aleister Crowley* (North Atlantic Books, 2010) p. 160.

'he would endure ...' Lawrence Sutin, *Do What Thou Wilt: A Life of Aleister Crowley*, p. 241.

'carrying some fifty pounds ...' Ibid.

'These individuals were ...' Ibid., p. 251.

'In one stroke ...' www.seanscreenplays.com/BETENOIRECD/Articles1

'Scarlet Woman play ...' Sutin, *Do What Thou Wilt: A Life of Aleister Crowley*, p. 274.

'officially described as ...' Deghy & Waterhouse, *Café Royal: Ninety Years of Bohemia*, p. 181.

'Aleister Crowley's "cesspool of vice"' *John Bull*, 24 March 1923.

'The main room of the "Abbey" ...' Ibid.

'at a horrible hotel in Russell Square ...' Crowley, *The Confessions of Aleister Crowley*, p. 889.

'She was tiny ...' Sally Fiber, *The Fitzroy: The Autobiography of a London Tavern* (Temple House Books, 1995), p. 27.

'full panoply of a Scottish chieftain' Deghy & Waterhouse, *Café Royal: Ninety Years of Bohemia*, p. 178.

'If he frightened her ...' Ibid., p. 180.

'a fertile territory for lovers' Virginia Nicholson, *Singled Out: How Two Million Women Survived Without Men after the First World War* (Penguin, 2008), p 246.

'homosexual women felt accepted ...' Ibid., p. 258.

'a soccer-playing, rag-minded undergraduate ...' Deghy & Waterhouse, *Café Royal: Ninety Years of Bohemia*, p. 180.

'his ghostly white face ...' Ibid., p. 181.

'The responses of husband and wife ...' Sutin, *Do What Thou Wilt: A Life of Aleister Crowley*, p. 302.

'Even before the Lovedays arrived ...' Deghy & Waterhouse, *Café Royal: Ninety Years of Bohemia*, p. 181.

'the toxic effect ...' Sutin, *Do What Thou Wilt: A Life of Aleister Crowley*, p. 303.

'a cat that frequented the Abbey ...' Ibid., p. 304.

'a frail youth with ...' Kaczynski, *Perdurabo: The Life of Aleister Crowley*, p. 380.

'at a glance that ...' Crowley, *The Confessions of Aleister Crowley*, p. 917.

'Betty May found him in bed ...' Kaczynski, *Perdurabo: The Life of Aleister Crowley*, p. 391.

8 The Crowley Connection Part II

'I don't charge Crowley with causing Raoul's death ...' Kaczynski, *Perdurabo: The Life of Aleister Crowley*, p. 392.

'According to the *Sunday Express* ...' Jeremy Lewis, *Shades of Greene: One Generation of an English Family* (Jonathan Cape, 2010), p. 55.

'the Café Royal seemed unusually crowded …' Deghy & Waterhouse, *Café Royal: Ninety Years of Bohemia*, p. 182.

'had at last been damaged beyond repair' Sutin, *Do What Thou Wilt: A Life of Aleister Crowley*, p. 308.

'the underlying reason …' Frayling, *The Face of Tutankhamun*, p. 41.

'The answer, for those who had the ears …' Ibid.

'Oxford [University] was electrified …' Lewis, *Shades of Greene: One Generation of an English Family*, p. 56.

'North Africa had served Crowley …' Sutin, *Do What Thou Wilt: A Life of Aleister Crowley*, p. 309.

'It is the beginning of the end …' Aleister Crowley, *The Magical Diaries of Aleister Crowley 1923* (Samuel Weiser, 1981), p. 16.

'He had lost both his Abbey …' Sutin, *Do What Thou Wilt: A Life of Aleister Crowley*, p. 311.

'She gave lavish parties …' Goodman, *Murder on Several Occasions*, p. 9.

'Lord Carnarvon accepted their invitation …' Rose, *Scandal at the Savoy*, p. 48.

'gripped by the prevailing Tutankhamun fever' Ibid., p. 49.

'Clad in a riding habit …' Ibid., p. 52.

'had fired her pistol …' Goodman, *Murder on Several Occasions*, p. 46.

'agreed with Marshall Hall …' Ibid., p. 44.

'suggested that when the pistol …' *Murder Casebook: Shots in the Dark*, p. 3081.

'The building, one of the highest in London …' Stanley Jackson, *The Savoy: A Century of Taste* (Muller, 1990), p. 39.

'no doubt chosen for its Egyptian linkage' Sutin, *Do What Thou Wilt: A Life of Aleister Crowley*, p. 381.

'paraded a Jew, an Indian …' www.cornelius93.com/Epistle-BeastlyLifeofAleistey Crowley-PartII.html.

'present woman emissary in London' *John Bull*, 10 March 1923.

'leaving behind an emotionally and financially bereft Hirsig' Sutin, *Do What Thou Wilt: A Life of Aleister Crowley*, p. 316.

'In her magical diaries of this period …' Ibid., p. 319.

'who would, within weeks …' Ibid.

'The reason for these bizarre developments …' Rose, *Scandal at the Savoy*, p. 186.

'lived, prosperously and unspectacularly …' Goodman, *Murder on Several Occasions*, p. 50.

'earned his contempt for lacking …' Sutin, *Do What Thou Wilt: A Life of Aleister Crowley*, p. 346.

'Like another diabolist …' Deghy & Waterhouse, *Café Royal: Ninety Years of Bohemia*, p. 178.

'to the delight of …' Crowley, *The Confessions of Aleister Crowley*, p. 648.

'There is another strange account …' Sutin, *Do What Thou Wilt: A Life of Aleister Crowley*, p. 346.

'He [Crowley] believed that he possessed …' Ibid.

'The assembled gentility taking tea …' www.conspiracyarchive.com/NWO/Secret_Societies.htm.

'that marked his final exit ...' Deghy & Waterhouse, *Café Royal: Ninety Years of Bohemia*, p. 185.

'Once again a private dining-room had been booked ...' Ibid.

9 The Crowley Connection Part III

'One day [Thomas] and Theodora Fitzgibbon ...' Barry Miles, *London Calling: A Countercultural History of London Since 1945* (Atlantic, 2010), p. 30.

'Whether I should be ...' www.billheidrick.com/tlc2000/tlc0500.htm.

'sharply satiric self-portrait in verse' Sutin, *Do What Thou Wilt: A Life of Aleister Crowley*, p. 352.

'Some of their names ...' Ibid., p. 357.

'Are you familiar with the words ...' Kaczynski, *Perdurabo: The Life of Aleister Crowley*, p. 473.

'On the third day ...' Deghy & Waterhouse, *Café Royal: Ninety Years of Bohemia*, p. 183.

'Still, there was a bright spot ...' www.cornelius93.com/Epistle-BeastlyLifeofAlei steyCrowley-PartII.html.

'a diary entry over three years later ...' Sutin, *Do What Thou Wilt: A Life of Aleister Crowley*, p. 373.

'When the Black Magic case ...' Deghy & Waterhouse, *Café Royal: Ninety Years of Bohemia*, p. 183.

'small trust payments ...' Sutin, *Do What Thou Wilt: A Life of Aleister Crowley*, p. 374.

'the last phase of the Beast's story ...' Deghy & Waterhouse, *Café Royal: Ninety Years of Bohemia*, p. 184.

'In 1937, when Crowley had decided ...' Ibid.

'Crowley launched his own ...' Sutin, *Do What Thou Wilt: A Life of Aleister Crowley*, p. 385.

'the Beast proceeded ...' Ibid., p. 395.

'It was also here at 93 Jermyn Street ...' www.luminist.org/archives/knowingac.htm.

'When her book was finally ...' www.cornelius93.com/Epistle-BeastlyLifeofAleis teyCrowley-PartII.html.

10 Aleister Crowley and Jack the Ripper

'repeated from cronies and rivals ...' Paul Woods & Gavin Baddeley, *Saucy Jack* (Ian Allan, 2009), p. 175.

'Frenchmen are "notoriously the worst linguists in the world" ...' Ibid., 179.

'His most dogged accuser ...' Ibid., 181.

'Harris establishes that his suspect ...' Ibid.

'He was suffering from neurasthenia ...' Ibid.

'story later repeated ...' Ibid., p. 184.

'occult apprenticeship' Ibid., p. 185.

'Levi was certainly a highly influential ...' Ibid.

'Journalist Christopher Smith has concocted ...' Ibid.

'Nigel Cawthorne's overheated true-crime paperback ...' Ibid., p. 175.

'From this point Crowley ...' Paul Roland, *The Crimes of Jack the Ripper: An Investigation into the World's Most Intriguing Unsolved Case* (Arcturus foulsham, 2006), p. 156.

'Though he was a customer at the Fitzroy ...' Fiber, *The Fitzroy: The Autobiography of a London Tavern*, p. 27.

'evade detection after shooting an assailant in India' Sutin, *Do What Thou Wilt: A Life of Aleister Crowley*, p. 371.

'*The unorthodox congregation* ...' Woods & Baddeley, *Saucy Jack*, p. 173.

11 The Aftermath: Howard Carter, Allies and the Ones Who Got Away

'was not unique for his era ...' Collins & Ogilvie-Herald, *Tutankhamun: The Exodus Conspiracy*, p. 92.

'It is certain, had he lived ...' Ibid., p. 91.

'after he was named ...' Ibid., p. 94.

'bigoted portrayal of Fahmy Bey ...' '*Savoy Stories*' – *Time Out: London For Visitors*, Spring/Summer 2010, p. 7.

'for a few days following ...' Goodman, *Murder on Several Occasions*, p. 50.

'and Professor Percy Edward Newberry ...' Rupert Furneaux, *The World's Strangest Mysteries: Happenings that have Intrigued and Baffled Millions* (Odhams, 1961), p. 91.

'among the book-reading public of the day ...' www.dooyoo.co.uk/printed-books/brideshead-revisited-evelyn-waugh/252080/.

'reminiscent of ... Sir Francis Dashwood's Hellfire Club ...' Ibid.

'The climate and food nearly ...' Nina Hamnett, *Laughing Torso: Reminiscences of Nina Hamnett* (Kessinger, 2004), p. 177.

'A great deal has been written ...' www.dooyoo.co.uk/printed-books/brideshead-revisited-evelyn-waugh/252080/.

'Evelyn Waugh may have participated ...' Ibid.

'it is possible that ...' Ibid.

'had been a particularly retrograde step' Frayling, *The Face of Tutankhamun*, p. 35.

'began to frequent the Café Royal ...' Evelyn Waugh, *A Little Learning: The First Volume of an Autobiography* (Chapman & Hall), p. 211.

'template for Le Chiffre ...' Jake Arnott, 'Aleister Crowley's lives', *Daily Telegraph*, 30 May 2009.

'W. Somerset Maugham's *The Magician* ...' Ibid.

'He lives retired from society ...' www.freakytrigger.co.uk/ft/2009/02/hauntography-lost-hearts/, 18 February 2009.

'And, amazingly, the commanding officer ...' Phil Carradice, '*Evan Morgan of Tredegar House*' – *BBC Wales History*, 30 December 2010.

12 A Curse Returns

'As if the world of the pharaoh's ...' Rachel Campbell Johnson, 'Tutankhamun at the O2 Centre', *The Times*, 13 November 2007.

'a gay, speed-addicted, devil-worshipping ...' David Gritten, 'Joe Meek: he topped the charts and then himself', *Daily Telegraph*, 15 June 2009.

'psychologically unstable ...' Ibid.

'[he] had another visitor ...' Kate Hodges, 'Joe Meek', *Bizarre Magazine*, February 2005.

'Local restaurant worker Anwar Khan ...' news.bbc.co.uk/1/hi/uk/1166667.stm, 13 February 2001.

'In 1946 [the year before Crowley's death], George Orwell ...' Simon Read, *Dark City: Crime in Wartime London* (Ian Allan, 2010), p. 9.

Index

Other titles published by The History Press

Jack the Ripper: Scotland Yard Investigates
STEWART P. EVANS & DONALD RUMBELOW

£14.99

Join two leading Ripper experts that have joined forces to treat the case of the Ripper's East End murders like a police investigation. Using their unparalleled knowledge of the murders and their professional experience as police officers, they uncover clues about this darkly fascinating case that have remained undetected for over a hundred years.

978-0-7509-4229-4

Victorian CSI
WILLIAM GUY, DAVID FERRIER & WILLIAM SMITH

£12.99

Based on the final edition of William A. Guy's *Principles of Forensic Medicine*, this guide could instruct a detective on the victim's cause of death – or whether they were dead at all. With original woodcuts, case studies and notes on identifying the corpse and walking the crime scene, Victorian CSI will fascinate lovers of crime fiction and of true crime alike.

978-0-7524-5513-6

Greater London Murders:
33 True Stories of Revenge, Jealousy, Greed & Lust
LINDA STRATMANN

£14.99

This compendium brings together thirty-three murderous tales – one from each of the capital's boroughs – that not only shocked the City but made headline news across the country. This carefully researched, well-illustrated and enthralling text will appeal to both those interested in the history of Greater London's history and true-crime fans.

978-0-7524-5124-4

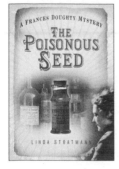

The Poisonous Seed: A Frances Doughty Mystery
LINDA STRATMANN

£8.99

When a customer of William Doughty's chemist shop dies of strychnine poisoning after drinking medicine he dispensed, William is blamed, and the family faces ruin. William's daughter, nineteen year old Frances, determines to redeem her ailing father's reputation and save the business. She soon becomes convinced that the death was murder, but unable to convince the police, she turns detective.

978-0-7524-6118-2

Visit our website and discover thousands of other History Press books.

www.thehistorypress.co.uk